'Gavin EDINBURGH
death in the sink estates of Brit
that most of us only glimpse in l
the kind of people that we fear (
indeed, a bright afternoon.'   *Observer*

'The British *Wire*'   BBC Radio 5 Live

'In focusing on three cities, Knight tries to highlight major issues in teen criminality: drug addicted, absent or ineffectual parenting, gun culture, the profit motive and gangster chic. His research is impressive. He spent two years embedded with the police in these cities, and uncovers the sort of stories that never make the news. A Somalian child soldier who relives the civil war on the streets of London, Glaswegian gang fights in Easterhouse, and homeless Sikh heroin addicts living in bin sheds . . . *Hood Rat* does raise some deeply troubling and interesting questions.'   *Scotsman*

'Gavin Knight spent two years with anti-gang units in London, Manchester and Glasgow in order to write his gripping new book'   *Esquire*

'In its approach and style, Gavin Knight's *Hood Rat* follows the New Journalism that revolutionised the form in the 1960s . . . This book is not only a disturbing, significant portrait of the present, but a snapshot of Britain's future if this trend continues to escalate . . . The pace of *Hood Rat* is spurred on by Knight's economy of detail and staccato sentences, which thankfully avoid the slang and colloquialisms found on the lips of those he encounters. His experience crosses two worlds: he does not report simply on the gangs, but also on those entrusted with the powers to bring about justice and change.'   *Literary Review*

'A rollicking tale'   *Big Issue in the North*

'Its pace is thrillerish and there are passages of undeniable tension.'   *Sunday Times*

'A challenging read . . . The author vividly shows a world where drugs hook young boys into gangs, where posturing and "respect" is all, so one gang murder escalates into revenge killings on both sides.'   *We Love This Book*

'If more non-fiction books were like this I'd be reading more of them but for now I'll just eagerly await Gavin Knight's next project.'   Ric's Reviews

'Journalist Gavin Knight spent two years embedded with under-cover police to tell these three very different stories of real-life street crime . . . fast-paced, gripping and visceral'   *Metro*

'The book is a step forward for British true-crime.'   3AM

'An excellent and unputdownable true-crime book . . . Names may be changed but everything else here is true. And in much the same way *Wire* creator David Simon and Roberto *"Gomorrah"* Saviano lifted the lid on Baltimore and Naples, so Knight (embed-ded with undercover police and underworld contacts for years) employs a series of interlocking, novelistic narratives to present an immediate and immersive study of brutalised youth from London to Glasgow "who'll live and die in a square mile", doomed by peer-pressure – or their own treacherous postcode. Though remaining profoundly political, there are no pat solutions or easy analyses on offer – just shocking stories and statistics . . . and perhaps a shard of hope too.'   *Word* Magazine

'Britain's *Gomorrah*'   *Independent*

'A searing and powerful story. And it's real'   *Irish Business Post*

'To understand the unholy chaos that rages within the hearts of urban poor youth and how they have been disenfranchised by globalisation you can do far worse than picking up Gavin Knight's *Hood Rat*'   *Business Standard India*

'A gripping, terrifying exposure of a much-discussed – but never explained – part of Britain. A must-read for anyone who wants to understand our deeply fractured society'

Owen Jones, author of *Chavs*

HOOD RAT

Gavin Knight has written for the *Guardian*, *Newsweek*, *Esquire*, *The Times*, *Prospect* and many other publications. Over a two-year period he was regularly embedded with police units in inner-city London, Manchester and Glasgow. He also spent time with dozens of violent criminals involved in gang and gun crime.
Hood Rat is his first book.

Hood Rat is a work of non-fiction.
Various names, nicknames, times, dates and
identifying personal characteristics have been
changed, to protect people, and a couple of
very minor characters created from
composites of several people.

GAVIN KNIGHT

HOOD RAT

PICADOR

To A and I

First published 2011 in paperback by Picador

This revised and updated edition published 2012 by Picador
an imprint of Pan Macmillan, a division of Macmillan Publishers Limited
Pan Macmillan, 20 New Wharf Road, London N1 9RR
Basingstoke and Oxford
Associated companies throughout the world
www.panmacmillan.com

ISBN 978-0-330-52308-0

1 3 5 7 9 8 6 4 2

A CIP catalogue record for this book is available from
the British Library.

Printed and bound by CPI Group (UK) Ltd, Croydon, CR0 4YY

Author's Note

Over one hundred hours of digital tape went into the interviews I did for *Hood Rat*. The accounts of events and reported speech were written up in a fictional style, using the present tense. This technique has its roots in the New Journalism of the 1960s.

I would like to thank the many different sources on the frontline of inner-city crime who voluntarily gave me information. Particular thanks to Karyn McCluskey, who spoke to me at length about her work with the Violence Reduction Unit in Glasgow alongside her inspiring co-director Detective Chief Superintendent John Carnochan. Dr Christine Goodall from Medics Against Violence detailed the trauma of victims of gang violence she has treated over twelve years. Karyn, John and Christine are passionately committed to preventing violence in Scotland. I was fortunate to talk to 'Cathy' and her colleagues, dedicated social workers in the East End of Glasgow. They allowed me to spend time with their cases, including 'Kenny'. I'm grateful to members of the community in Easterhouse and officers of Strathclyde Police's B Division who I accompanied as they targeted gang fights in Glasgow's East End.

In London, 'Pilgrim' kindly shared his life story with me over several meetings. 'Hardeep', 'Jas' and 'Kam' showed me the truth about addiction and crime in Southall. Jama told me about his tireless work with Southall's Somali community and introduced me to 'Troll'. I was embedded over time with a CID unit from the Met in Southall throughout a drug-surveillance operation against Somali dealers, which culminated in dawn raids.

I am especially grateful to Detective Constable 'Anders Svensson' from Greater Manchester Police, who met up with me on several occasions to patiently chronicle his work pursuing 'Merlin', 'Flow' and others. I also spent nights out with him and his colleagues from XCalibre on the streets of south Manchester.

I am very grateful to Kate Harvey, my brilliant, incisive editor at Picador, and to my agent, Will Francis at Janklow & Nesbitt, who was an excellent sounding board for ideas.

There are many others, too numerous to mention here, who took the time to talk to me, often anonymously. These include victims of knife and gun crime and their families, youth workers, charities, criminals, ex-offenders and current and former gang members. In amongst the violence and despair were stories of longing and undefeated human promise. They gave a true account of fractured communities blighted by crime. Abandoned by the economy, media, politicians and social infrastructure, they built a violent alternative world for themselves. *Hood Rat* is a journey into that world.

MANCHESTER

1: Web

A gang member from Moss Side shivers in his car outside Strangeways Prison gatehouse. He has been ordered to pick up an old associate, Whippet, who is being released after serving three and a half years for dealing crack cocaine and heroin. It's December. It's snowing, cloaking the red-brick watchtower which rises over north Manchester. He scrapes ice off the inside of the windscreen with his gloved knuckles and makes out another man waiting, a big guy, early forties, who stands smoking in a black polo shirt with short sleeves. 'You cold?' he calls out. The big guy turns his head and sucks smoke through his teeth. 'Half Norwegian,' he grins back. The man's head is shaven, his teeth stained and chipped, but his frame is broad, as if he works out. He finishes his cigarette and disappears inside the gatehouse. When he comes out Whippet is with him. The gang member leans on his horn and beckons him over. Whippet looks the other way and keeps walking. The big guy pushes him into a car and drives off at speed, tyres hissing on the sleety road.

The car tears around the ring road and heads north on the M6, the city thinning out, towards Lancaster and Kendal in the direction of the Scottish border. The big guy, Anders Svensson, has been a detective for twenty-three years, and can sense that something is troubling his companion. Whippet's muttering to himself, running his hand back and forward over his Jamie Foxx buzz cut. 'I don't need no babysitter,' he says, glaring ahead. The side of his mouth twists back as if snagged by a fish hook. 'I'm respected. Old school.'

Svensson lights another cigarette, says nothing. He has investigated thirty murders and worked the ganglands of south Manchester so long and hard that the job is wired into his blood. He notices how Whippet taps his upper lip and keeps glancing in the wing mirror. Under the prison swagger, he's terrified.

Svensson knows he's a good cop. Over the years he's had chief constable recommendations and the respect and backing of most of the senior officers in his division. But he's never taken up the offer of a promotion: he joined up to be a cop, to stay in the trenches. He is still a DC, working with much younger men who don't understand what he does and are sometimes jealous; he tries not to let them piss him off. Don't hate me because you ain't me. That kind of thing. What sets him apart as a good detective is his guile and the ability to get under the skin of criminals like Whippet.

'Will you call up your old crew?' Svensson asks. 'Merlin?'

Whippet rubs his eyes at the mention of Merlin's name. He shakes his head.

'Fuck him, man. Them thugs are no friends of mine. They're just haters,' he says. 'I want to spend some time with Amber. Amber and the kids. People who care about me.'

As the countryside around them opens up, Svensson listens to Whippet make promises. He's heard them before, many times. They're rarely a testament to the transformative powers of prison, and usually last as long as the licence conditions. Perhaps something shows on his face, because Whippet jabs a finger at him.

'This time is for real,' he growls. 'You know where I've been for three years? Every day someone telling you when to take a piss. No way I'm going back.'

For two years before his sentence, Whippet was busy robbing and torturing drug-dealers to make a name for himself. He's a middle-ranking predator. Despite the glamour the kids associate with the hustler lifestyle, most of the dealers Svensson knows are scraping by and living with their mums. Whippet was barely making ends meet before his conviction. There are only one or two who ever make any serious money and have the sense to move away from gang life.

But every fifteen years there comes along an individual of such outstanding criminal ability he inspires total fear in the other predators. Like every detective, Svensson is a hunter, and hunters are only interested in big game. He has read all the books on Sutcliffe. He remembers the quote by Ian Brady in *The Gates of Janus*, that a serial killer is like a great white shark cruising through society and the rest of us are fish. Whippet is just fish. Out there in the dark corners of south Manchester lurk the people that Whippet is afraid of. Svensson knows he can use this fear.

He knows a few other things about Whippet. Intelligence suggests Whippet has been involved in more than drug-dealing. He's got a temper on him, too: as a kid he once tried to smash his way out of a young offenders' institution with a sledgehammer. Whippet's victims have all left behind relatives and friends who hate him, would like to see him dead or locked up permanently. Svensson has been careful to talk to all of them over the last couple of months. He goes round for a brew with the victim's sisters or beans on toast with their mums. Whippet is the topic of conversation. Before long they are competing to tell him stories about the savage things he has done: the blowtorch, the soldering iron. Svensson acts unsurprised, as though he has heard it all already, and chips in with his own details, so when he leaves they are under the impression they haven't told him anything new. He builds up a picture of which old associates Whippet is still rolling with, whose orders he is following. And two names keep coming up. Names Svensson knows well.

Flow and Merlin.

Svensson has been tracking this pair for twelve years, since 1994. Merlin is the boss of the Gooch gang, Flow the enforcer. Flow is what US law enforcement calls an ultra-violent impact player. When he is around, he catalyses brutal incidents. Flow has recognized in recent years he has a rare ability to kill someone and walk away. He has developed a reputation as a stone-cold killer. He can do things that most people would find abhorrent, like close-up headshots, and be untouched by them; he doesn't need to psych himself up. You could meet Flow an hour after he's pulled the trigger, have a drink with him and find him charming, be none the wiser. You would think he's a sound lad, a nice lad. Svensson regularly talks to gang members who have murdered people, and he can see the strain etched on their faces. With Flow there is nothing. He has a pale, childlike face and wide-open eyes. He's a boyish twenty-seven, with a short military haircut. Thick eyebrows are raised and dark lashes blink as if he is mildly, pleasantly surprised the whole time. There's a strange earnestness about him.

Flow has – or had – two brothers. One was bottled in the city centre for being related to him. The other, Dean, a young DJ and amateur footballer, was killed for the same offence while Flow was in jail. He was shot in the stomach as he left his favourite club at 1 a.m. He was with friends, including Flow's girlfriend, Kerry. Over his time in prison, Flow has formed a mental picture of who he thinks was responsible. Word was it was the Longsight Crew. While the kids on bikes retaliate the next day with chaotic, random acts of revenge, Flow waits, and thinks, and blinks. It's been five years. In that time he's amassed a collection of sophisticated, high-powered weaponry. Three days after Flow was sentenced last time, Svensson went to visit his mum, Gemma. She made him beans on toast. He looked over at her as he sawed through the soggy bread. What do you say to a mother who has one son in the ground and another in prison?

Merlin's a different matter. It doesn't take most people long to twig that he's a psychopath. Merlin has used Flow's talents to stake his claim to vast areas of Old Trafford, Moss Side and Fallowfield. His shadow now extends over most of south Manchester. The secret of Merlin's success is his ability to exert absolute control over the people around him, something Svensson has never seen on this scale before. Merlin is thirty-one and rumoured to be making serious money. Over the last four years he has set up a well-organized network of foot-soldiers selling crack cocaine and heroin. The profits are used to buy handguns, shotguns and automatic weapons, including a 7.62 mm machine gun, which he wrapped in plastic and stowed in the attic of a female bag-head. He earns £700,000 a year. This is £668,000 more than Svensson. On the other hand, the more murders there are, the more overtime Svensson clocks up. Merlin isn't one of those players who eventually move away from the drugs, despite the inevitable time inside on the rare occasions Svensson's colleagues can make something – anything – stick. It excites him too much. Merlin and Flow are big game. They haven't been out on licence long and already they are the prime suspects behind two recent gang murders. A drive-by and a follow-up killing that was so brazen it shocked the whole city.

The problem, Svensson knows, because he's encountered it again and again, is that when Merlin is behind a crime it's impossible to find a witness to come forward. They start seeing Flow in every stairwell, at the bottom of every alleyway. Svensson wants to build a case that will put both of them away for a long time. That's why he's giving Whippet a lift.

Now, speeding north through the whirling snow as the afternoon darkens, Svensson only has to mention Flow's name and Whippet grows pale and weary. When he was in prison he heard that Flow was going to kill him because he'd kidnapped and tortured the wrong guy, a dealer connected to Merlin.

'All I want now is to spend time with my kids,' Whippet croaks. Svensson adopts a paternal tone.

'You'll be under curfew at the bail hostel. Your licence prevents you from entering Manchester. You can't go to Legends in Ashton. Or JJs. Can't go to the Arch Bar in Chorlton.'

'Legends?' Whippet laughs. 'One foot in there and I'm dead.'

'No one knows where we're going,' Svensson says.

Whippet looks at the passing road signs, twitchy and paranoid. Over the last two hours he feels he's been eye-balled by every driver on the M6. They are drawing close to the Scottish border. There isn't much time left: Svensson knows that if he's going to get anything useful out of Whippet, he needs to put the pressure on.

'We're already tracking Merlin and trying to take him off the streets. It would be easier if we knew which mobile he is using at the moment.'

They listen to the throb of the exhaust as he changes gear. He cracked it on a muddy track in Buxton. Right now, Whippet's willing to do anything that will stop him being shot. No one will know it came from him. It could come from anywhere. What's the big deal about a mobile number? He lolls his head back, closes his eyes. He can't snitch on Merlin. He'd never sleep again.

Left alone in the bail hostel, Whippet's paranoia starts to bite. There are more surveillance cameras in each room than in the Big Brother house. He is under a strict curfew. His thoughts keep returning to the associate at the prison gates. Will the word go around that Whippet disappeared with a cop? Just like a grass. The longer he lies low, the more suspicious they will become. So on an impulse, he rings one of Merlin's lieutenants. He moans about being taken off to the bail hostel.

'Where's the hostel?' the lieutenant asks.

Whippet has to think fast. If he tells the lieutenant he runs the risk of Merlin sending someone to harm him. But if he doesn't reveal his whereabouts, then Merlin will know immediately that he is hiding something. Whippet takes a deep breath.

'Carlisle,' he says.

When he ends the call Whippet feels dread creeping over him. Why did he ring? For a moment he was safe. Now Merlin can find him. He goes to his room, and examines the lock. It's a single Yale that would give way after a few determined, powerful kicks; there's no deadbolt. So he methodically drags all the furniture in the room against the door. Barricaded, he sits on the floor, listens to the cold wind rattling around the awnings of the building, and waits for Flow to come and kill him.

•

On the drive back, Svensson can't stop thinking about how he needs Merlin's mobile number. The gang murders were so blatant, so brazen, they reeked of Merlin and Flow. If a mobile number could be linked to the crime scene, they would have enough to secure warrants for fresh arrests. This is how Svensson likes to work. None of the other cops really know what he does, nor do they need to know. He disappears deep into the community for days and weeks on end. When Svensson walks onto an estate a young lookout warns his superiors by mobile. 'XCalibre are here,' he tells them. 'Which one?' they ask. 'The main one,' the kid replies. Yet Svensson has never laid eyes on this lookout before.

Svensson is an old-fashioned cop, a law unto himself. Some detectives will recite a long list of 'Trace/Interview/ Eliminate' names to their superior officer to justify how they spent their day. They will spend hours preparing an 'interview plan' for a suspect. Interview plan? Svensson has bought himself a little more breathing room than that. No one asks about his methods, because he is known to get results.

One of his three mobiles rings. It's not one he uses for informants, so he flicks it onto speaker. It's his wife.

'Can you pick up Jessica from Stockport later?' she asks.

'No problem.'

This job has meant he has had to put his own life on hold for long periods. It has cost him one marriage and put the current one under strain. The hours don't help. For someone who is not involved it becomes a chore to listen to him talking about the world where he spends most of his waking hours. The connections, the concentric rings of dealers, enforcers, informers, victims, surrounding the big players. He remembers the time his first wife kept asking him to leave the office so he could pick her up to go to her friend's wedding. She made him promise he would be away in forty-five minutes. Thirty-five minutes later he was standing over a body in Moss Side. It was a cold day like today and the bullet holes were clogged with frozen blood. 'I can't leave. I have a shooting,' he told her. It happens once, you can get away with it. But not when it happens again and again and again.

'What are you getting her for her birthday?' she asks.

'Some Miley Cyrus thing,' he says. 'She's the biggest Hannah Montana fan ever.'

They laugh, then he rings off. He has too much on his mind to chat. The first time he was married he had to leave his wife to go on an overnight surveillance job in Milton Keynes. The job escalated and he came back nine days later. He was in the car most of the time with an attractive female trainee detective who kept reading the manual for her exam. If he was totally honest he would say he's always had a bit of an eye. In the early days he used to meet loads of girls. But these days he doesn't tend to meet anyone outside the gang community. There were even times in the early days when cops and ex-girlfriends of gang members would end up shagging. One detective told him that he woke up in bed with a gangster's girlfriend and didn't know what he was more afraid of – the gangster coming through the door or the police. That hasn't happened for a long time. On the rare occasions he meets girls for a drink and tells them what he does for a living, they're interested. It's a bit of ego-massage. It's the same skill he uses with his informants – reading people, judging their body language, seeing what he can get away with. He's on friendlier terms with his ex-wife now. He sees his kids when he's not doing a row of three-to-eleven shifts. His son stays over at his place in Buxton on the edge of the Peak District with his wife and their daughter. His first wife is a cop and has married another cop.

When Svensson arrives back from Carlisle, the night shift is underway in south Manchester. A police helicopter hovers over the Alexandra Park Estate, where the Princess

Parkway marks the dividing line between the warring gangs, the Gooch and the Doddington. The Gooch foot-soldiers jostle to gain favour with Merlin, their manipulative, self-styled general. He gives the order and across town someone takes a bullet. Merlin grew up in the streets belonging to the Longsight Crew, an affiliate of the Doddington. But he chose to side with the Gooch, so his street pals from Longsight became his sworn enemies. Flow is right about who shot his brother. They have been fighting for almost twenty years. Although they keep it hushed up, the cops have a spy plane which watches the whole area as if it was a war zone.

The urban war in south Manchester is an abandoned, forgotten one: a desolate inner city, steeped in gun crime, gangs and drugs. Tit-for-tat violence. No sooner do the police cut off the heads of one faction than the gangs regenerate themselves. They imprison the gang leaders and create a vacuum for a rival gang to move into, and the cycle repeats itself, over and over. Younger men compete in acts of brutality to move up the ranks and fill their ex-leader's vacant shoes. When the cops look for witnesses they find a community living in such fear that no one speaks out. Crimes go unreported. Svensson's gang unit, XCalibre, has used intelligence to cover a twenty-foot 'wall' with a hundred and eighty gang members' faces and street names. They commit these faces to memory as they patrol the estates of Moss Side, Old Trafford and Longsight.

The gang members use military tactics too. The police spy plane will pick up an infrared image of a group of four masked, hooded riders moving on mountain bikes in a diamond formation through the streets of Moss Side. The formation is a classic Gooch tactic for scouting a forward area, and signals that a raid is in progress. The one at the front is the scout. The ones on the outside are outriders who will starburst when they encounter trouble. They aim to confuse their enemies, whether they encounter a rival gang or the police. The instinct is to follow the riders who burst away and ignore the one they are protecting in the middle. But he is the carrier. He's the one with the gun.

The gangs' tactics are evolving. Now the assassins strike at night, in ski masks and hoods. To prevent the police gaining valuable physical evidence, they have become increasingly forensic-aware. They wash their bikes down with petrol to remove DNA traces. They fire their handguns into buckets of sand so the grains are sucked back up the barrel to remove any firearm-discharge residues around the muzzle and breech that a ballistics expert might pick up. Many gang members are in jail because of ballistics evidence. The sand thing doesn't work. Other tactics, like the use of latex gloves to hide fingerprints, are more effective.

Svensson eases the car out of the late-night traffic and into a quiet walled street. Towering wire gates open automatically as he approaches: XCalibre headquarters. He finds a space between a battered unmarked Mondeo and a bulletproof Tactical Aid Unit van. Inside he heads to the canteen. At the counter he recognizes from behind the retro navy polo shirt and suede Chukka boots of the new arrival from the Covert Source Management Unit. The lad dresses like James Bond and cannot wait to gain control of Svensson's informants. Quickly, he ducks back out and heads down to the operations room. No one knows how

Svensson has built up his web of intelligence and informants, but the slick, fresh-faced recruits from CSM want to lay their hands on them. These days Svensson spends as much time keeping his network secret from other cops as he does protecting it from criminals.

•

At the Carlisle bail hostel Whippet dreams about Merlin. He's jumpy. Slammed doors make him flinch. Over the next few days he's enrolled into programmes to help him back on his feet, to ease the transition from prison to the world outside. He does not break the rules of the curfew. Weeks pass, but the fear that Merlin is coming for him stays, and stays. He has headaches and can't sleep. He leaps out of bed at night when the pipes in the walls thump, imagining he's hearing the grate of a key in the lock. Repeatedly he pleads to be moved.

'You have a visitor,' his handler tells him.

Svensson stands at the door in a black fleece, grinning. Whippet, despite himself, is pleased to see him.

'Get your things,' Svensson says. 'They're relocating you to another bail hostel, in Northumbria.' As Whippet gathers his stuff together, Svensson brings over two mugs of tea and sits on the edge of his bed. Whippet takes one and slurps greedily.

'I'm giving it up. I promise you. This is it,' Whippet says. Svensson doesn't say a thing, but he notices how worn out Whippet is looking, gaunt and thin.

'Still think he's coming after you?' Svensson says at last.

Whippet nods. He doesn't even bother to hide it now. Svensson leans forward on his knees.

'Let me tell you a story.'

This is what Whippet doesn't know. A few weeks ago Merlin was forced off the road in the early morning, some way from his manor, out on the A666 between Bolton and Blackburn. He was in a minicab with a girl. In the driver's rear-view mirror he saw four cops burst out of the other car. They wore body armour and face masks. Merlin knew in a second that his freedom was about to end and he scrabbled for the door. He heard a shot. An aluminium canister hissed around his feet and white gas engulfed him. He erupted out, tackling the first man headlong, his whole body shaking. Immediately a muscular forearm whipped around his neck, pulling his head back into a choke hold. He struck upwards at his attacker's jaw. But the cops had come prepared. Merlin's eyes and throat burned. He writhed around in a rage, tears blinding him, and the cops pinned his arms and pressed his face against the tarmac.

Whippet listens intently, sipping his brew, his stiff shoulders dropping down and the tautness in his back easing.

'He'll big himself up about that,' he chuckles. 'How they didn't use no pepper spray or nightsticks or ASP. They needed a can of fucking tear gas to bring him down. Like they were facing a rioting crowd.'

This is the news he's been waiting for. But Svensson hasn't finished.

The same morning, seventy-one miles away, Flow was asleep with his girlfriend in her flat near Nottingham. Outside in the dark, under the window of her bedroom, fifteen armed police in riot gear edged along the wall. They crouched like sprinters and pulled down the visors of their helmets. This was the Tactical Firearms Unit, specialists in breaking doors and rapid entry. The description of Flow in the briefing an hour earlier had unnerved some of them, and their blood was up. With them were two trained paramedics, also in riot gear and flameproof outfits. Usually it happens fast. Jemmy to open the door a fraction, slide in the high-powered hydraulic clamp, splinter the wooden door frame, then a well-built cop will lunge forward, swinging a heavy metal ramming block – the cops refer to it as 'the enforcer'. This time they have a hostage negotiator with them. They surround the house and he calls out Flow's name. Flow knows how this ends. He does not want his family to hear the door smashed down, feet thunder up the stairs as they shout, 'Armed police!' So he walks out calmly with his hands up.

Whippet shakes his head and whistles.

'Since you are serious about leaving the streets,' Svensson says, 'we'll rehouse you and your family outside Manchester. All you have to do is suggest somewhere. Any ideas?'

'Wrexham,' Whippet says. North Wales, fifty miles outside the city.

'I'll see what I can do.'

•

They move in August 2008. Whippet has two kids to support, and he takes a course to become a qualified mechanic. He doesn't venture back into Manchester. It begins to look like he wants to reform, to settle down. But Svensson is waiting and watching him. The conditions of his licence still apply. If he breaks them, Whippet will find himself caught in Svensson's web.

With Merlin and Flow in custody, the Murder Squad celebrate. Svensson is still uneasy. He drives out to his house in Buxton and goes riding out into the Peak District. In his garage he lifts weights. His ex-wife calls to ask about him taking his son for the weekend. On the way to his daughter's school he gets stuck in traffic and his mind returns to the trial. It will last months, cost millions and be one of the most significant in Manchester's gang history. Any witnesses will have to be protected around the clock, speak using voice-changers. He isn't convinced the current evidence is strong enough. The forensics aren't compelling. There's some DNA evidence, but it's thin. There is testimony from criminal associates about the guns being wrapped in plastic and stowed in a loft. But it isn't enough – he worries that Merlin and Flow won't be behind bars for long. They could launch an appeal for a retrial on this lack of evidence. Svensson needs to delve further back, look into other unsolved crimes. He wants the trial to prove they presided over a reign of murder. He needs Whippet.

Back in Wrexham, though, something strange has happened to Whippet. With the news of Merlin's arrest, a weight has fallen from his shoulders. He stops feeling fearful. Some of his old bravado and swagger is coming back. As he walks out he starts to roll his shoulders and hold himself a bit taller. That October, he comes off licence. Svensson starts to hear rumours. He sits in a betting shop in Fallowfield watching the greyhound track, waiting. A skinny guy, Femi, in an Adidas shell suit and cornrows, shuffles in. Svensson gives him a cigarette, and the two head to the door. Femi is happy to talk about Whippet. He still has the scars on his inner thigh from the last time he saw him.

'Bastard's out in Wrexham, is he?' Femi says. 'With his baby-mother and little ones.'

Svensson says nothing. News travels fast. When Svensson talks to these lads – it doesn't work so well with the girls – he likes to pepper the conversation with moments of uncomfortable silence. It makes them open up, blurt out something, anything, to fill the space. For the lads their lifestyle is a choice. Respect is important to them. An armed robber takes his ill-gotten gains, buys himself an Xbox and takes it home, but they want something more, some sort of recognition of what they are, of the risks they take. They drop the odd word. Sometimes it's 'Whippet'. Svensson says he will do everything in his power to protect them. They know if there's Personally Identifiable Information in court and the judge rules that the source has to be divulged then Svensson would rather that the job is dropped than give them away.

'I heard that he showed up at a party in Manchester,' the lad goes on.

'Yeah?' Svensson asks.

'Beat the shit out a drug-dealer. Nicked his wad,' the lad says.

Svensson nods, doesn't ask him to elaborate. This is enough for now. One or two of the younger uniform cops make the mistake of pushing it too early. Svensson took a colleague round to the house of a mother and girlfriend of a known gang member who was in jail. They sat down and had a brew with them. Svensson asked them about a recent birthday party, chewing the fat, chat chat chat. Soon they were outdoing each other to give him information about the players they knew. The young cop couldn't believe it. He sat there in silence soaking it up, his eyes darting between Svensson and the two women. Then he leant across the table, like it was an interrogation, and demanded, 'Right, what can you tell me about Whippet?' They all clammed up. 'I'm not a grass,' one snapped back, folding her arms. And Svensson was thinking, Fucking shut up. So he stopped taking his colleagues along.

Svensson is always looking for a chance to open up a new line of intelligence. A couple of days later, he's gliding through the rain when his radio crackles. There's a shooting in a pub car park. Other units are racing to the scene, so Svensson checks his watch and heads to Manchester Royal Infirmary's A&E. He stands outside the fire door, invisible in the dark, and peers in. There's two girls waiting. One, lanky and wide-eyed with an expensive weave, presses her lips together and rubs her eyebrow. Keeping up appearances, Svensson thinks. He waits and soon enough she comes outside for a smoke. She flips open her clamshell, glances over her shoulder and punches a number. Then she spies Svensson and rings off.

'You all right?' he says.

'Who the fuck are you?'

He offers her a cigarette. He has to think on his feet, there isn't one way of doing it. He knows that her Mr Wonderful is lying shot or stabbed in triage inside. This is a good moment to approach her as a source. She might tell him to fuck off, but they rarely do. In ten minutes he leaves with her address. Now he's into the area of field craft. It's about nurturing.

His sources of information always want something in return. The majority of informers are with the Covert Source Management Unit, and are put on contracts, receive payments. Svensson's sources all fall into another category. They are what is known as 'confidential contacts'. They don't get paid: what they usually want is a certain individual out of their lives for good. Or revenge for being raped or beaten.

The next day Svensson is sitting in his car smoking. He's watching the girl's house in Ashton Road, waiting for her to return. He is about to drive away when he sees her, round the corner, eyes down. She goes into number eight. Svensson pulls his collar up and walks down the row of terraced houses after her. Graffiti on the walls heralds all the 'fallen soldiers'. Grime music blares from an upstairs window. He recognizes the track as Dizzee Rascal's 'Suk My Dick'. These girls have bought into the image of gang life that rappers like 50 Cent or Akon present, where women are treated like princesses, driven in Aston Martins and Playboy cigarette speedboats and bought expensive presents. But the reality isn't like that. The reality is being chased by the police, ten men from the Tactical Support Group in visors and helmets charging in the front door of your council house at 5 a.m. Being beaten, being left alone for days.

Svensson knocks on a door and she opens it a crack.

'Chanelle?' he says softly.

She has a frozen, cowed look in her eyes. He has seen this look before.

'What do you want?'

'Is your mum in?'

She shakes her head. Soon they are talking over a cup of tea in the flat she shares with her mum. A lot of Svensson's skill is getting these informants to trust him enough to talk. And the women do trust him, they trust him to keep them out of danger. One or two even fall in love with him, or what they think he represents, which is the ability to keep them safe. His best informants are girlfriends. They sense something empathetic in Svensson. Today he won't press her for intel on the Gooch. Today's about building rapport.

'Why did you become a cop?' Chanelle asks him.

Svensson shrugs. This sort of thing comes easily to him. 'My dad was a violent man. He beat up my mother. To get out of the house I took up judo. The judo instructor was a cop.' Before he leaves he tells her to put his name in her phone as 'Jackie' and when she sends him a text to put a kiss at the end, so he knows it's her.

Svensson's driving his son back from school the first time Chanelle calls him. A bad moment, but he has to take it. The traffic is hairy so he tells his son he's going to put something on speaker phone and he has to keep silent. The boy's mother and stepdad are both cops so he knows the drill.

'While Aaron's in hospital, I haven't got no one to protect me,' she says. Her voice is ragged and choked, like she's been crying. Svensson stays silent and glances at his son. The boy sits and listens and says nothing. He is twelve.

'This dealer friend of his comes round every week now,' she says. 'He's a fucking animal. I wish someone would merk him.'

The dealer visits Chanelle on a weekly basis, off his head, and assaults her in front of her kid sister. Svensson grits his teeth, listens.

'I just want it to stop. I want him out of my life.'

When she rings off, the boy looks up at his dad. Svensson feels his fury subside. His son is far too young to overhear that kind of detail.

'Mum just interviews people,' his son says. 'My stepdad just drives round in a Panda car. But you're Ross Kemp.'

He spends the next few weeks building Chanelle as a source. She only knows about low-level Gooch footsoldiers, but she becomes part of the web, the one he's built so that anything that gets caught on the edges about Merlin and the Gooch and what they are doing and where he is will come back to him via different routes. One evening when he's on a late he has a breakthrough. An informant rings him with Merlin's mobile number. Svensson switches phones, calls a colleague and slowly recites the number.

'I want you to check this number from 4 p.m. to 7 p.m. last 17th June,' he says. 'Locations, whereabouts. Try to track a route for the caller. Also check cell-site location from 2 p.m. onwards on 27th July. Tell me where he went – Moss Side, Cheadle Heath area, Chorlton.'

The analyst immediately recognizes the times and locations of the two murders.

'Whose phone is that?' he asks.

'The bad wizard.'

Mobile-phone computers keep tabs on the antennae through which mobile signals are routed for billing purposes. These are called cell-sites and they can pinpoint, via triangulation, the location of the caller at any given time.

'OK, Anders. Anything else?'

Svensson thinks for a moment.

'Yeah. Tell me significant periods that he doesn't call Flow's number.'

'That he doesn't call?'

'They usually call each other several times a day. If they're not calling, then chances are they're together.'

2: Before

Flow waits by the window, silently watching Michael. It's 2005 and he's just out of jail. Michael, a retired cop with a silver peak of hair, checks on him as he glances through Flow's file. He's been released early for being a model prisoner and seems to be turning things around for himself. At all times he seems calm and soft-spoken. He has to shade his eyes, but makes out Flow's muscular outline, his big shaven head. Broken blinds clatter, trucks rumble by the window. He puts a cap on his pen. When he looks up again Flow is right on top of him, looking down. Michael didn't even hear him move. He hands Michael a polystyrene cup of coffee. Michael leans back in his chair, with a practised ease of manner acquired from years in a desk job.

'One Gooch lad has stopped going to school because he has to walk through Doddington territory to get there,' he tells Flow. Michael works out of this office trying to turn ex-offenders and young lads away from gang crime. He feels paternal towards these lads, whose fathers have disappeared or are at best 'McDonald's dads', taking them out for a cheeseburger once in a blue moon. He has brought his own daughter up with old-fashioned discipline. She's an IT expert with the Royal Signals. 'So we provided a taxi for him, so he could keep up his schoolwork,' he says proudly.

Flow nods thoughtfully, trying to concentrate. He knows all about Michael's taxis. The gang members have been pulling the wool over Michael's eyes for some time now, taking cabs across town when they want to, claiming it's for a 'school project'. One Gooch lad told Flow it was 'the best cab company in the city'.

'We work with the council and youth workers,' Michael goes on, gesturing to two people who sit next to him. 'Giving them help with jobs or rehousing them. Loads of different partners all work together on this.'

Michael knows his work has its limitations. Even though he is retired, the kids are wary that he's just mining them for intelligence to feed back to the XCalibre cops. They prefer to talk to their own, older ex-gang members. This is why he needs people like Flow, because he is respected. He stops talking. Another truck thunders by, sending ripples through their coffee. The 'Youngers' only listen to someone like Flow, who is high up in the gang hierarchy. He would be a valuable asset to have. A major coup for Michael. So much money has been poured into this scheme that it can't be allowed to fail.

'If you could talk to them about what prison is really like,' Michael says, looking Flow in the eye. 'How you decided to make the switch. And leave the streets.'

'Easy,' Flow says, nodding slowly. To him it sounds like a piece of piss. All he has to do is keep this nonsense up for a couple of months and he'll be a free man. They look pleased with his answer. The meeting breaks up. Michael takes his jacket from behind the door and escorts Flow downstairs where his probation officer is waiting for him.

On the landing he remembers something and swivels round to face Flow.

'Can you come in tomorrow?' he asks quietly.

'Why's that, then?' Flow asks, narrowing his eyes and cocking his head.

'Because the police want to speak to you, from Manchester.'

Flow's smile sinks away and his eyes darken. The blood is thudding in his temples.

'Who?' he says.

'Well, it'll be someone from XCalibre,' Michael replies with a shrug.

'Svensson?' he asks, scowling. 'I'm not talking to that fucker.'

'It's not him,' Michael says, growing slightly uneasy.

He is newly aware of how thick Flow's bull neck is, how his shoulders and upper arms present a wall of muscle. Flow's eyes bore right through him. Michael adjusts his gaze.

'You'll be here?'

'Yeah, course I will,' Flow says.

Then he walks out of the door and never comes back. That's why at the start of 2006 Flow is on the run, and Svensson is determined to hunt him down.

•

Moss Side is not, as outsiders think, a mass of soulless tower blocks. It is rows of two-storey terraced houses, with gardens. The streets are etched on Svensson's memory as he cruises past a house where they recovered several rifles and handguns and a car where they did an armed strike, officers surrounding it with weapons out. He slows down, eases into second and scours the dark outer fringes of Alexandra Park, looking for silhouetted figures darting between the blackened trees. In the daytime the park sees joggers, dog-walkers and families feeding the ducks. At night it is used as a short cut by Gooch gang members who want to avoid venturing into Moss Side. The Fallowfield Man Dem, a Gooch affiliate, often cut through it too. It can kick off if they are spotted by the opposition. Svensson strains to see one shadow moving in the distance. The trail on Flow has run dry. The only intelligence Svensson has so far is that he is selling drugs in the Gorton area, robbing other drug-dealers.

He tries to put himself in Flow's shoes. What would his next move be? He pictures Flow in prison, getting chummy with someone on his wing. The other inmate knows of Flow's reputation as a brutal enforcer. He also knows that you can only grow and control your drug business through extreme violence. Flow can dispense it fast and efficiently, without thinking twice. The associate tells Flow that he could use his muscle in their burgeoning drug operation in Gorton. Gorton is close to his old haunts, but far enough for him not to be recognized on the street. But it is only when Flow is on the run that he returns to the offer. Any act he commits must remain under the radar, and Gorton fits this.

Flow hears rumours from local kids of the faint smell of cannabis coming from a deserted building. He stakes it out early in the morning. Two tired Vietnamese guys arrive.

Look as rough as a robber's dog. Illegals looking after the house. The windows have been blacked out. Flow returns at night with his tools. He snaps the lock open and moves down the shabby corridor. The electricity meter has a nail banged into it to divert current without alerting the main grid and strong white light comes from under the door. He grips his gun and creeps in. There are rows of plants under the glare of hydroponic lights. He hacks them down, clears them out and bundles them into black bin liners. He will be able to sell them on for £3,000 on the streets. It will not be reported.

Flow can establish contacts with a buyer quite easily. He is used to commanding respect from his local foot-soldiers, but these new kids in Gorton don't recognize him. After only four years away, the place is full of fresh, younger faces. They are as young as thirteen, all trying to step up and make a name for themselves. He does not go back to Moss Side in case someone sights him, but here in Gorton he can walk and people don't even know who he is.

'Where you from?' one of the kids asks him, as he hands over money for the bin liners.

'Prison,' Flow replies.

'Who's your general?'

'Merlin.'

'Merlin and Flow? You know them two?'

Right away the kid is babbling out a story about Flow, without even knowing who he's talking to. Flow smiles but says nothing. It suits him. His one of these names that exist in the ether, legends of the past. He will just bide his time until Merlin comes out and then they'll cook up some plans together. He is happy for now just to sit tight, make a bit of money.

As the year goes on, the intelligence Svensson is getting back tells him very little about Flow's movements. He knows the young kids don't recognize him; he too has noticed the age group dropping, younger and younger kids dealing in the street, stepping up to be foot-soldiers. And now the US names are coming in too – Old Trafford Cripz, Moss Side Bloods. Svensson hates computers but these kids are all using the latest gadgets, filming sexual assaults on their smartphones, uploading brutal hazings onto YouTube, writing taunts on the Facebook pages of deceased teenage rivals. What they all know of Flow and Merlin is the folklore of how they were arrested in 2001. Like something out of a Tarantino movie, they were relaxing in body armour, surrounded by a bevy of gang girls, weaponry and ammunition, including a Skorpion sub-machine gun. They even had their jeans pockets altered to make them like gun holsters. They are like heroes to the kids. Later, when the police photos of Flow and Merlin went up, people alleged family connections to them. Flow and Merlin can strut about with their armoury of weapons, but Svensson smiles when he hears this story. It was an anonymous tip-off that led to the arrest. 'Never did find out who made that anonymous call,' he thinks to himself, grinning.

On Saturday 9 September 2006, fifteen-year-old Jessie James is murdered in Broadfield Park. The city is in uproar. Not even a gang member, but brutally gunned down on his bike. Every cop is desperate to solve this one and extra police are working round the clock trying to find the killer. It's the fourth shooting that year. All the pressure is on the force to try something new. Loads of damaging headlines. XCalibre, the new gang unit, is created in October and Svensson, with his powerful intelligence network, is drafted in. The heat on the murder does not let up. Every month the papers run a photo of the kid, a mention of his school record. Every day in Svensson's office they're all in black body armour and T-shirts, working the phones, crumpled greasy cartons on the desk.

Svensson scopes out the park. It's a small, dark, deserted square with thick tall boles, overshadowed by a gym building where the gang members work out. He scours the perimeter. There is no one around. What actually happened here? He spins the wheel and eases the Q-car, lights off, through a narrow opening in the railings and into the park. Twigs crack under the wheels as it rolls forward along the path to the centre. He comes to rest at the spot near where the boy went down. A dark, lonely place to die. By dawn the next day it was chaos. Suited-up SOCO officers with tents combing the crime scene. Blue-and-white-tape cordon flickering from tree to tree. Then the media circus. Camera crews and unshaven reporters in long coats camping out on the family's doorstep. The poor mother shut inside. Amid arrangements for a public wake, between the interviews and press statements, trying to find space to grieve.

Now Svensson peers through his windscreen in the darkness. No one is even aware his car is there, its black silhouette merges with the trees. He tries to imagine the scene that night. There is a low wall behind a mound, an almost military piece of cover for a crouching gunman. The ballistics report suggests that this is where the shooter started. He hails the kid from behind that wall. The boy edges nearer. Does he know the killer or is he stepping up to some kind of taunt? It is after midnight, not a good time to be out on your bike if you are a teenager. As he cycles up he is shot three times with a semi-automatic handgun. A witness said that he saw flashes of gunfire moving backwards, as if the shooter was firing on the move like a retreating soldier. He could still hit his target. That puts him a cut above most of the kids out there. Most of them shoot themselves in the foot while stationary. If they ever use a Mac-10 it's like a high-pressure hose, spraying all over the place. This gunman knew what he was doing. Then there is the business of the final shot. Someone stood over Jessie as he lay on the ground and fired into his chest. Who does that to a fifteen-year-old kid? This man was a stone-cold killer. Svensson stares out as the wind threshes the matted foliage.

Jessie's innocent. His mother denies there's any link to his older brother Elmo, serving seven years for robbery and possession of an imitation firearm. Svensson went to interview him in prison. Elmo shook his head and moralized.

'I'm not the sort of person who goes around threatening people with firearms.'

'What were you convicted of, Elmo?' Svensson asked softly.

'Robbery.'

'What did you use to threaten the victim?'

'A gun.'

'Well, then you are the kind of person who threatens people with firearms,' he said. Elmo glowered back at him.

'Go easy on Elmo,' another officer tells Svensson later. 'He's part of Jessie's family. He's a victim.'

'He's an armed robber, that's what he is.'

Svensson turns the car around and eases out through the railings. He heads towards Fallowfield, drives past some kids wearing black RIP T-shirts with a photo of the recently killed teenager. He is irritated by this current trend. It's all part of the fashion, the lifestyle choice of becoming a gang member. Most of these kids probably didn't even know the lad. He slows down until they level with his window.

'Mates of his, are you?' Svensson calls out.

'Used to know him back in the day,' says one cockily, flicking his fingers at Svensson.

'Back in the day? He was only fucking fifteen when he died.'

Svensson finishes his shift, drops off the police hire car. He punches in the code and the heavy metal bars slowly ease open. He sprints up the stairs, through swing doors, another door code. He can see an L-shape where the numbers have been worn away. The office is deserted. It smells of sweat. A muffin sits in a plastic Asda box. Body armour is slung over chairs. The wall of gang members stares down at him balefully.

He makes himself scrabble through the daily log. Svensson is no fan of all the paperwork the job now demands, all the computers: the latest is that he can't even write out a statement unless he is trained on some new IT system.

By the time he heads home it is 2.30 a.m. He has to clear his mind of criminals and so he takes a beer from the fridge and leafs through an old copy of *Top Gear*. One day he will buy himself a Caterham, he thinks. Then he takes off his shoes and goes upstairs, showers and creeps in beside his wife. She is already asleep with her body turned away from him towards the wall. She wears the silver lace silk slip he bought for her on her birthday several years ago. Her hair has fallen over her face, which is buried in the duvet. Svensson's lower back sears with pain as he climbs in next to her.

He is lost in a dream. He approaches a glass box. It has black bars through it like a cell. Inside it there's an armed man. As he gets closer he can see the man is Flow. He has a gun trained on someone on the floor. He is threatening the person. Svensson is outside, trying to get into the glass box. He is trying to smash it but it isn't breaking. Flow isn't even looking at him. He is just doing what he is doing. He beats harder on the side of the box. Whoever is lying there is dead.

He wakes with a start. His heart racing and the room is silent except for his wife's breathing, deep and steady. He looks at the clock on the bedside table. It's 5.30 a.m. Outside he can hear a fierce wind rattling in the trees. Since Flow has been on the run Svensson keeps having the same dream. The dream repeats itself. He can't get at Flow. It's a continuous frustration. He gets up and goes downstairs, sits under the lamp and leafs through a school essay his daughter has written about heroes. He expects it to be about a teen pop idol or Miley Cyrus, but the title is 'My Dad'.

As he stares at the words he notices that his hand is trembling. He watches the paper flimmer and realizes he needs to slow down. They tease him in the office, that those two, Merlin and Flow, are an obsession for him. Particularly Flow. He will not sleep properly until Flow's back in jail. Svensson worked murder inquiries from 1997 to '99 where Flow was a 'person of interest' to the police. He was called in for questioning. One victim was killed by a close-up headshot. Flow was released due to lack of evidence. The killer was never found. It made Svensson angry that he is still on the streets. He will not be at peace as long as he is out there doing what he does. It's only a matter of time before he kills again.

The next day Svensson drives out on the ring road to the south-east of Manchester. He turns off and keeps going until he reaches Kimberley, outside Nottingham. It is an affluent area compared to the Alexandra Park Estate. Like Didsbury. He stops opposite a row of terraced houses, crosses over and rings the bell. A pretty blonde girl answers the door. She nods at him without smiling. Inside two small girls are watching telly.

'Hello, Kerry,' Svensson says.

'He's not been here,' she sighs.

Svensson raises an eyebrow, offers her a cigarette. Kerry is not the usual gang girl. She knew Flow when they were kids. She was next to Flow's brother Dean when he was killed. Kerry gave evidence, with Flow's permission, and was moved out to Kimberley with her identity changed. He feels sorry for her, because she does love Flow. She is not one of those girls who find it all attractive and exciting, who come from a decent background, who live in houses in Stockport.

'Look, have you seen him, not seen him?'

'Try his other fucking women. Try that Sonia.'

He cheats a bit. Not much. There's a girl he stays with up there. But otherwise he doesn't treat Kerry badly, never batters her, never threatens her. He just isn't there. Svensson thinks Flow cares about his family. He is one of those who never takes it home. It is pointless searching Kerry's house because he never brings any guns or drugs back, never has gangster mates round. You'd like Flow as your neighbour. He is a normal quiet guy. He doesn't have parties.

You'll get certain gang members going round the bars in town giving it biggun. Flow doesn't do that. The difference between him and Whippet is that Whippet needs to bulk himself up, take steroids and brag the whole time. Whippet's violent because for him it's a power thing. Whereas Flow is more of a man, at ease with who he is.

Svensson stands with Kerry on the doorstep and looks into her sad brown eyes. He grinds his cigarette into the pavement. He needs to make her relax, so that her guard will drop and she will let something slip. He asks her about Kimberley. She tells him that she'll take the kids into Nottingham for a special day out. He talks about his young daughter's birthday party and asks her about her kid. This works. He can see Flow's girls over her shoulder.

'She's started having nightmares now. And she doesn't sleep well.'

'What's she having nightmares about?'

'Oh, nothing. But it's not helping her.'

Svensson flashes her a look. 'What's not helping her, Kerry?'

She starts to chew on her lower lip and cannot look him in the eye.

'Flow's not been here, has he?'

At that moment he knows the truth. It doesn't matter what she says now, he can read her, the way she folds her arms, tucks her hair behind her ear. Over the years he has learnt to trust his intuition. He keeps the same calm, soft tone, trying not to alert her that he has caught her out. Then five minutes later, when her little girl calls for her, he slips away to his car. It is only three miles back to the city. He turns the dial to a pirate-radio station playing grime.

Back at headquarters he sits on the desk behind two colleagues who are typing up forms. They swivel their chairs round to listen. He tells them his hunch.

'All you have to do is sit on the house and he'll call.'

'Kimberley is off our patch, mate,' another cop tells him, leaning back and folding his hands behind his head. 'You'll have to go through Nottinghamshire constabulary.'

Svensson eases into a spare desk and rummages around for the number. A younger officer, tapping efficiently on her keyboard, eyes his noisy rustling and pulls the number for Nottingham's Force Intelligence Bureau out of the computer, scribbles it on a Post-it and slaps it on his screen. They exchange a smile. He calls Nottingham and gets through to a DS.

'We need your help to bring in a wanted man,' he says. 'We need to survey a girl's flat long enough to trap him.'

The DS says nothing, as if he is distracted or writing something down.

'Can't report a full team,' then, after a pause, 'it'll cost too much.'

Svensson starts to tell him Flow's criminal history.

'We've got our own criminals,' the DS says.

Svensson rubs his forehead with his fingertips. He glances at the female detective and rolls his eyes. More fucking red tape. In his mind the clock is ticking. Merlin is still inside and he has to find Flow before he is released. Together they are far too dangerous.

'We'll even go and do it ourselves,' Svensson protests. 'Our office will go and camp in Nottingham for a week and he'll come. He's having contact with the kids.'

The DS says he will see what he can do and will call Svensson back. Svensson sits and waits for the call. He takes out a folder and begins leafing through an investigation into arms coming into Manchester from Turkey and Central Europe. A man in a lock-up in Ordsall is converting Russian Baikal 9mm semi-automatic handguns and selling them in 'kits' with ammunition. It's like a supermarket, he thinks. His phone rings. It's the DS from Nottingham.

'I spoke to the lad who pulls the purse-strings here,' says the DS. 'He says no.'

Svensson closes his eyes and says nothing.

'We can offer you something,' the DS continues. 'We'll put a camera car outside his house.'

'A camera car?' Svensson sighs. 'They may as well put a Panda car outside his house.'

'No one is in it,' the DS protests. 'A lot of them cars have about six cameras.'

'He lives down a quiet road. If there is a car suddenly on his road, he'll clock it. Flow is too switched on.'

'If you look at them you wouldn't see it.'

So the first camera car is parked outside the flat of Flow's girl in Kimberley. Usually they have one camera out the side, one in the doorbox, from behind the grille. This one has a refrigerator thing on top of it. The camera is inside. It only has one camera. They park the car up. It starts recording pictures. It is there for about twenty minutes and then a pair of boxer shorts is put over the camera.

•

March 2007 arrives. Still no sign of Flow, and Merlin is due for release. Svensson walks into the station, his head bowed against driving rain. An icy wind cuts his fingers and knuckles to the marrow. Black crows peck at a torn sack. The trees' leafless branches are sharp like snapped chicken bones. This is the moment Svensson is dreading. He looks up at the wall of A4 photos of gang members, arranged in a military hierarchy. It runs the length of the main operations room. At the top are the faces of Merlin and Flow, and on Merlin's face is a yellow Post-it with the word 'Licence'.

Beneath Merlin are the names of Trench, Pacman and others. Last month Trench launched an attack on the Doddington. It was like the Wild West. He raided their territory with a cohort of ten kids on bikes. He and his lieutenant, Miller, rode out in body armour. Once they would have been on horses, carving up the cattle trail, brandishing silver Peacemakers. Now, they are twenty-first-century urban barbarians, with mountain bikes, body armour and semi-automatic pistols, their territorial sorties over a few streets of high-density housing. Trench, a wiry trigger-happy character who dreamed of taking Merlin's mantle, did not succeed. They came up against concerted gunfire from the other end of the street and his kids on bikes fled. His lieutenant was hit twice in the legs. Trench limped to a nearby ambulance. A bullet fell on the floor as the paramedic tended his injury. Svensson did the interview himself.

'How did you get a bullet in your foot?' he asked.

'I was returning fire.'

'How were you standing, like this?'

Svensson lifted one foot out in front of him pointing a two-fingered gun at his toe, and accused him of shooting himself in the foot. The bullet is straight down through his shoe. They laughed at the time, but Merlin will not be able to let this stand. The Gooch have been made to look weak. This botched raid has seen the young Doddington high-fiving each other for weeks.

The public were shaken by Trench's shoot-out but that is nothing to what Merlin is capable of. Svensson knows that he has one last chance to try to keep the streets safe. Merlin's up for a series of hearings before a panel of cops, council and probation officers. If he breaks his licence conditions he can face a severe sentence. But smart criminals know how to play the panel. Merlin is smarter than most. Svensson goes in knowing it will be tough for him to convince them. He looks at Michael in his bright-coloured fleece and Timberlands, like he's off hiking in Ambleside. He's a nice guy but he's no detective. They are laughing over the morning newspaper. He takes his seat.

'Merlin is the most significant gang release the city has ever seen,' he says. Faces round the table stare at him. There's a faint burning smell from a glass pot of coffee as it simmers on an old plastic machine. 'If he isn't managed properly then people will die.'

'He has asked to go to a funeral which is in his exclusion zone,' says a senior officer. 'We've decided to keep an eye on him at the funeral.'

'You're wasting your time,' Svensson says, closing his eyes and shaking his head. There are always funerals to go to. Gang-bangers are being shot or riding motorbikes into stationary trucks. This is just an excuse for Merlin to meet a contact, make a move. 'You're absolutely wasting your time.'

The surveillance unit take up their observation positions discreetly at the funeral. They deploy eight cars in the unit, tucked away in back streets, staying in contact over different radio channels. Merlin arrives. He appears not to have noticed them. Between the eight cars they keep reporting Merlin's position over different channels, easily keeping an eyeball. Then, halfway through the funeral, they lose him. He disappears. Twenty minutes later he is back again.

After the funeral Svensson goes to see Merlin. He stares Svensson down, tracking him with his whole head, the eyes face front. It's as if he knows the channels of Svensson's mind. When he lets his eyes drop first, Merlin breaks into an ugly smile, his widely spaced teeth rimmed by a wiry beard. He can see how arrogantly Merlin plays the game, his unshakable confidence.

'One more thing. How's Flow?' Svensson asks at the end.

'Who?' Merlin replies.

'Fuck off.'

'Why would Flow come and see me? You follow me everywhere.'

'I don't follow you everywhere.'

'Your people do.'

'Don't flatter yourself, Merlin.'

'They followed me to that funeral.'

'How do you know?'

Merlin reels off a list of cars. He'd clocked five out of eight. Svensson knows that in the twenty minutes he was gone Merlin would have got his hands on something.

At the second meeting, Merlin's probation officer is the first to speak.

'Probation are encouraged that he has found a job in a friend's shop.'

Svensson stares into the middle distance. 'What did he say?' he asks drily.

'He came to us and said: "There's a guy who has a super-market up in Eccles who is looking for a shelf-stacker. This mate of mine who delivers milk has mentioned that he knows me. I can start work straight away." '

Clever bastard, Svensson thinks. Merlin knows that if he starts working his conditions have to be relaxed.

'That is encouraging, then,' says another one, looking impressed.

'His licence conditions shouldn't change,' Svensson insists. 'Nothing about what is being said makes any sense.'

'We have to give him something,' says the probation officer. 'He's got himself a job.'

Svensson lets out an involuntary laugh. He can't believe what he is hearing.

'Let's think about this,' he says, throwing his arms out wide. 'I run a shop and the guy I buy milk off says to me, "A mate of mine is in a bail hostel – can he come and stack shelves for you? He's been in prison for possession of a machine gun." '

The probation team don't seem to think this is unusual. Michael looks round the table and then directly at Svensson. He raises his hand for emphasis.

'Anders, how will this look if we don't reward ex-offenders for finding work after release?' he says. 'It's difficult enough to convince a sixteen-year-old lad who comes out with no qualifications to become a plasterer. "This is what you'll do. You'll be picked up at seven o'clock in the morning, you'll work all day long and you'll get £120 at the end of it. Then in the future you'll be able to have your own business." Then he sees his mate, who's got girls hanging off him, gold hanging off him, doesn't get out of bed till lunchtime.'

Another twenty minutes of discussion, the others start collecting their papers together. Svensson realizes they have made their minds up. He goes to the door and puts on his jacket.

This is a disaster. He starts to make surprise visits to the shop, but Merlin is never there. He is always 'at the cash and carry'.

'OK, I'll fucking wait for him,' Svensson says. He stands in the doorway and lights a cigarette. When Merlin appears he nods towards a shelf. There is a load of Guinness stacked on a wall with one can of Carlsberg in the middle.

'You've not stacked them very well, have you?' Svensson says.

'I'm not here to stack shelves,' Merlin says in a menacing tone.

'Oh?' Svensson says drily. 'What's your position now, then?'

'Till security.'

The rumour is that Merlin is there as protection: there has been a murder at the supermarket over an ongoing dispute between gangs up in Bolton. The bloke who owns the shop has bought a flat near the centre for £26,000 cash and he lets Merlin use it. Like you do with your shelf-stackers, Svensson thinks bitterly. Normal rent is £700 a month but he lets him have it for £300. He fully furnishes it, but it is all Merlin's stuff.

It's been three months and on a daily basis Merlin is playing the game. He's going to work, going to the gym, going to the bail hostel. He's a model resident at the hostel, shares a room with a guy. Even though he's in his flat in the day. And so on 13th June despite Svensson's opposition Merlin has his licence conditions eased again. He can roam the streets. An Audi with tinted windows has been hired for his release. He gathers his elders round him.

The Gooch are seen as weak, they tell him. He hears how Trench's incursion was met with rapid return fire from the Young Doddington, with Trench and his henchman being shot twice. Now their street general is back. Trench has found a place to stash weapons. Gang girls live with their parents and are no good for this. He has found someone who is not going to be curious. Sandy Mitchell is a heroin and crack user who used to buy drugs off them, and they reckon she is so out of it that she won't notice they are coming to and fro with bags of heavy objects. Her attic becomes the place to store all their guns, including a machine gun, wrapped in plastic.

In the early evening of 17th June, Merlin is just prowling around in the car with his lieutenants, Trench and Pacman. Beside them they have dark clothing, balaclavas and weapons. Merlin sits in the back behind tinted glass. These are his streets and he will claim them back. At around six fifteen a Mégane drives past them. Merlin glowers at the driver and narrows his eyes. He is familiar.

'Longsight Crew. Right next to us.'

Merlin calls Flow. He tells him that there is a guy who is in the Longsight Crew, who just had the misfortune to drive past him in Levenshulme. Flow swears through his teeth. They are the ones he still blames for his brother's shooting. He rings off. It is six twenty. Merlin calls him back. Why doesn't he just ice him right now? He's driving around in a red Mégane, easy to spot.

'Take the fucker out,' Flow says softly.

Merlin gives the order to his lieutenants. They pull down their balaclavas and pull on black gloves. They pull the safety catches back from their weapons. Merlin calls Flow again. They are ready. They're going to draw up level at the lights and fire through the window. Flow calls back at six thirty-one. Merlin is near Bickerdike Court. The Renault Mégane floats by and is captured on CCTV.

Antoine Gayle, twenty-four, has that afternoon taken a mate to the Job Centre and visited his girlfriend. He's just become a father, weeks before. Then he's been back to the cul-de-sac in Longsight with red-brick terraced houses where he lives with his parents. Now he is heading towards the centre of Manchester with two friends. Calvin in the front passenger seat. Ryan in the rear.

As his car slows down to turn left into Dennison Road, a silver Audi pulls along its offside. Witnesses later describe seeing three people inside, all wearing dark clothing. A rear passenger window winds down and a gun is pointed at close range by a male with a cloth covering his face and wearing gloves. Seven shots are fired. Three of them hit Antoine. Calvin is also hit, by a bullet which passes through his right hand. Antoine's hands slacken on the wheel and he slumps forward. His body weight nudges the steering round and the Renault crashes into an electrical box at the side of the road. The killers speed off in the silver Audi in the direction of the city centre.

Members of the public rush to help. One calls 999. Another tries to stem the blood-flow. Time is critical. An ambulance from Manchester Royal Infirmary races to the scene. Paramedics fight to keep Antoine Gayle alive. One shot hit his right upper arm. Another bullet went into his right upper back near his shoulder. The third penetrated his chest. The first two shots are puncture wounds, but it is the third bullet that has done the most damage: it has injured his liver, heart and lungs and causes massive internal bleeding. On his arrival at Manchester Royal Infirmary, Antoine is pronounced dead. He was just out for a drink. His week-old daughter will learn of her father only from stories and photos. His mum hears the news while she's still at work and collapses.

Some distance away Merlin takes off his balaclava, calmly exhilarated. Later that evening he checks into the bail hostel and signs in. He has not broken his curfew, is still working as a shelf-stacker and is the perfect hostel resident.

News of the killing spreads through the gang community. A gang girl hears it and says she is going to buy some cigarettes, slips out to the shop. She looks behind her. No one is following. She crosses through some railings into a small park. It's empty. She takes up her phone and presses the number that says 'Jackie'.

Svensson is at home in Buxton when the call comes in. He has left work at 4 p.m. and is watching TV with his wife. He recognizes the ringtone as for informants, and darts into the kitchen to answer it.

'There's been a shooting,' the girl tells him. 'A drive-by. Do you know who did it?'

She is worried that the killer is her boyfriend. He says he will find out what he can. When he returns to the living room, his wife doesn't look up from the TV. When his phone is going and there are women calling him, it can get difficult. The way these gang girls live, when they get someone like Svensson who does not abuse them, they phone him at ridiculous times of the day. One girl phoned him last week at two o'clock in the morning. She'd just found out that her boyfriend in prison was threatening to kill her, that one of her family members was speaking to him and passing information about her life. She was hysterical. The first person she decided to phone was Svensson. He's not a father-figure or brother. He's like a mate. They forget what he does for a living.

Svensson phones a lad on duty at the office.

'Got a call,' he says. Then he checks himself. It is eight thirty. The shooting was at six forty-five. He is not supposed to be running informants: they are all looked after centrally now. He quickly covers his tracks. 'From a concerned member of the community. Said a lad was shot in a drive-by. Do you know who it was?'

'It's Antoine.'

'Is he dead?' Svensson asks.

'Yeah.'

Svensson knows in his bones that this is a Merlin and Flow assassination. Antoine Gayle has links to the Longsight Crew, who killed Flow's brother. A drive-by is their style of hit. He goes back in and sits down heavily next to his wife.

Whippet once said to Svensson that going to the bar and ordering a Coke is the same emotional height that Merlin would reach when killing someone. It just doesn't bother him in the slightest. The process you go through of ordering the Coke, putting your money on the bar – that's about as excited as he gets. He could have sat there with the financial backing he had, bought guns, given them to the kids, and said go and do it. And they would have done it for him, because he had that charisma. But he loves it.

Merlin and Flow are like brothers, from growing up together. Whippet was the first one selling drugs. Then Merlin started and within four weeks he'd made four times the profit. He's a smart, ruthless entrepreneur. If he ran a legitimate business he'd be a millionaire.

'I fucking told them,' Svensson says. He does not need to explain.

At Longsight station the next morning the investigation is already underway. The ballistics expert crawls around and picks up in her tweezers seven cartridge cases in Anson Road, which leads to the city centre. All are confirmed as fired from the same 9mm gun. In addition, they recover seven fired bullets of the same calibre as the cartridge cases. Three are from Antoine Gayle's body, one from his clothing and three from the Renault Mégane itself: one from the rubber seal of the driver's window, one from the front passenger seat, and one from inside the front passenger door. These were all fired from the same gun, a converted Russian Baikal self-loading pistol.

The silver Audi has vanished off the face of the earth. It was a ghost car. It is never seen again.

Svensson goes out to gather intelligence on the Monday. It is the funeral of Delroy Minton, a Gooch member and associate of Trench's. Delroy was killed on a motorbike with a wrap of ten rocks of crack up his arse. By the time they put him in the ground he is in seven body bags. Svensson tails the cortège from Fallowfield up to Gorton cemetery and goes to the church on the way. A queue of cars form behind Svensson as they come out. Svensson mentally takes note of who they are.

Suddenly an Audi RS4 sharks into the queue and he recognizes it as belonging to one of Merlin's associates, Shredder. Four in it, windows up. He's sure two of them are Merlin and Flow. It just jumps into the cortège. Svensson is desperate to get closer, but he is jammed in now at the head. He cranes to watch the cars ease, one by one, into the cemetery. When the Audi goes in it drives right up to the grave. The windows open. They don't get out. They are safer in the car, as they aren't sure what capability the cops have. The light catches something as it is thrown into the grave. The windows come up again. A chill runs through Svensson as he realizes what he has witnessed. They've just got rid of the gun that killed Antoine, he thinks. Who would look for it there? He would never get a warrant to go digging up a grave. It is a classic Merlin sleight of hand: Delroy has died and they've put one in the ground for him. What better place to get rid of the gun? There's so many people round the grave. They'd have wrapped it. Part of him wants to run up there and jump in and scrabble round and find it, but if he is wrong the outcry would be deafening.

His knuckles are white where he grips the wheel. He is aching for another cigarette. He waits for an opportunity to stop the car: Flow is wanted, he can't associate with Merlin; Merlin is in his exclusion zone. But no senior officer is going to say, 'Get that car while it's in the cemetery.' Svensson notices that just outside there's a little crossroads so that the cars are coming out bit by bit. The Audi only has to nudge past the entrance and he can take them. But as if sensing something, it stops and waits. When the way is clear it takes off like a fucking bullet.

In the incident room on Tuesday, Svensson looks over a DVD of the funeral. Merlin's lieutenants are there: Shredder, Deven, Fleet, Pacman.

He can see all the elements of the murder investigation coming together, but he is frustrated. A detective inspector is directing a team who are inputting everything into a bank of computers. He reels off the actions, allocating them to cops. Highest priority is tracing the car. They wait for the results of the post-mortem. This is all about gathering evidence now: it needs to hold up in the court room.

Then on Wednesday Merlin does one from the bail hostel. He goes out in the morning and never comes back. They are both on the run now.

'That just fucking confirms it,' Svensson angrily tells the team. They don't need to be sitting down and saying, 'Right, Antoine's Longsight Crew so it's likely to be Gooch, who's active in the Gooch at the moment?' Svensson has been getting phone calls since Sunday throwing people in for it. All Merlin's group are named. The first ones Svensson hears are Trench and Pacman. Apparently Pacman is seen disposing of a pair of gloves. Svensson wonders if Pacman was given the order by Merlin, whether Pacman was the one who pulled the trigger. It's too early to say.

It's down to the SIO to draw up a list of suspects. His focus is also on managing how information is passed on to the *Manchester Evening News* and members of the press. They have to be careful not to alert any suspects early on.

The others make progress on the Audi.

'What do we have?'

'We have a partial reg.'

'Two partial regs.'

'We know it is an Audi A8.'

Through the Police National Computer they do a speculative search and it throws up three silver Audi A8s. They work through to try to establish which one it is. Finding the advert. Where it appeared. Who sold it. Soon they discover it was bought in Luton.

There are eight syndicates, murder investigation teams. There are two that specialize in gang-related killings. Initially each team has forty detectives and support staff. Most of the intelligence comes at the beginning. There are people out gathering CCTV from the murder scene all the way through the city. Once they pick it up people try to view it as quickly as they can. They know the time – six forty-five – so can narrow it down. They plot the route all the way through the city. It's manpower-intensive. To get footage of the Audi on Deansgate heading that way, moving up Deansgate with it to find if there are cameras up there, looking at more footage to try to pick it up again. The team tracks the car all the way through the city up to Cheetham Hill. Svensson looks long and hard at each frame on the chance that there might be a picture of who's inside. He is struck by one shot. The killers' car alongside Gayle's car when the killing is taking place.

Svensson prefers to work the streets. The split-second decisions, reading people, drawing them out. This is what he is good at. On the morning of Antoine Gayle's funeral his phone rings again. It is one of his girl informants.

'A neighbour told me they were out looking for body armour,' she says.

You can buy body armour on the Internet, you used to

be able to buy it in Army & Navy stores. They were looking for other people's body armour to use that day.

'Who was it?' Svensson asks.

'Pacman. Not sure how many people he's asked.'

Pacman is known to pose around in plated Kevlar like he is Omar from *The Wire*. Svensson punches the roof of his car. Would they really be that brazen to attack a funeral? It has never happened before. He mentions this to the office. Someone in the office says: 'They don't attack funerals.'

Svensson shakes his head. 'You can't underestimate who you're dealing with.'

3: Wake

Svensson squints into the low sun as he walks beside the cortège in body armour and trackie bottoms. The hard Kevlar covering of the armour does not breathe and underneath his skin is prickly and drenched in sweat. It is difficult policing gang funerals. There are about three hundred mourners on the move, who've come to bury Antoine Gayle. Tensions are high. Three shootings that week already. He keeps his eye out for motorbikes arriving suddenly. Anyone who shouldn't be there. Anyone from the opposition.

Svensson sees a car prowl around the perimeter. It doesn't look quite right.

'Black Golf. Reg SJ8 912K,' he says into his radio.

The cops type it into the Police National Computer, which crunches through several databases with over a hundred million vehicle records.

'It's clean. Nothing coming up.'

Svensson glances back, but the car's gone. Gang members used to use their own wheels. But to combat the computer it's hire cars now. Always from the same hire companies. Same fucking tinted windows. You've no idea who's behind the tinted windows, unless you have a hunch. Some kids whose mum is worried about sunburn, a boy racer hiding his cheap upholstery or a multi-murderer

with an automatic weapon. Electric window whirs down.
Bam.

Svensson stays with the cortège. It moves slowly from
the church at Longsight to Manchester cemetery. There are
six police from Svensson's office plus the other uniforms
around.

'All right, Anders.'

He turns to see a middle-aged lady with cornrows and a
black dress.

'Hello, Princess. Love your hair like that.'

Many of the mourners know Svensson and his unit
anyway. They wave, come over and chat. They like the
cops being there because it offers them a bit of security.
While they are there predators stay outside the perimeter
or retreat. He glimpses an informant. She slides her eyes
quickly away. A sullen teenager in a chain pops in front of
him.

'We don't need no police presence. Let us grieve in
peace, man.'

There are all ages. Older women in formal, brighter
colours. Teenage girls in white school shirts pulling faces
at risqué texts. They all look forward to jerk chicken, rice
and peas. Some smile and laugh at stories of the dead man.
Old friends catch up.

Svensson is with another cop, Dermot, a lad who works
in Liverpool, knows different people. Dermot nods to a
handsome black guy, early twenties, with close-cropped
hair, a shiny forehead and sad, sleepy eyes.

'Kyle. This is Anders.'

Svensson has never got to know Kyle, but he knows
of him. Kyle considers himself to be influential in the

Longsight Crew. He was involved in a running battle in the corridors of Manchester Royal Infirmary, with the Gooch. Terrified nurses barricaded themselves and patients behind doors. Gang members went on the rampage using trolleys as battering rams. Kyle did twenty months for it. Svensson's intrigued. Kyle nods slowly at him and smiles at Dermot.

'Fuck, haven't you retired yet?' Dermot jokes. Kyle's been keeping away from his old haunts, staying with his three kids and pregnant girlfriend, Nicole, who joins them. Svensson is distracted for a moment by Kyle's sister, Talitha, who is slim and pretty with full lips. She could be a model, he thinks. Maybe she is a model. He has to force himself to focus. He's heard that Merlin's trigger-happy lieutenant, Trench, has been asking about Kyle's whereabouts recently. Three drive-by shootings this week. Kyle's taking a risk, venturing back to pay his respects.

'When is little Kyle due?' Dermot nods at the bump.

'It's a girl,' says the mother. 'We have little Kyles already.'

Dermot widens his eyes in mock-surprise at the tiny people peering shyly from behind their father's legs. Svensson winks at the kids. Kyle brushes a wasp from his black leather coat. Only twenty-three, Svensson thinks, and four kids. Fuck me. But round here every twenty-three-year-old has history. Out of habit he chews over Kyle's profile in his head. It's all coming back to him. Brother Dexter shot dead in 2000 at the end of a Mac-10 machine pistol – a drug turf killing. That would have hit teenage Kyle pretty hard. That's the way it all starts.

Then a few years later, when Kyle was nineteen, something very strange happened. He is out with his mates in a reggae night at a lap-dancing club in Stockport. They pile into the toilets. Kyle, his nineteen-year-old pal, Wes, and two others. Wes holds in his open palm a four-inch miniature metal gun. Looks like a lighter. Has a button on it like you're popping a car door. Next thing Wes's slumped back on the cistern with a hole in his head. He was wearing body armour. Did it go off in his hand? Those key fobs are lethal. Or did someone else push the button? It remains unsolved. An open verdict. Wes's mother Linda looked Svensson straight in the eye, gripped his arm and said she knew who killed her son. It was one of his friends, she said. They lied at the inquest. But then she was a mother stricken with grief. It's unusual to take out one of your own soldiers, it weakens your crew.

Svensson squints at Kyle. His download is complete. Dermot wraps up his banter, pats him on the shoulder and they slip away. Svensson tracks the back of Kyle's head as the crowd swallows him up. He's a good target, he thinks.

They make new friends, chat to mourners they've never met, people who might normally be anti-police. The coffin is lowered into the grave. A lone woman wails and flings a fist of dirt on the lid. Antoine's friends toast him, splash a bit of brandy over him and upend bottles of Dragon Stout firmly in the earth by the grave. It's about showing respect, having a last drink on the dead man. The taste in flowers isn't the best ever, Svensson thinks, as he looks at the big letters spelling out the deceased's street name stuck on the side of his grave.

The crowd trickles away now. They follow each other

to the West Indian Centre. The family are near the door, shaking hands, nodding, eyes closed.

Svensson cracks his neck, digs his fingers into his knotted shoulder. It's a long day, these funerals. He's been there right through, is finding it harder to concentrate. Seven hours is too long. He's tired now. His eyes sting. The lids feel sticky. He stays at the wake from two till about nine. At the West Indian Centre they put police cars at either end of the road to stop any trouble. He is grateful when word comes to set up an observation point. He sinks heavily into the car next to Dermot.

'It's all right when we're sat here,' Svensson says, rubbing his eyes. 'When they're on the move you need about ten eyes in your head to keep track of it all.'

Dermot nods. He's a good laugh usually and Svensson's looking forward to a bit of banter. He can tell Dermot's not on his best form today, though. He keeps ringing his phone every twenty minutes, being bumped straight to voicemail.

'Fuck.'

He slaps the handset on his knee and sighs angrily through his nose.

'What's up, Dermot?' Svensson asks, lighting a cigarette and winding down the window.

'Just been caught out by the girlfriend.'

'Oh yeah?' Svensson says drily, raising an eyebrow. 'How'd she find out?'

'She found my photo on a dating website,' Dermot sighs, lolling his head back and closing his eyes. 'Under a different name.'

Svensson screws his face up and wrestles to keep in a laugh. It is priceless. He looks across at Dermot, in disbelief. Dermot chuckles too, but wearily. He knows he's fucked up.

'Do you want me to phone her, Dermot?' Svensson asks.

'Yeah, phone her, phone her.'

So Svensson calls. He tries his calm, measured voice. 'I'm sorry to hear what's going on. I know he thinks the world of you.'

But she isn't right in the head.

'You know what a cock he is,' he continues, trying to talk her round. 'Can't keep it in his trousers. But I don't think he's done anything.'

Svensson's relationships are much the same. Marriage number two's not in great shape. It's all the late shifts, the constant late-night phone calls, the overtime. Most women don't want to spend dinner talking about how many times a gun has been passed around, or know that you lie in bed thinking about a case, or that the reason you haven't listened to a word she's said was because you'd just had a hunch that Scarz shot so and so.

The mourners drift past the car. Svensson sees a kid he knows and slips out.

'All right, buddy. Where they going to now?'

'It's like the unofficial wake,' he shrugs with a half-smile. He looks defensive. The kids around him are louder and jumpier. They've been drinking all day and look daggers at Svensson. One grips his friend's jacket, yanks him away.

'Yeah. *Un*-official. No police.'

Back in the car his radio crackles. 'You can stand down,' comes the order.

Svensson drops his eyes to his watch. It's an hour later than he told his wife he'd be back. He's already on a yellow card. He hurtles the car back like they're giving chase. Punches in the entry codes, tears open the Velcro on his body armour and hooks it on the back of a chair.

'Suppose they'll be all right,' Dermot says. 'The opposition won't know the cops have pulled back.'

Svensson weighs it up. 'They might have spotters,' he says, mock-texting with his thumb. Then he unhooks his personal radio. The radio is supposed to remain locked up at the end of every day. They are on a secure net and if one gets lost or falls into the wrong hands, it's not good. He hesitates, listening to the crackle of the static. Dermot's got him thinking now. What if they do have spotters? Without a radio he will have no idea what is happening at the wake. Looking from side to side, he slips it into his pocket. Then he heads home.

He unlocks the door and steps in. The kids must be asleep upstairs. He sees the back of Sarah's head in front of the telly. A bottle of her favourite Chardonnay is already half-empty. He joins her. She doesn't look away from the screen.

'How've you been, love?' he asks, warily.

'It's been a hard day. Kids fighting again,' she says quietly. She throws a hand out in frustration. 'Another really difficult day.'

Svensson sits tight. To chat might risk a row. Better to let her give him the cold shoulder, focus on the movie. His sole tactic in this marriage is 'rope a dope', the one Ali used in the George Forman fight. Lie back against the ropes and soak up the blows, eventually she'll grow tired.

He keeps the radio in the kitchen on low. Then pops out and listens to it. It crackles and scratches during key scenes. She glowers at him. Why does he need that bloody thing on? It's past ten in the evening. But Svensson is drawn back to his radio, and keeps switching it on to listen for the next two hours.

Midnight approaches at the wake without incident. A shoal of mourners, now drunk on brandy, collect outside the Gayle family's house. They are hemmed in on three sides by two-storey terraces with the council's hanging baskets outside. At the entrance of the close, gang members sit in cars, carrying out their own security detail. Some older women, who chatted with the cops earlier, bundle protesting children inside. In the kitchen they tut at the mountain of dishes and roll up their sleeves to scrub the pots. Puff Daddy and Faith Evans' 'I'll Be Missing You' plays over.

Kyle is still there, enjoying seeing his old crew. A pretty teenage schoolgirl holds her mobile up for him to listen to a track.

A car jerks to a stop at the top of the close. It's a green Honda Legend. A second car, light blue, draws up next to it. The passenger front window of the Honda is wound down, but there seems to be no one inside. Just darkness. Tinted windows in the back. They have a clear angle towards the crowd of mourners milling around. A woman pulling out of the street sees them in her rear-view mirror and takes her foot off the clutch. On the first floor of the house, Antoine Gayle's partner hears a noise like fire-works. The school girl also hears it. Pap pap pap. She sees the crowd scuttle and clamber inside over the baby gate. She turns to see Kyle. He looks like he's been winded. He doubles over.

'What's wrong, Kyle?' she asks. Then she sees the blood. It is coming from his mouth.

'Help me,' he rasps. 'I've been shot.'

The girl shouts for help. She clamps a hand over her mouth. 'Just breathe,' she says, 'It'll be all right.'

People run towards him, but he collapses. Blood soaks out through a single hole in his shirt. The night fills with screams. Bullets rip into the nearest row of mourners. Glass flies into the air and falls on women and children who flatten themselves on the ground. They crawl crab-like for the door. Others jump blindly over a nearby wall. The shooters appear to be firing indiscriminately at them. Bullets zing as they ricochet off the wall, piercing the metal of a row of parked cars. Inside one young mother ducks beneath the dashboard with one arm still tugging at the child seat. Another mourner yelps. He is hit twice in his left leg. Kyle is dragged across the street into the house.

The gang members who were on security detail spring into action. But the cars are long gone. They are pumped up, ready for revenge: this is so brazen it cannot stand. They've been muttering all day about Antoine Gayle's murder. Now they have to put together a counter-strike.

The police radio crackles on Svensson's kitchen table.

'There's been a shooting at Walcott Close.'

There are still a few police officers parked up in nearby streets. They now converge on the scene. One officer looks up to see two cars travelling towards him. One of them is a light-blue Audi A4. The driver has his face covered and the front passenger is wearing a balaclava. Another officer is parked up on Ladybarn Road, not far away. He sees two cars racing past. One is a flash of light blue. The other is a Honda. The Honda's headlights are not even turned on. While his instinct is to head to the scene of the shooting, his mind races. These are the shooters. It's a drive-by. He crunches the ignition and the engine roars. He spins the car around and floors the accelerator. As he tears after them, he strains to pick out a number plate. There's rain on the windscreen. It's risky. High-speed pursuit requires 100 per cent concentration. If he hit a pedestrian he'd kill them. The car sharks right. High-speed cornering is hairy. He cranes forward over the wheel, looking for the corner of the kerb, then wrenches the wheel down hard. Stay with them, he keeps thinking. These aren't some bag-snatchers. They're armed murderers and a danger to the public.

He manages a few blocks but without tail-lights it's just impossible. The car's a grey blur in the night.

'Lost them,' he blurts into his radio. 'Heading in direction of Kingsway.'

The gunmen in the back report that they're shaken off the cops. However another police officer picks them out as they travel towards Kingsway. As they race past, he yanks his neck round, desperately craning to make out the registration number. He clocks the first four digits – S831. But the rest are lost. Now he too gives chase, but it's too late. They are moving too fast. Through the rear window the gunmen watch as they lose a second police tail. The Honda vanishes into the darkness. The driver earns his money that night.

Kyle has a gunshot wound to his chest. He's in really bad shape as he's carefully borne to a car and driven to Manchester Royal Infirmary. His friend at the wheel glances with horror at the blood leaking from his ears, nose and mouth. At the other end trauma doctors race him into theatre. They discover the bullet has damaged his heart and liver. His right lung is punctured. They fight for him for half an hour. It's too late. His mother and pregnant wife cradle him. His sister Talitha's pretty face is now twisted with grief. She grips her mother's hand. To lose two sons to the gun is too much for any mother to bear, and Dexter, Kyle's brother, was killed in 2000. The group cannot leave the body. They sit shattered in a side room. The song 'I'll Be Missing You' is put on again and Puff Daddy sings for the shot rapper B.I.G. One mourner angrily paces the corridor. 'They just don't attack a funeral. It's ain't right.'

Svensson leans over his police radio in the kitchen, stunned by what he just heard.

'Kyle Lewis is deceased.'

'Fuck. Me,' he says aloud. He can't believe he was watching telly when the actual attack happened. He strides into the living room and stands in Sarah's line of vision. She looks at him wearily and listens as he blurts out what has happened. She's a cop too and has soaked up so much of Svensson's work she could probably go on *Mastermind* with Merlin's criminal history as her chosen subject. He bolts out of the room and calls the office.

'Can you phone me?' he asks the operator.

'No I can't,' the operator snaps back. 'It's getting busy and they'll just transmit it over the air.'

Svensson has had this when he's been working other murders and people call in. He shouldn't distract the other cops who are out there now, in the field. But he can't help himself. He needs to know. He calls the office, anyone who is working, trying to get info.

He hears the TV fall silent. The empty bottle rattles into the bin. Dishwasher door opens and closes. Then he hears her footsteps on the stairs. She doesn't say goodnight. She knows their weekend plans will now happen without him, which means more tantrums for her to deal with. He has no capacity to listen to how exhausting her day has been so she leaves him sitting up listening to his police radio on his own.

As they transmit events, he shakes his head in disbelief, paces up and down the kitchen. Upstairs he hears the bath running, the door lock. She is chatting to her mum on the phone. Svensson grabs his keys and drives off, turning the music high. He heads into HQ, where a new office is already being set up. They're wheeling in chairs, installing PCs. It seems like yesterday they did this for the Antoine Gayle investigation. A new file is quickly created on the HOLMES database. They need HOLMES. Every piece of DNA fibre, grainy CCTV footage, statements, vehicles and intel will go in that system. It was all because the tip-off for the Yorkshire Ripper had been lost in a filing tray in the incident room.

'All our efforts are focused now on tracing the two cars,' the officer tells him.

'What have we got?' Svensson asks. It all sounds familiar.

'A green Honda Legend, closely followed by a light-coloured Audi,' the officer says. 'We're looking at the CCTV now.'

Svensson finds Dermot and they drive down to the site, stopping at the end of Walcott Close. Here Svensson has a clear view of the crime scene. It is a cul-de-sac, so there was no escape once you were in there. The fluttering cordon is guarded by policemen in bulletproof jackets, and scene-of-crime analysts go about their business in white plastic boiler suits. He looks at the place where Kyle Lewis fell down.

'They said that the killers were firing indiscriminately,' Svensson tells Dermot.

'Yes, into the crowd.'

'They did well to hit him from where they were,' Svensson says, raising both eyebrows.

He thinks how Flow has a personal beef against the Longsight Crew for his brother's murder.

'Reckon you were right about spotters?' Dermot asks.

Svensson remembers the young girls texting on their mobiles. 'They must have tracked the progress of the cortège,' he replies.

He closes his eyes. He can see Merlin, receiving the all-clear, pulling down his balaclava like an executioner's hood. Pacman, also masked up, guns the engine. The cars pull up at speed, empty their weapons into the crowd. From that range they manage to kill a known gang member. No women are shot. No children are injured. Then the drivers leave at high speed and outrun two police cars. The people in the cars must have known exactly what they were doing.

'Imagine the adrenalin that must have been going through them cars,' he says.

Dermot looks at him strangely and keeps quiet. It strikes him as a weird thing to say.

Witness reports come in. Svensson starts to fillet them, building a picture in his head. The Honda crosses Kingsway then they abandon the car in Burnage. Just after midnight a witness on the street sees a group of men burst out of one car and pile into another parked up on Firethorn Avenue. It is the Audi A4. It then drove off at speed. The strange thing he remembered was that they didn't turn the headlights on. Two of the team try to leg it on foot. Those dark gunnels in Moss Side were designed with fleeing criminals in mind. A nightmare for cops. You chase the outriders on their bikes down one lone road, through concentric rings, but find there's no exit for cars and you have to chase on foot. It is like entering a fortress. It knits the community together, but also isolates them. Svensson once found himself chasing a criminal. He tackled him and sent them both sprawling through a wooden gate, pinned his knife arm. The assailant tried to break away but Svensson kept his grip and ran him along towards a low wall. As the runner went to jump it, Svensson yanked him down, so his knees smashed hard into the wall and he crashed to the ground. He got a warning for that. But it stopped the guy in his tracks.

The two men seen running on the night of the shooting cut through one of the rear gardens and back towards a third car which is parked on the avenue. The driver keeps gunning the engine, cursing and slamming his palm against the wheel, desperate not to sit around a second longer than he has to. Witnesses hear the car revving before it speeds out of the street, leaving the men behind. They have to outrun the cops now, closing in around them like baying dogs cornering their quarry. The two men are young and fit but they aren't fast enough. A police car appears, and they wheel around in panic, searching for any place to hide. One man launches himself over a fence and lies flat on the ground. The other squats down, hunched up behind a parked car. The first man realizes in a beat that he is in danger of being discovered. He leaps up and jumps back over the fence. But he is tiring. The adrenalin coursing through him clouds his judgement. In the dark he doesn't see the barbed wire running along the top of the fence. As his face grazes over it his balaclava snags and is torn off. He is revealed now, exposed to any witness or cop who sees him. The two men hurl themselves down Firethorn Avenue across Avon Road and into the driveway of some flats opposite. A police officer pursues one, sees him accelerate away across the road, opening up a distance between them that will be difficult to close. The cop swears in frustration as he watches the killers climb over another fence, out of sight. They are gone. The officer turns back. On Firethorn Avenue he sees a row of cars. There is something about one of them that does not look right, parked as it is at a slight angle. As if the driver left in a hurry. He rests the palm of his hand on top of the bonnet. He can still feel the warmth of the engine. He takes a note of the number and make. He calls it in over his radio. Control lets him know that this Honda Legend was seen leaving the scene of the shooting. It is one of the murder cars.

The dog unit is called in, to see if they can pick a scent. As the handler drives across town in his van, he glances at the grille behind him, where a two-year-old Alsatian sways with the motion of the car, its pink tongue lolling out. At the scene he creaks open the door and the Alsatian leaps out, padding quickly over to the abandoned Honda. It sniffs the wheels, the door and interior seats and upholstery. It does not take long. The dog is away, straining on the lead as her nose glides over the grass of the garden of 4 Firethorn Avenue, across Avon Road, along the edge of a fence and past the bungalows behind. The dog stops at the last bungalow and scrabbles at the fence, which leads into the rear garden. An officer pores over the ground with his torch. He sees something. He stops and lowers himself carefully and presses his fingers into the cold earth. There in front of him is a footprint, all that remains of the fleeing men. It is evidence. An examination of the fence shows it has sagged inward under the weight of a body. He shines the torch around it and discovers a black rag draped on the wire. It is the balaclava. It is carefully bagged by Scene of Crime analysts, who spirit it away for DNA examination. They have something at last.

The murder team painstakingly works through the real drudge of the murder investigation – the Trace Interview Eliminate lists, the CCTV footage of the cars. When the trial comes there will be so many exhibits, eight thousand in the court room, that they will assign a police officer to look after them all.

'It is just the audacity of it,' Svensson tells his senior officer. 'To shoot someone and then, six weeks later, to shoot the mourners at his funeral.'

He can remember the grisliest days of the IRA and the Troubles, when a grenade was thrown into a crowd of mourners. Then at another funeral the cortège boxed in two undercover soldiers in a car. The mob surrounded them, caved the windscreen in to get at them, dragged them out. He remembers the footage of the incensed crowd. How the soldiers were beaten up and then shot, at a funeral where the priest blessed the dead. Svensson is picking up tremors from his web. The intelligence is now so strong that he feels it is compelling. He goes back to his senior officer and tells him what he has. The senior officer listens gravely, staring up under his eyebrows at Svensson. He makes swift notes in his book.

'Forget what evidence we've got for Merlin and Flow on the jobs,' Svensson says. 'Just get them in custody.'

The senior officer says nothing. Then he gives him a small nod. With Operation Silverstone green-lit, money is no longer an obstacle. They let Nottingham know that Flow is wanted for two murders. This time there's no red tape. A team sits on his house. Svensson is keen for news. A day goes by and nothing. No sign of him. Then two more days pass. Nothing. Svensson wonders if Flow is staying away. It's just too soon after the murder. He doesn't do time well. He might be more cautious than the others. At the end of the fifth day the surveillance team report in.

Still no sign of him. Svensson puts the phone down. 'Fuck!' He rubs his eyes. He's got a bad feeling about this now. Flow must have read the headlines. He knows the heat is on.

Then on the sixth day he appears. Nottingham's Tactical Firearms Unit are called in. Svensson later describes it to Whippet at his bail hostel. They call out his name: 'Flow. Armed police.' He is inside with Kerry and the kids. He looks out the window and can see fifteen cops with firearms. They are training weapons on his house. He's not going to kick off at home, his kids are there. He's not going to come charging out the door and go down in a hail of bullets like Butch Cassidy and the Sundance Kid. He kisses Kerry, who is wide-eyed and scared. He hugs his daughters. They are confused and frightened. He knew in his heart that one day this day would come. He must move quickly now. He comes down and opens the door. Then he walks out, into the August dawn, with his hands up.

A team are watching Merlin that night too. They see him walking with an attractive mixed-race girl, leaning close to her, whispering in her ear. He hails a minicab. The cops tail it as it moves off in the direction of the A666 to the North. For Merlin they deploy a far more radical technique. He is not surrounded by a wife and kids so he has nothing to lose. He could try anything. He is likely to be armed and a hostage situation is likely to ensue to secure his escape, either with the driver or the girl. They must act with lightning speed to subdue him. On the A666 the taxi rolls along, as Merlin leans back, his arm draped around the girl's shoulders.

'What the fuck!' the driver calls out.

A police Land Rover Discovery sharks in front of the car, blocking it in. Another looms behind, tailgating them. The cab driver doesn't know where to go and is forced into a hard stop. They sense there are other police cars around them too. A dark figure appears at the side window and aims directly at the passengers with some kind of weapon. The girl screams. There is a deafening bang as a tear-gas canister smashes the glass and roars in through the window. It is a high-risk tactic. The car has to be stationary. When they practice they use chalk cartridges to replicate CS gas. A cop was killed on a training exercise and it went to inquest. With Merlin it's especially dangerous because of the girl and the taxi driver. But he is such extreme high risk to the public that they get the go-ahead. There is a narrow margin of error. Other officers swarm around the car as it quickly fills with smoke. Merlin is disorientated, can't see. The taxi driver flails around, blinded. The girl's screaming and choking, clasping her throat. They tear open the door and wrestle Merlin out. He must not be given the chance to take the girl or the driver hostage.

'OK, buddy, thanks for letting me know.' Svensson puts down his phone. He closes his eyes. Both Merlin and Flow are back in custody. The guards arrive to search Merlin and find him in his cell feverishly chewing something. They force open his mouth and dislodge a piece of paper. It is from his back pocket and has a soggy phone number on it. It proves to be incriminating.

Svensson knows there is a race against time now to gather enough evidence for the case to stack up. Sandy Mitchell is taken in for questioning.

'What can you tell us about the firearms on your premises?'

She looks hunted. She runs over things in her head. She remembers her brother telling her off when he found the machine gun in the roof.

'I did move it,' she says.

'So you handled the firearm yourself?'

'I told my son to move it.'

They put a photo in front of her. It's Trench.

'How do you know him?'

'Used to buy my gear off him. Years ago.'

'Was he round at your house much?'

She thinks about him and his pals lugging heavy plastic bags up and down the stairs. How they used to chop the gear up on her table.

'He told me to move it. Put it in the woods.'

The detectives lean over and look her in the eye.

'Are you aware of the penalty for possession of a firearm?' they ask her softly. She shakes her head. He goes on to explain about Section 5 prohibited weapons.

'It's one thing to have a shotgun in your cupboard, but having a machine gun in your attic is quite a different scenario. You face a much longer sentence. Mandatory minimums.'

Inside Pendleton station, Svensson sits and waits for Flow to be brought in from Strangeways to be interviewed for the murders. Next to him sits one of the murder-investigation team. Flow's got a jumpsuit on because he is Cat-A. It's like a kind of jester's suit. He's got handcuffs on, pulling his wrists tightly together in front of him. He nods at Svensson.

'Fancy seeing you here,' Svensson says drily. Flow looks at him. His face does not move a flicker.

The MIT cop coughs, keen to follow procedure. 'Have you got any marks, scars, tattoos since you were last arrested?' he says.

Flow shakes his head.

'Yeah, you have, you've got Never Take Me Alive tattooed on your shoulder,' says Svensson. 'September 2006 you had that done.'

Flow smiles.

'Any more?' the cop says.

'No,' says Flow.

'What about Original Outlaw you had tattooed up your arm in Rampton,' says Svensson.

Svensson knows that 'Never take me alive' is a line from a gangster song. It was done in Nottingham. The tattooist took a picture of it as he was doing it and put it on his website. Svensson, ever the detective, tracked it down.

'Fuck me, what else can you tell me about myself?' Flow says, screwing up his face in disbelief.

The cop asks him another question.

'Ask Anders,' says Flow.

Afterwards, Svensson goes for a chat alone in the cells with Flow.

'Do you want anything?' he says.

'Could you get us something to eat?' Flow says. 'I've got some money in my property. The food is shit.'

'What do you fancy?'

'Cheese and onion pie and chips.'

The two men eat together in the cell. Svensson has had better cheese and onion pies, but it isn't bad. It is general chat. It is not like Flow would let anything slip, he doesn't underestimate him. He is far too switched on for that. They have known each other over thirteen years. They go back.

4: Trial

Merlin and Flow cast such a long shadow over Manchester's underworld that everyone worries that the jurors will be intimidated. The witnesses are scared. Given the wall of silence it is unbelievable they stepped up. They are using such high-tech voice-changing technology Merlin won't even know their sex. Ten-year-old Mancunian kids can name the Gooch before they can name any figure from history. So the trial is moved to Liverpool Crown Court.

Svensson sits in the gallery with the relatives of the deceased. He stares across the court room at the defendants.

Merlin taunts the victims' families. He could walk a few paces across the court room and be an arm's length away. His crew are so pumped up: they stick their chests out, berate the judge for the injustice of this trial. They smirk. They share a crude joke. They see Kyle's mother's head sink into her shoulders, and they laugh. Merlin himself is arrogant and appears to love the stage he is on. He is no stranger to the court room. His answers ring out defiantly. The evidence against him is damning.

Far more chilling to Svensson is Flow's demeanour. He just stares calmly ahead. His defence hinges on the assertion that he wasn't in the cars. He looks as if the proceedings do not really involve him, so the jury might forget he is even there. But in his silence Svensson can detect the icy calm of a killer. It makes him nervous. Sometimes Flow catches Talitha's eye, or looks at Svensson. But no emotion passes over his face. It is eerie to think he, Talitha and Kyle all used to play in the streets together, when they were kids.

Svensson hears that a shit-hot criminal barrister is due to prosecute. He has high hopes but then again the evidence may not stand up. Flow remains his biggest concern.

The pair are charged on two counts of conspiracy to murder; the sentence, if they are convicted, could be over thirty years in jail. The first charge is for Antoine. The second for Kyle, six weeks later. When the hearings break for lunch, Svensson eats with Kyle's family. The chat turns from Kyle to the crowd he used to hang with. Svensson is protective of them, enjoys their company, but the more they relax, the more he is aware that the gossip they tell him is high-grade intelligence that he can use. As usual he pretends to know less than he does, raising his eyebrows until they are competing to give him morsels of information. He gets on well with Kyle's sister Kemi, remains intrigued by Talitha. Kyle's mother looks older. She seems to have shrunk somehow. Talitha presses her knuckles as she sits next to her, trying to be strong for her mum.

She has now had two of her brothers killed in gang-related shootings. It is bad enough to lose one. When Kyle died it was like being hit by a train. She felt a pressure in her chest and the colour drained out of each day. Now she has to look at the men who shot him, joking, being cocky and arrogant like they've lived their life in a court room.

Svensson deals with so many girls who are deep into gang life, he is keen to know how Talitha has stayed so decent.

'How did you keep out of the life?'

'I was never attracted to that type of man,' she shrugs. 'I was always more of a girly girl. I like my reading.'

Oprah Winfrey is her hero and she follows her book club. When she was off work on a Sunday she could read a whole book through.

'What are you into?'

'I like autobiographies,' she says. 'And Virginia Andrews. You know *Flowers in the Attic*?'

Svensson has heard of Julie Andrews, but not this one. Sounds like a girl's book. He reads a lot of true crime himself. She tells him how Kyle went downhill after his brother Dexter was shot. She tries to come to terms with her loss by deciding it is more a male thing to be led down the spiral of craving revenge. For her losing Dexter just reaffirmed that it was much more dangerous to be a young man, all the threats and pressures you faced. She still walks around those streets and feels safe, just because she's a girl. Svensson knows that Kyle's friend Wes was shot in the head wearing body armour in a toilet in a lap-dancing club. Wes's mother blames the murder on his friends. Kyle's grave is just down from Wes's. When someone defaced it, two cops tidied it up. He keeps this all to himself. As they walk back to the court, he lags behind the others with Talitha.

In the car park, they run into a group of Gooch kids. They are Merlin's lieutenants, there to support their general. They clock the family and scowl. One flicks away his cigarette and taunts them. They start to approach, their mouths twisted with threats. Another makes lewd hand gestures, falls in behind. Svensson puts himself between them, blocks their path. He says their names quietly. They know him. He stands there, like granite. When they have gone he comes over.

'At the end of the day,' he says as he lights the family's cigarettes, 'I'm part of the biggest gang in Manchester.'

Sandy testifies that Merlin's gang stored weapons in her attic, that she saw them carrying heavy objects down from there in bags. Her brother went up there and discovered a machine gun wrapped in plastic. He was not pleased and told her to be careful. Svensson watches her as she shakily delivers her evidence. The defence will question her reliability, he thinks, make her out to be a rattling old bag-head. Other key witnesses are kept under armed guard in a neighbouring hotel, with an armed-response vehicle parked nearby. They are former criminal associates of the defendants. How much can the jury rely on the evidence of some old gang-banger with a grudge? The defence will pick holes in their testimony.

Merlin and Flow appear with five associates. One of them is Trench, who Svensson hopes will be the loose cannon. His intelligence suggests that Trench resents Merlin being the leader and has been overheard saying that they are on the same level. He used to be close to an associate who is frightened enough now to be collaborating with the cops. Trench starts to worry what this witness will say in court. The day before his testimony he makes a high-risk move. He's got himself a mobile and calls the witness in his hotel room.

'Fuck Merlin,' he whispers. 'I don't care about that fucker no more.'

The witness listens uneasily. Trench goes on to dob Merlin in. The witness glances nervously down at the digital counter on the recording equipment and the leads running to his phone. The cops have provided him with this high-tech stuff. They guessed Trench'll call.

It is played out the next day. Merlin listens to it stony-faced.

Trench claims that he has flu and skips court.

It becomes clear though that the piece of evidence that will damn Merlin is not the witness testimony, but the mobile phones. The case against him hinges on proving that he was in the murder vehicle. The prosecution barrister shows the jury the route the car took, pieced together from CCTV footage and eyewitness accounts. Then he shows them how calls from Merlin's mobile phone, around the time of the murder, mirror exactly the car's route. Triangulation data can pinpoint their exact place and time. The picture the jury have is of Merlin on his phone several times after he's just shot Kyle dead at the wake.

Merlin huddles down with his defence team. He shrugs it off. His entire defence is that it is not him on the phone. He was never in the car. It's not even his phone.

'How do you plan to persuade the jury the phone isn't even your phone?' his defence lawyer asks.

Merlin cooks up a load of ideas, but his defence team just shake their heads. They are not sure if they can use this. Merlin glowers across the table. These people work for him, but they are ignoring his advice. He is used to absolute control. He tortures people who step out of line.

He has overseen a huge criminal empire in south Manchester. These pussies in their suits and ties are not going to let him sleepwalk into a thirty-year sentence.

So he fires them all.

From now on he will present his own defence. Every day now the relatives of the deceased have to endure Merlin strutting around the court like he's Tom Cruise in *A Few Good Men*.

A month into the trial an eyewitness describes the actual murder. Kyle's family listen to a graphic description of how Kyle died, how he had blood coming out of his mouth and nose. His older sister, Kemi, finds it too much. She bursts through the doors into the corridor of the Crown Court and doubles over on a bench, sobbing. Svensson goes after her. He has grown closer to Kemi than Talitha. She's more his type and finds her easy company. In the corridor he runs into a local uniform cop. 'No sympathy for her,' the cop mutters.

Svensson squares up to him.

'They're just as much victims as the guy who was shot,' he says through clenched teeth. 'You fucking cock.'

He walks over to where she is hunched up and sits next to her.

Two months go by and Svensson is spending so much time in Liverpool that he never visits the office. One evening he pops in. On seeing Svensson a young guy spins his chair around and stands up.

'I don't know if any of you know DC Anders Svensson. Let me introduce you.'

He offers sarcastic introductions to the others. But the

trial drags on. There are eight thousand forensic ex-hibits. It lasts six months. When it finally ends it has cost £5 million.

In the final days Merlin rises to his feet to make his own closing statement for the defence, summing up all that has gone before. He has to deal with the two murders in order, first Antoine Gayle, then Kyle six weeks later.

'Ladies and gentlemen,' he begins. 'I did not kill Antoine Gayle.'

Fucking hell, Svensson thinks. This is going to be good. But this opening, he will later tell colleagues, represents the peak of Merlin's summing-up. He carries on for four and half days. His main points about why the mobile phones are not his are questioned by the judge. He claims that he was not in the car but still seems to know exactly who was calling who. At the beginning he refers to Svensson as 'the officer in the court'. The next day it becomes 'Detective Constable Anders Svensson'. By the end, as they near day four, it is just 'Anders'. The judge and those in attendance in the court are growing impatient. On the fifth day, in the morning, the judge has had enough.

'You told us that you were reaching the end, but you have only spoken about Antoine Gayle,' he says. 'You have not even got on to the second murder. How much longer do you intend to carry on?'

'I'm about halfway through, your honour,' replies Merlin.

'I'm afraid not,' the judge sighs, taking off his glasses and rubbing his nose. 'You have to finish by one o'clock.'

Merlin looks up at the court clock. It shows a quarter to one. Fifteen fucking minutes. He has no time to go through the defence he has prepared on the second murder and just says, 'I did not kill Kyle Lewis either,' before he sits down.

The judge directs the jury in the points of law in a smooth, deliberate speech.

'The defendant claims that this mobile phone is not his phone and that he did not use it,' he says, peering at his notes. 'The jury may ask themselves why, during this time, ninety-three calls were made from this phone to the defendant's mother.'

They shuffle out.

Since they've been arrested the streets have been quieter. Gun crime has dropped by 92 per cent. The Greater Manchester Police decide to make capital of it. The Home Secretary, Jacqui Smith, duly arrives to give a press conference with police chiefs. But the judge rules it would prejudice the trial if the jury connect the story with Merlin and Flow. Nonetheless the word 'Gooch' appears in a newspaper which is seen near a jury member. Svensson cannot believe it. Outside the court room he lights up a cigarette and glowers into the traffic. For six months he has been driving to Liverpool, and now there might have to be a retrial.

He goes home and spends a furious night smoking and watching random TV shows. He can't sleep. But by the time he staggers in the next day the crisis is averted. Objections to the reporting are dismissed and the jury can safely continue to consider their verdict.

Svensson does pre-recorded interviews for the press. No one is absolutely sure of the verdict, so he does one for not guilty, one for guilty.

When the jury file out one by one, he looks across at the family. Talitha is not there. She is at work in town. Kemi is there, with her mother. The foreman holds a piece of paper, which is trembling slightly. Then he is told to stand up. Svensson sits motionless. He stares across the court at Flow. He was never a man of words like Merlin, never entrepreneurial. His defence hinges on keeping silent. Svensson senses he has secrets, stretching back years, that will never come to trial. Flow discovered early in life he had an efficient talent for violence. It is Flow's first charge, the murder of Antoine Gayle.

'Have you reached a verdict on which you are all agreed?'

'No.'

Svensson cannot believe it – a hung jury. This is his worst fear. They could be back on the streets in days. He cranes forward to study Flow's face. There is nothing, not even a flicker.

Then the second charge comes up. Kyle Lewis.

'Guilty.'

Flow's eyes are black and unblinking, like a basilisk. Svensson wonders if he is really prepared for the shock of a thirty-year sentence. Then he sees it. A twitch in his temple. It is like watching a mighty bull whose flank suddenly judders. Then it is gone. Flow sits back, cool, unflustered, legs wide apart.

Svensson's old boss, one of the best detectives he worked for, believed that one detective should concentrate on one or two criminals. Merlin and Flow were allocated to Svensson. They are his life's work. His eyes pass to Merlin, who stares straight back at him. He has presided over a reign of murder for over a decade, Svensson thinks. He cannot believe that it might finally be about to come to an end.

The foreman is again asked for his verdict.

'Guilty.'

Merlin's gaze does not leave Svensson's. He has a message for him. He clearly mouths the words: 'Are you happy now?'

Svensson hears blood thud in his temples. He cannot stay in the court and listen to the other verdicts for Trench and the associates. He makes his way into the corridor and paces around in a daze. He pushes through the double wooden doors into the daylight. Then he pulls a cigarette out and lights it. He draws the smoke in and lets it pour out the side of his mouth, through gritted teeth. Fifteen years of work and finally they have been taken off the streets for good. His phone starts to ring. It is a senior officer who is about to go into a meeting and wants to know the verdicts. The officer hasn't spoken to Svensson for almost a year now. The victims' families file out through the double doors.

'Guilty,' they tell him. 'All of them.'

Merlin and Flow are sentenced to thirty-five years each. Flow will launch an appeal.

When Svensson heads home it is dark. He makes out the barren hills of Buxton where an empty house awaits him. His second marriage of eight years has ended. His wife has left with their daughter. Some evenings now Svensson ventures into town and stays out drinking late. One night, another cop retires at forty-eight and Svensson and a colleague get so wasted they end up singing a duet in a karaoke bar. The other cop staggers home to his wife and daughter. Left alone, Svensson picks up a girl. At home, in his bed, he sees that her entire back is tattooed with a dragon from the nape of the neck to the top of her buttocks. He is so amazed he takes a photo on his phone and shows it to colleagues the next day.

Some nights, rather than go home, he goes drinking in a lap-dancing club in town.

He remains uneasy. Even after months he sees Merlin's face in the dark glowering cockily across the court at him and asking, 'Are you happy now?' He gets up and closes the window. In the other room, he can hear his ringtone, the one he uses for informants. When he answers it, thudding rap music blares out. A girl is screaming. She sounds like she is in a car. Then he recognizes it is Chanelle. Her new boyfriend, an eighteen-year-old drug-dealing thug, must have cranked up the stereo to drown out her voice. She yells at Svensson to help her, but her words are garbled in the din. Svensson knows her boyfriend just had a few friends over to watch an action movie. He got off his face, battered her and burnt her neck with a cigarette. He threatened to tell the Gooch that she had been talking to the police. The phone suddenly goes dead. He must have snatched it and thrown it out the window.

Svensson puts his phone down and lies down. He worries about her with this new thug. He also thinks about Whippet who is up on a new drugs charge. He's put a lot of work in bringing him to justice. After the car chase he's also up for dangerous driving, but he needs a guilty verdict on the drug charge to take him off the streets. The landing light is on. He climbs out of bed again and stares out the window at the silhouette of the trees. Can't he ever give it a rest?

Svensson's ex allows him to hold a party for his daughter, Jessica, who is turning fourteen. A crowd of teenagers turn up and crank up Miley Cyrus. Jessica swigs from a Smirnoff ice and goes up to her brother. 'Do you want one, Tom?'

Tom is an eccentric, lanky twelve-year-old man, in a bow tie. 'No thanks.'

'What do you drink?'

'I prefer a sweet sherry.'

Svensson roars with laughter. He ducks into the kitchen so they can't see. He loves it how seriously they take things at that age. Jessica frowns back at Tom, like he's a freak.

'Do you prefer it dry?' he asks, puzzled.

He looks at them and thinks about Chanelle and how vulnerable she is.

His phone rings. The officer at the other end tells him that Whippet has been let off his drugs charge. Svensson is livid. How can he be found not guilty of selling drugs to an undercover cop? Turns out that Whippet directed the deal, he didn't actually hand the drugs over himself. It allows his defence enough to plant a sliver of doubt. It bugs him for the rest of the party.

Next morning he slams the car into gear and spins it round. After Merlin and Flow, he was expecting that Whippet's trial would go the same way. For the rest of the day he is unable to concentrate on other things. It never seems to end. All the violence and rage keep rising like a great sea. Later that afternoon he drives around Moss Side and visits some informants. No one has heard anything about Whippet, or his plans.

A year since the trial ended and Svensson has been visiting Merlin and Flow regularly in prison. When he goes to see Merlin he takes a huge cop along who can lift heavy weights but says nothing. He doesn't know if Merlin will try something. He has nothing to lose, after all. When he was in Strangeways, he had a freelance solicitor come in and assist him on an appeal. They put the legal files through the X-ray and there was a ten-inch blade there. This time, Merlin throws his arms out and pulls him into a hug. As they sit down, Svensson can see the cuts where another inmate bit his nose. It was an Asian kid who Merlin never got on with. The kid had stabbed Merlin in the neck and it left a mark. They ran into each other in dispersal at Long Lartin. In a last-ditch attempt to save himself he bit Merlin's nose.

'Fancy seeing you here,' Svensson jokes as he sits down.

'You live to see me here.'

They talk for a while. Svensson finds out that Whippet has been in touch with Merlin and mentioned that Svensson is after him.

'If Svensson's after you, then you're fucked,' Merlin tells him.

Svensson takes it as a compliment. As the interview draws to a close, he asks Merlin what he misses the most. Merlin thinks for a second. 'McDonald's.'

As he leaves the prison gates, Svensson decides that he will go and visit Merlin on the day he retires, in four years' time.

Flow does not hug him. Svensson decides it is because he does not want to crease his Armani top. His prison regime means the inmates can wear their own things. He is focused on his appeal, so he is behaving himself. Svensson can sense defeat in his eyes now, like he knows it is hopeless. Unlike Merlin, who let the doors lock behind him and said, 'Right, lads, let's get on with it,' Flow cannot do time well. Svensson thinks he won't make it. To do a few years and come out in your twenties, that is one thing. But to meet Kerry and his kids and know he will never be there to see them grow up, that when he comes out his daughter will be forty-two, that is hard. After the trial they put up posters of his young face all etched and lined and sagging. 'Growing old in prison' was the caption. His family tried to sue saying it was an infringement of his human rights. He will spend the rest of his life here and for Svensson this should be enough. But still he looks across the visiting table and thinks: What else have you got away with?

Whippet is the last one of the group who is going to be back on the streets. When Svensson sees him he is stunned: he's been bulking himself up and his five foot eleven frame carries a forty-five-inch chest. He has cornrows. He speaks quietly and Svensson is reminded of Flow for a second. But he's not as clever as Flow.

'I never did anything to anyone who wasn't in the game,' Whippet says.

Svensson has heard this old morality tale before. Whippet is good at making people feel sorry for him.

If you hadn't been in here when they killed Kyle Lewis, Svensson thinks, you would have been in one of them cars.

After he leaves the prison he heads out to see Whippet's wife in Wrexham. She hugs him and invites him in.

'You're going to fall for him again, aren't you,' he tells her. 'I can hear it in your voice.'

As he drives away he watches her in the mirror. The probation panel will do little to stop Whippet seeking revenge. He has already sold them the line about how he is a real gang member who has lived the life, that the kids will listen to him.

The end of the week comes and Svensson is preoccupied with a firearms warrant. He hears he will not be supported by the Tactical Aid Unit, the heavy brigade who specialize in forced entry. Two gang nominals are downstairs in custody awaiting interview after a fight at a garage. Half of XCalibre are up climbing Helvellyn in the Lake District on a team-building course with German cops so Svensson asks his gaffer, the detective inspector, to come along. The gaffer nods and wraps a bulletproof vest on over his shirt, tie and jacket. They drive over to Longsight Police Station to try to rustle up some more bodies. Svensson briefs a team of police in dark blues as a girl hands out the purple plastic gloves for searching the crime scene. She looks about half Svensson's age.

The convoy draws up. He starts directing his team around the house.

'Gaffer, you're on doors. Wixsy, you do light duties. Terry, you cover the back gate.'

He bangs on the door. Nothing. A gaunt Doberman plays with some young kids in the close. A bleary-eyed guy, all henched on his arms, appears at a neighbour's window.

Svensson turns his back to the door and hammers it hard with his heel. The noise brings a woman in a dressing gown, with her hair up in a towel, padding across the street. With a mother's irritation she strides off to fetch her daughter. Svensson despatches a young policewoman behind her.

The daughter soon appears, trotting at speed. 'Don't break my door!' she pleads, wrenching out her keys. She lets them in and they disperse in a systematic search.

'I have a lot of male visitors,' she keeps saying. Svensson squints at her. She is laying down her defence before anything is found. The others turf out the wardrobes, empty her laundry bags, go through drawers. Svensson goes straight for her mobile phones and letters. He finds a note about a relative.

'Says here that he is praying that once he's inside he won't be put on K-wing, the same wing as the Gooch.'

The Gaffer stares at him blankly as if to say – it's a bit thin.

'She is mixing with the right crowd, anyway,' Svensson shrugs, folding the letter. A young cop is sent up into the loft, because he is the lightest. He sways a flashlight around, and unwraps objects.

'I've got something,' he says.

'What is it?'

'Firearm.'

They can hear a quaver in his voice. He's over with them from another unit, and hasn't found a gun before. It is wrapped in plastic.

'OK, come down, we'll leave it for Firearms.'

Big Ray and his team wear dark-blue overalls and are

armed. On one hip is a yellow Taser and on the other a gun. In the van they have a loaded rifle. The gun that is found is photographed. Svensson pores over it. He has a bet with one of his colleagues what type it is.

'Definitely a Baikal.'

'Is that your final answer?'

'Baikal 9mm.'

Actually the analysis shows it's a Russian Tokarev. Svensson starts to work his intelligence sources to find out more details. He gets a call from a policeman in the Source Handling Unit, who gives him some information.

'Fucking hell, you're good you are,' Svensson says, walking into the corridor. 'You are not the useless wanker people say you are. I've been defending you all day.'

His informant's phone rings. It is a girl he hasn't spoken to for a while. The word is out on the streets about the gun being found already.

'It was put down for Whippet,' she says. 'It's waiting for him when he comes out.'

'Fuck me,' Svensson says as he hangs up. As soon as Whippet hits the streets he is likely to lay hands on a fully loaded weapon. At night, on lates, Svensson can see a change in the activity on the streets now that Merlin's power has been lifted. The kids are more assertive. He drives round a corner and there are two dozen of them having a fight, six to seventeen, with four of them on bikes. Two girls are belting the shit out of each other, swinging roundhouse punches and jabs. As one girl drags the other along the ground by her hair, the kids cheer them on, thrilled. Svensson steps out the car and walks over. One youngster's face lights up. 'XCalibre!' he gasps.

He waits for them to calm down and disperse.

The imprisonment of Merlin may mark the end of the old-school-style street general. Ten years ago it was all about the high-level drug-dealers, older gang members brutally exploiting the younger ones. They taught them that all that counts is who can become the most brutal, the most violent, the most feared. Now the drug trade has become fragmented the violence is all the kids are left with. The older gang members who want to make money in organized crime, fraud or money-laundering can't control them. They are too chaotic, too volatile. A twelve-year-old cannot wait to step up, shoot a general, and get a reputation for himself. It's like *X Factor*. Svensson thinks of all the hard work they have put in over the years, only to create this vacuum. It's like Iraq – you take out the brutal dictator and all you are left with is chaos and guerrilla warfare. The threshold of when it is acceptable to shoot someone dead has gone. Violence kicks off in seconds. There was a hierarchy, but now it comes down to who has the gun, the strongest punch or the loudest voice.

Svensson drives out into Moss Side, with a young lad, Steve, who is out with them for a week or two, on loan from their sister outfit, the Organized Crime Unit. Their new gaffer is also from Organized Crime. The investigations are longer there, it is more of a desk job. Svensson is impressed with this lad, Steve, and thinks he would be good for the unit. He wonders if he could do a recruiting number on him. He clocks Steve examining the intelligence wall. Steve asks about the key gang members, who the important ones are, about Merlin and Flow. 'I go on about them two. I do go on about them a lot but you can't underestimate the fucking impact they had,' Svensson says.

'Do they still run out while they're inside? When they're that big they do.'

'Merlin does. Intelligence suggests he organized a robbery of a sizeable shipment of coke from one of the Liverpool lads last September.'

From the window a couple of teenagers sit on a sign and scowl them up. The lights of fried-chicken outlets flash by. A new Golf with tinted windows roars past, bass pumping.

'This sounds dramatic, this, but when I went to see him, I don't know, I've lost count of how many gang members I've seen in prison. But you see them two. Specially him, specially Merlin. It's just pure evil, he really is. He just does not fucking care. He would not have stopped. Forget gangs in Manchester. Anywhere else in British criminal history where a funeral has been attacked.'

They draw level with the Zaku cafe in old Moss Side, not far from the Claremont Road. Outside some teenage Somalis loll against the wall. There's a strong Somali community round here. Svensson recognizes these as gang members from the Rusholme Crips, a Somali gang allied to the Gooch. He notices two of them are high from chewing khat sticks, which are sold from the flat near the cafe. Their talk is garbled nonsense, their eyes are burning. Their gang is now at war with the Doddington. Their tactic is to ride out in overwhelming numbers, behind Doddington lines to cause as much damage as possible. They call it an incursion. The locals find it terrifying. The Somali threat only emerged at the time Merlin and Flow went on the rampage.

'God knows what will happen when this lot get access to firearms,' Svensson sighs as they drive off.

'If the Somalians are beefing with the Doddington, how do they go around that area without getting grief off them?'

'They just go en masse, mate. Fifteen, sixteen of them come down, in an incursion.'

He rubs his eyes. It has been a long day. He's been up early taking a coachload of German cops in their formal uniforms out on a tour of Moss Side. At the end of it they only gave him a thermal mug. First time they came he at least got a wooden plaque.

'They race through that park there on their mountain bikes,' he says. 'If we are after someone and try to box it off, they are through it way before us.'

Steve is shocked to find there is a shooting story for almost every street. They ease into Quinney Crescent. Svensson slows the car and jabs at a gate with his thumb.

'Two brothers who were Gooch lads were fucked off with a prolific drug-dealer. He was stood by this gate here. And they brought a lad up, a hired hit man, to come and do him. They pull up there to point out the mark. Hit man apparently says, "Fuck it, I'll do him now." Gets out the car goes up to him. Dealer says to him, "You can't shoot me, I'm the Man Dem, I'm a made man." And he lifts his fucking top up and he's got a vest on so the hit man goes and puts three in his head.'

He and the lad chuckle. It's a funny story. Svensson has loads of them.

'If your best line of defence is your covert bulletproof vest, don't fucking show it off.'

They don't use hit men now, though. It doesn't give anyone kudos to hire a hit man rather than shoot someone themselves. What bugs Svensson is that some of the houses round there, off the beaten track, in Chalk Road as you head into Whalley Range, are really stunning. Even on the Alexandra Park Estate, the ones that look out directly onto the park have a gorgeous view. Millions have been pumped in to the area, knocking down derelict houses, building new ones.

Next they drive up into Hulme. You've got all the Swampies, subversives, people who aren't too keen on soap. They lived up a tree for five years then they let them design it themselves.

'It's well weird,' says Steve looking up at the wooden walkways and bridges in the air and rows and rows of caravans in the street. The proper Swampy season is still nearby. Svensson remembers how during the Commonwealth Games all the shit-house bands were parked nose in and they'd take the registration plates off, so he'd be up there at night trying to locate a vehicle.

'I bet the water rates here are very cheap,' he says. 'They'll often go and tie themselves to the Hulme Arch and bring traffic to a standstill, complaining about capitalism. As long as they have their Nike trainers on to climb up.' A gangly guy walks past in a tight seventies leather jacket, frizzy hair, drainpipes and thick glasses.

'It's amazing, isn't it,' Svensson says. 'He must have looked in the mirror and thought, I'm going to pull tonight.'

Back near the Alexandra Road, he points out the boundary between the Gooch and the Doddington. Steve peers into the dark at the front line. There is nothing but a tree and a wall that leads on to the Alexandra Road. He thinks about one mother who looks after the gang members. She has always been there for them. She took Merlin in when the cops were after him. One night Svensson chased a Gooch lad into her house and confronted her.

'He's been here all night. Yeah, he's been fingering our Tina, smell his fingers.'

Tina was her sixteen-year-old daughter. He also remembers that when she had a birthday party for her she was worried about a drive-by so she tried to keep everyone in the house. Svensson was sat in the car keeping watch and this mother brought some food out for them, bless her. She knew there was CCTV there. She brought a can of Stella over, the top was off and she dropped it in the car so it went all over. It stank of beer for days.

'Was there a shooting here?' the lad asks, still keen to learn.

Svensson is silent. So many shootings come back to him in operational details only, names, makes of cars, types of weapons, even the striation marks on the bullet casing. Then he has to remember all the different motives. An argument over a car stereo, an argument over a jacket, a girl, a pair of trainers. Steve can tell he is tired now. They are both on until 1 a.m. and then they'll do the log.

'Justin Maynard was the one who was shot here, by two Gooch lads. They saw him, then went off and came back with ballies on. It was sad that one.'

He has to keep the laddish banter going: that's what makes the hours driving around on a late pass by. Jokes about how their colleague Terry will only eat a kebab that has fallen on the floor for less than five seconds, about his Merseyside roots that he plays up by slipping into an Irish accent. They rib Jenkins because he looks like Marti Pellow. They rib Svensson that he is obsessed with Merlin and Flow, so at Christmas they gave him an 'I love Merlin and Flow' T-shirt. But for once, Svensson can't make any more jokes. He suddenly feels battle-weary.

'I was working and I found him, lying on the pavement. He only lived up the road and his mum turned up. As a detective he was a piece of evidence now. There was no point in trying to run him to hospital, the fucker was dead. And all she wanted to do was pick her baby up. I still speak to her, I sometimes see her wandering around late at night, pissed out of her head.'

'Was she like that before?'

'Since, mate. Since then. She'll just go to kids on the street and say, "Go home, go home. They took my son." That's when you start getting the compassion for it.'

'Yeah. We're all the same at the end of the day. If you grew up in the middle of Moss Side you'd probably be doing it yourself.'

'Mate, I was nose to nose with a copper during that last trial. Kemi Miller, Kyle's older sister, had just heard a witness say that she'd found her brother with blood pouring out of every orifice on his face. She's come out the court crying. This uniform man is sat there and he went, "No sympathy for her." Had to square up to him. It's no fucking wonder these people don't want to talk to you.'

Svensson's voice is quieter now, down to a croak. The younger lad shakes his head. Svensson cracks his neck from side to side.

'It's that thing when you're a kid, you grow up, you play on your bike. You do what your mates do.'

When he started working the streets they fired rockets at the cops out of the doors on Bonfire Night. When there were laser pens, you would be driving around with red dots all over you. It's all changed now. It's live. He took a new DI on a tour and ran into a lad carrying a Mac-10 in one hand and a handgun in the other. Mad fuck. But whenever he goes away on a job Svensson misses Moss Side. He wonders what he will do when he retires. Maybe he will just come and drive round here.

•

It's the Chief Constable's Excellence Awards and Svensson thinks they will be in with a chance. His work in the community speaks for itself, how he's built up his intelligence network. The conviction and sentencing of Merlin and Flow have got to still count for something.

He remembers when he got his first Commissioner's recommendation. He was a young man in his early twenties. He'd stopped a car, with a guy with a long coat on, and found a shotgun in the back. He said he was heading to a meet. Thinking on his feet, Svensson put the coat on and drove off in the car. When he hit the High Street two guys ran out to him and jumped in. They had just robbed a bank and he was their getaway. It was after that he became a detective.

His police radio crackles on the seat next to him.

'Male with firearm arrested in Longsight.' He leaves his desk and goes down to the custody desk to ID him when he is taken out of the van. He might recognize him. For a cop to arrest a gang member in possession of a firearm is like winning the European Cup. Svensson needs to get the measure of him, look him in the eyes. Revenge is an emotional state, he can understand that. It's the ones with the dead eyes that worry him. They are dangerous. They could be a young Flow. Somewhere out there another stone-cold killer is being forged. He is likely to be soft-spoken, calm and confident. Behind the desk is an attractive custody sergeant, Wixsy's girlfriend. Wixsy really is punching above his weight.

His phone rings. It is his mate Pete, who he has agreed to meet before the awards do.

'What time are we meeting up?' Svensson asks.

'Half four,' Pete says.

'Fucking hell, half four? We'll be legless.'

Svensson turns up at a bar in town in his tuxedo. Despite pressure he stays on the wine because if he mixes he'll feel horrendous. His plan is to have a glass of wine, bottle of water, glass of wine. That lasts for one bottle of water. He is half-cut by the time they get there. Pete thinks he's a cert for the communication award. But when it is announced, they give it to someone who had interacted with the young Somali community.

'I can't believe we didn't get one,' the lad says, deflated.

'Nor me,' says Svensson. 'They are very politically awarded this time.'

'Cannot fucking believe this,' the kid says again, filling a large wine glass up to the brim.

'It's just the nature of the beast, Pete. Community-based thing.'

They get very, very badly drunk. Pete falls on his arse in front of the chief constable and police authority. He tries to get up and pulls the table over. It is his fault, Svensson thinks. Pete has to go and see the detective super within the week. It was a good do, nice meal, quite civilized. Svensson is in the press club until five o'clock. He's never been in there sober. He can remember being with a girl in a black dress, then waking up in his hotel alone. Took his contact lenses out, how he did that he doesn't know. He has a missed call back at five in the morning. He reckons he'd left about half four and she was checking he got back all right. He was struggling to walk and talk.

He looks at his calendar. Whippet will be out in a matter of days. It will not take him long to find another loaded firearm. He rubs his eyes and stands up. His lower back aches now and his legs feel stiff. He goes to the garage and does some weights. Then he picks up his third phone and makes a call.

LONDON

5: Birthday

It's a funny thing how Pilgrim's dad always knows when he's going to do something. The old man pauses at the front door, trying to figure out how another afternoon ended up in a carpet of discarded Ladbrokes slips at his feet. He is silhouetted against the hallway light, stares out at the car waiting, engine warm. Inside are two young black guys, known thugs in shell suits, who glower back at him. He brought his son over from Jamaica at the age of eight, out of a life without electricity or water, and now here the boy is on his nineteenth birthday, a fully-fledged man gangster. He is baffled how this happened. Pilgrim thunders down the stairs and brushes straight past him, rolling his shoulders as he storms out to the car. Something is being planned for later, a man's amount of trouble is brewing.

'Son, be careful,' he says.

At the sound of his father's reedy drawl Pilgrim turns. He scuffs the dust with his foot. His snake-eyes Avirex T-shirt shows his henched core, his bull neck. If he can credit his old man with anything, it is a canny sense for trouble. He always calls Pilgrim to check on him, just as he is tooling up for a robbery. It's the only thing he has any sense about, Pilgrim thinks. He gambles all his foreman's wages on the horses and gives the small change to Pilgrim's stepmum and stepbrother. Pilgrim has made his own living on the streets, ever since he was old enough to wash his pants in the bath.

'Yo, birthday boy, where we heading?' Steps yells from the car. He is twenty-one, lighter skin, muscular build, always in dark clothing. A joker. His arm lolls outside, thick silver ring rapping on the black bodywork. He's keen to keep it moving, show off his chrome rim-spinners. Pilgrim shoots his father a wide grin.

'Old Street,' he says.

His father drops his eyes. Pilgrim shrugs, jumps in the car. They're celebrating his birthday.

'Hey,' Steps says. He punches Pilgrim on the shoulder. 'How often will you see us three in one car?'

Pilgrim looks at him, then at Ribz in the back. Ribz is five foot four with famous green eyes that give him his reputation as a ladies' man. His dad is black but he gets the eyes from his Indian mum.

'It never happens,' Ribz grins. 'The dream team together.'

It is true. Every gang has three wanted guys at the top who never meet up with each other. Never more. It's impossible to have more than three like that at the top. But here they are, top guys from three gangs together. Holly Street, Rowdy Bunch and Love of Money all in the same car. They are running Hackney now. They have the hood on lock. Forget Pembury, Forget London Fields. They can't even talk to Pilgrim. No one can. Not even in the Premier League.

The city is laid out before them like a vast smouldering war zone. It's divided into the great battlefields – South,

North, East, West, a very different London from the posters on the wall in childhood Jamaica, no mention of Missus Queen, the Commonwealth, Madame Tussauds or the gold replicas of Big Ben that sat on his granny's mantelpiece. Each region competes with tales of brutal warriors feared across several postcodes for their violence. Sparks was a ruthless gang leader who could knock out anyone with one punch of his anvil of a right jab. Three hundred and fifty people came to his funeral, to show respect. There was nothing more honourable for a young man than to be a soldier and ferociously guard his ends against incursions, protecting the drug revenue. A bus driver kidnapped and tortured with a steam iron for five days, horrifically burnt all over his body, his genitals seared – all for an unpaid drug debt. There were tales of impenetrable fortresses like Stonebridge in Brent, with black towers so high a small child had fallen to its death, and where an eight-month-old baby was left crawling for sixteen hours amongst the bullet-riddled bodies of his mother, aunt and sixty-two-year-old stepfather. Broadwater Farm in Haringey where fierce riots raged and a policeman had his head hacked off with a machete. Or Brixton where cops shot a stocky Rasta four times who was holding up a gun-shaped novelty lighter to someone's head. These were the tales that were told of London. To be feared is to be respected. We're not afraid of death. We've got your back. This is the street code. Step up and be a good soldier.

'We don't go up to Carnival no more,' Pilgrim says.

Not since that man died in 2000. A group of them stamped on a guy's head, threw a wheelie bin on him and killed him, just for a chain. It was a bit silly but that's the way it goes.

'You're in prison I'm on road, you're on road I'm in prison,' Ribz sighs from the back.

'Friends always missing each other like that.'

'Apart from back in the '90s when everyone was outside,' Pilgrim says.

You might see them late one summer night or something, smoking under the trees in the park. Or when they come back from country, or wherever they are where they meet up. Have a little chat, pretend you all like each other. Sure you all tossed coins in the street together when you were kids, but that doesn't mean you can trust them now. If trouble comes for you those guys will be gone.

'You won't see it happen ever again,' Steps says grimly, glowering through the windscreen like he has a death wish. Unless someone gets murdered, Pilgrim thinks, and everyone has to come back for the funeral. If one of them was merked, they would all big up how they were going to kill other people, but they wouldn't bother. Steps always pretends he's up for violence until it comes; his older brother is well known in the area. But apart from a funeral you will not get everyone in the same place. Pilgrim thinks about his father's words. He feels the gun pressing against the upholstery into the small of his back.

'Hold up,' Ribz yells, whacking the back of the seat so Steps' head snaps forward. Ribz lurches round and scopes out a wiry kid in a US aviation pilot's jacket, wading up the street with two lanky weasel mates on each shoulder. Steps wrenches the gears to second and slows so they can ID him properly. 'It's that fucker that blew up Elijah's A3.'

'It was a big thing for him, buying that car. He put a lot of work in,' Pilgrim says. He and Elijah have been friends since the minute they came to this country. They all know Elijah is a hard worker, a good dealer. You stay in the hood and deal, you make £500 to £1,000 a day if you are lucky. Elijah gets up seven thirty in the morning, takes the train to Colchester, Milton Keynes, wherever he can find his little spot where there's a bunch of drug addicts. He could be earning £5,000 a day, minus the £1,000 he needs to buy back his drugs tomorrow. So he's making £4,000 profit, paying £500 a week to one of his shotters and £350 if he has a driver. In the hood he sells 0.2 for £20, but in the country he can get £20 for 0.1. Plus the London heroin is purer, straight off the M25.

But once you start flossing, people get jealous. This guy was jealous of the A3, so he just set it alight one day. The petrol tank caught and it blew up. So Ribz now wants to kill someone, before they've even made it to the Old Street club.

They pull over and watch the three figures walk on down Lower Clapton Road, past torn, spilt sacks of rubbish, the neon strip lights of fast-food joints. There's a heat haze over the surface of the ponds. Up ahead they make out the domes of the Chimes Bar and Palace Pavilion against the skyline. It is clear where they are heading.

Pilgrim cannot believe the wheels have come off his birthday plans so quickly. It has become so bad in the last few years that to go inside Palace Pavilion is like a trip to the Death Star. Six gangland executions in Lower and Upper Clapton Road, in two years. More likely to hear gunshots here in the murder mile than anywhere else in

Britain. The police loiter round the corner, in their ARVs, knowing the call-out will come soon enough. These cop sharp-shooters don't need to take the safeties off their Glock 17 self-loading pistols and Heckler and Koch MP5 carbines before they'll have to lurch into the club's car park to close down the latest shoot-out. They are 90 per cent accurate shooters, which is more than you can say for the Tinies and Babies, twelve-year-old wannabe gangsters out there, who'd splinter their own foot bones before they hit someone. And it's getting worse, racking up to a frenzy like Beirut. Across the road, a man is shot in the West Indian takeaway, Too Sweet, by an assassin in an Afro wig. Two days later two motorbikes swarm a guy in his Beamer convertible and block him off. They dismount and pump shots through the window, the driver twists out the door, ploughs face forward into the grit and trodden gum of the pavement, where he dies. A week later a forty-six-year-old pedestrian is beaten purple and hurled under the wheels of a passing Routemaster bus, crushed like a Big Mac carton. Why? Well, this guy was just unlucky. Same as Pilgrim was unlucky when he had to take his beats at home. Trouble will find you. It is waiting around the corner.

They park up outside the Pavilion. Chimes Bar is next door and mainly Jamaican. Palace Pavilion is for young kids into garage, hip hop and rap. Pilgrim phones the girl who works inside and tells her they are coming in. They sit and wait for the guy with the aviator jacket to roll in. After a while they realize he isn't going to show up.

'Must have clocked us as we were parking up and took off,' Ribz snaps, cracking the door open. The rubber seal sucks the air with a hiss.

'His friends are in there,' Pilgrim says. He saw the two lanky weasels going in. So they walk straight to the front of the line, ignoring the jeers as security, a fifteen-stone guy hopped out on steroids, bulked up with jail muscle, fresh out of Wandsworth, sees them coming and snaps the iron bar down to swing back the heavy metal door. Out of a cloud of sour sweat, mildewed damp and sweet hash smoke, a wall-eyed girl in a micro-skirt appears. She escorts them straight upstairs to the VIP area where it's quieter. Down on the dance floor the new kids are shoving into each other to Pharoahe Monch's 'Fuck You'. To the untrained eye it might look like a mass fight, but it's just the way the kids dance. As soon as the clubbers see them up there they know someone's going to get it. They all start nodding at Pilgrim, so nervous they nod three or four times until he sees them. Pilgrim squints into the mass, scouring their faces until he finds the two weasels, leaning on their elbows at the end of the bar. He jabs Ribz. 'Do what you're doing and get out of here.'

Pilgrim locks onto the two guys and they bristle. His eyes burn as he pictures the charred carcass of Elijah's A3. You don't fuck with a man's brand-new Audi. He wants these goons to suffer and feels the rage well. The clubbers are watching like there's a spotlight on them. They are known guys. When they are around, bad things happen.

'Whatever you feel he deserves,' Pilgrim says to Ribz, goading him on. They have already lost their strongest weapon, the element of surprise. Ribz leans on his fists, bragging about what he's going to do to those mother-fuckers, gassing himself up. He presses his back into the leather seat so he can feel the butt of the gun. Ribz keeps outside London selling drugs. He will only really fight if his back's against the wall. It makes him very dangerous in a fight because he'll try to end it as fast as possible with a knife, gun or CS gas.

The more Pilgrim listens, the more a bad feeling grows in him. In this game you cannot let the minutes slide by. There are other young thugs in the club who could have stripped their pieces and cleaned them with a fucking brush by now. He stands up and goes downstairs. He doesn't risk a trip to the john, even though he's bursting. He could be trapped in there with no room to manoeuvre and no escape route. So he finds a pillar and leans against the wall so it blocks him off. He feels better now.

He's been going to clubs since he was nine. It's eleven years since his dad brought him out of Jamaica to live in this hell-hole. He brought him to his new wife's cramped two-bedroom house to share a room with her son. They were horrified when he arrived with Pilgrim from the airport. 'When's he going back?' was all Pilgrim heard; these people never wanted him in their house. You took me from Jamaica and my mum and put me in hell here, he thought. His stepbrother's dad was still lurking around to buy his son new trainers, a computer, Game Boy and mountain bike. Pilgrim's dad lost his foreman's wages in the bookies and gave what was left to his stepmum. He was the last kid in Stoke Newington to get a Game Boy.

Arguments rage in the house over money. Pilgrim can't take living in his stepbrother's room after a while. Two young men in one cramped room, it's like a pressure cooker. He asks them if they could move him to his own room. The only other room is a cupboard where the freezer is kept. He moves in there. No windows, no nothing. Like Cinderella. But now he's in his own room he's happy. He's downstairs by the front door, he can slip in and out whenever he wants. Living in his own room, later on bringing girls in, sneaking them in and out of the house.

Pilgrim is probably one of the best fighters at his school. No one really wants to fight him on the streets. Even though he's in Stoke Newington, he hangs around in Pembury, and at thirteen, he is the leader of a Pembury gang. Now you hear London Fields and Tottenham, but then it was Pembury that was running the whole of Hackney, all the serious people, a few from Clapton. Pembury was the main place.

Pilgrim was well advanced in the street life when some forty-year-old white guy, Wolf, approached him. Wolf had been on the scene since the '80s. Pilgrim was fifteen, known as muscle that would come down, rob someone and beat them up. He was like a hit man. The trail of victims meant that London Fields Boys wanted his scalp. Wolf sought Pilgrim out, because he knew he was a feared guy.

'You are making a rep for yourself in the area,' Wolf told him when they met.

Pilgrim looked at his slack chicken neck, the white whiskers appearing on his chin. He did not fear this old guy at all. He calculated that no one did and that was why he needed Pilgrim. His reputation was well on the wane.

'But I can promise you the keys to the city,' Wolf went on slyly.

'What's in this for me?' Pilgrim snapped. 'What you got that I want?'

Wolf's eyes narrowed. His tiny black pupils stared back at the younger man, as he pumped on a roly. 'Access to guns,' Wolf said.

With long-standing links to organized crime, Wolf could supply Pilgrim's crew the one thing they needed to become more powerful. So they teamed up for a while. He sent Pilgrim out to collect money from promoters, the Turkish community and strip clubs on the pay roll. Pilgrim no longer had to pay to get into clubs. Any strip club that was on the pay roll: he would always do his research, find which night the promoters were on and turn up. The other clubbers clocked the bottles of champagne being brought to his table and his respect built up. Celebrities who liked to dabble in that lifestyle and feel dangerous for a night would approach him. Pilgrim was taking girls back every night to his room. They were surprised to find it was a cupboard with a freezer in it and no windows.

Pilgrim feels a strong grip close on his shoulder. He wheels round.

'Yo, Pilgrim. You all right?'

It's a local bad boy with a razor cut and a large gold chain, wanting to be seen saying hello to him. The kid slips away and into urgent hand-moves on the dance floor. An angry ragga track has come on. Pilgrim flashes a look around the club. No sign of the weasels. He peers round the pillar, catches a glimpse of them, their faces set, purposeful. Pilgrim floats back and fades into the crowd, works round the edge of the dance floor in the opposite direction, then upstairs to Ribz' booth.

'They're by the DJ box now. If we're going to do something, let's do it,' he says. 'We ain't got time to think.'

That is how Pilgrim likes to work. Do what you're doing and deal with the consequences after. The guys are now in position, scowling them up from the far wall like they know exactly what the next play is. They won't risk firing indoors. It's too crowded. They'll try to draw them outside. They have become the prey. Ribz is still talking, but Pilgrim ignores him. With all his talk, Ribz has now lost them the advantage. He feels his phone vibrating in his pocket.

'Where you at?' It was Lil Solja, one of the top Tottenham Boys. Pilgrim had forgotten that he'd arranged for Lil Solja to pick him up, take him to Tottenham for his birthday.

'Palace Pavilion,' Pilgrim says.

Pilgrim runs a risk having allies in the Tottenham Boys, given the long-standing beef with Hackney. But Lil Solja was in his class once. They got on well. The Tottenham Boys are not allowed near the Palace Pavilion. Their sullen A4 mugshots are pinned to every cork-board in the corridors of Hackney police with 'Wanted – Armed Robbery'. The most fresh-faced special or blues and twos glances at them on the way to the canteen. They are Turkish-speakers who will use knives held to people's throats, taxing the snooker halls and hookers' flats. But in Hackney, they are dead. Only the other day a Turkish guy was crawling along in heavy traffic when a pedestrian walked over and shot him six times through the window. He was stuck behind a bus at the junction of Lower Clapton Road. They executed him in broad daylight, on a sunny afternoon, in front of the milling women and kids.

'I'll call when I'm outside,' Lil Solja says.

Pilgrim shuts his phone. He gets up to leave the club.

Fuck this place, he thinks, as he heads downstairs again and tenses at every young black guy he passes. He has to get out without being seen. The shootings in recent months all seem to have been guys who were walking away from the Chimes Bar next door. Across the dance floor, there is a Younger who he knows, posing in sunglasses in front of two over-made-up teenage girls. Pilgrim can tell from his body language he is giving some macho account of a shoot-out that never happened, bigging himself up as the hero. Their eyes lock. The kid bristles. A Younger has to fall in line to an Elder like Pilgrim. He'll patrol borders, head out on incursions, collect debts, stash guns and even go to jail, all in the vain hope that one day he'll fill Pilgrim's shoes.

After ten minutes Pilgrim's phone rings again. It's Lil Solja. He sounds nervous. Loitering around the Chimes Bar, waiting for Pilgrim, is putting him at risk.

'You're taking too long.'

'I'm coming. I'm coming.'

'Don't come out the back,' Lil Solja says. 'Five oh are here. Meet us in Ferry Lane. That's where the party is.'

Lil Solja rings off. Pilgrim bears down on the Younger in the shades.

'Lend me those a minute, will you,' Pilgrim says, sliding them off the kid's nose and putting them on. The younger knows why he needs them, that he has to leave the club undetected. Despite Lil Solja's warning he comes out the front exit. The police are a risk, but a lesser one than being shot. As he homes in on the door, he sees a small table with flyers piled up, picks up two and buries his nose and mouth in them. Security snaps down the metal bolt on the fire door for him and Pilgrim pulls up the hood of his Avirex jacket and walks out. With the sunglasses, the flyers and hood no one can see who the hell he is. The heavy metal door slams behind him and the music fades to a dull thud. He senses in a second that something is not right. The car park is too still. Instinctively he looks down to his right.

There is a little kid, squatting on one knee with gloved hands around a snub-nosed gun, aiming right up at him. Pilgrim hears the bolt on the door snap shut again. He's fucked.

The nearest cover is a hundred-yard sprint across an empty space to hurl himself behind a row of cars. By the time he's reached for his own piece and brought it up to aim he'll have four shots in him. He only has one option. Yelling like a banshee, his arms thrown wide, he charges down the stairs right into the face of his shooter. The kid flinches for a second like he's facing a mad man and lets the barrel drop a nudge. He's caught off guard. It's only a second, but it is just long enough for Pilgrim to wrench his own gun from his waistband. He aims at the chest and pulls the trigger. Nothing happens. The gun has jammed. Pilgrim doesn't wait. Now he runs into the night. Pumping his arms like pistons, he sprints down the road and sidesteps jerkily like a quarterback he's seen on telly. Behind him he can hear pow pow pow as the kid discharges his weapon. A bullet whips into the leaves of a tree ahead. He cuts across to the pond. The sooner he merges into the darkness the better. The rapid fire rate tells him it's a semi-automatic. This is the moment, he thinks. His lungs are burning, there's a metallic taste in his mouth. He can barely lift his knees. It's like he's wading through waist-deep water. No way can he cover the distance from here to the pond and survive. He risks a glance behind at his shooter, but all he can see is the heat rising off the ground in shimmering waves. Six shots have gone off now.

There's another crack. Bam. Bam. He buckles and skitters. Something burns his hand. It's like hot wax. Like someone has pressed a steam iron against it.

'Fuh-uck!'

Pilgrim brings his hand up. It is all swollen up, looks like it's covered in cigarette ash. He wheels round. Several hooded figures come out of the shadows and bear down on him now. Many shoot-outs end like this, with some fool with a jammed gun in his hand. When they find his body, the cops' first guess is that the dead man was not brave enough in the heat of battle to return fire. Then they find out it was jammed. A lot of the kids out there are poor shots, who can't hit a moving target over a hundred yards away. That's why there are so many gunfights where someone is shot in the leg or winged. He has read in *The Art of War* the importance of tactics and weaponry. As his blood thuds in his temples, he knows his only hope is to fix his jammed weapon. He must be fast. The shooters may be out of range, but he can hear them covering the ground quickly. In a few seconds they will be close enough not to miss.

Pilgrim has taken time to look into how a gun works. His gun has a sock stretched over it, to stop any prints going on it. Under the sock is a 9mm Browning self-loading pistol. It's standard RAF issue. He bought it in the army shop in Bethnal Green, with blanks, for £100. He drilled and reactivated it himself. Cut the plastic thing off and then put the real bullet head in there. He went to the hardware shop and bought the pipe and put it back in. Then the brush and the clip and he was ready to go. All he had to do was buy the bullets, 9mm Parabellum cartridges. All the kids think they are ballistics experts, but they know shit. Most of the guns on the streets now are imitations, starter pistols, air guns that have been converted to fire live bullets. Pilgrim has become a technician. He knows that after you have fired it a few times the pipe will swell and when it swells and cools back down it gets smaller. It either jams or backfires on you. And you can hit your finger off. When people get their hand shot off it's because they've got a rebore and the pipe's been burnt out. Sometimes it can fuck up if you put too much gunpowder in it. Or because you haven't put the firing pin in. So many things can go wrong.

Pilgrim grips his Browning 9mm until he finds the catch. Every serrated part of a gun is a moving part. Sometimes when a gun jams the panicked shooter tries to force it, rubbing his fingers over the serrated edge, covering it in his DNA. It becomes a forensics' dream. Pilgrim pulls back the catch and tugs it to the right. The jammed bullet drops into the sock. He's seen too many guys sent to jail for leaving shell casings on the ground. An eagle-eyed Five Oh from ballistics picks up the casing with tweezers and sends it to the NABIS supercomputer to analyse. The striation marks are like a signature, like a fingerprint. Pilgrim cocks it again. It's ready to fire now. He can hear his shooter's feet thud on the hard ground, to his left. He wheels round, lifting his arm with the gun up and aims at the sound. There it is. He fires. The gun lets one off with a loud crack. The footsteps stop. Silence. Then he sees two figures duck down and scurry back to the alleyway. They thought he was unarmed, as he hadn't returned fire. Pilgrim closes one eye and tracks them as they run. He fires again. They accelerate and scatter like deer. Pilgrim turns, shoves the gun into his waistband and jogs into the lengthening shadows.

Half an hour later, Ribz' car pulls up two blocks away. Pilgrim steps out of an alley and slumps into the back. His hand aches like hell, but they wipe a wet rag over it and strap it up. There's no question he can go to hospital with a gunshot wound. Same if he'd been shanked in the leg. You can't afford to take something like that to A&E, as they report back to Five Oh. You have to sort it yourself.

Despite the pain, he can see the others are hungry for the tale, his front-line war story. This is the ritual they live for. Everything is built on reputation and Pilgrim has taken a bullet. Everyone wants to be feared, because to be feared is to be loved. Prison cells, juvenile courts, street corners echo with bragging and story-telling, as men are made.

Pilgrim's fingertips tremble as Ribz hands him an ice-cold bottle of Red Stripe. He takes two long swigs, wipes his mouth with his knuckles, then begins to tell them. Coming out with the shades on. Seeing the crouched shooter. The dash across the car park. Fixing the jammed gun. He splays his fingers and tries to hold his hand level. It is purple, swollen like it's infected.

'I looked back. I couldn't see the shooter,' he croaks. He feels dazed. 'All I could see was the heat-haze. Coming up in waves.'

'That wasn't no heat-haze,' Ribz says ominously. The others frown at him. He wasn't even there. 'It was the duppies coming for you.'

But Pilgrim doesn't do black magic. He doesn't smoke crack, doesn't usually drink. But most of all he doesn't believe that evil spirits come for you like something out of *Dr Who*.

'I can't stand all that voodoo shit,' he snaps.

'The duppies won't trouble you while you're alive,' Ribz jabbers on. 'But when you're close to death the duppy comes to claim your black ass. That's the heat-haze you saw. You were that close.'

Ribz holds up his index finger and thumb for emphasis, right under Pilgrim's nose. Pilgrim is angry now. Ribz is muscling in. This evening it is a shoot-out story, a one-on-one duel.

'That shit is for women who go and get themselves washed down with liquids, to do black magic,' he says. 'That's all nonsense. You know what is for real? That kid firing his shooter.'

'Let the man tell the story,' Steps says gravely.

At the end they are quiet for a moment. He has their attention.

'Every kid in Hackney says they've been in a shoot-out,' Steps sighs. 'When they're in a shoot-out with their friends and fifteen or thirty people – that ain't a shoot-out. One on one with another gun man, shoot or be shot. That is respect, man.'

Then they pull over and drop Pilgrim off. His hand is throbbing like a truck rolled over it. He feels a wave of nausea. He is dog-tired. Once inside the words 'That is respect, man' echo round his empty room. From the car window Ribz holds his fist aloft like some Black Power salute. Rain thuds on the bonnet as the car pulls away. Pilgrim did not tell them that when he fired at the shooters he didn't want to kill anyone. He just wanted them to fuck off and leave him alone. Through the wall he hears a shrill smoke alarm. Then he realizes it is the persistent cry of a small baby, waking up hungry. Its mother's voice soothes and calms it, until the wail dies down. His own mother has been dead three years now. Five foot nothing but the bravest woman he met. He used to talk to her all the time on the phone. Then when he came back from visiting her in Jamaica his father and stepmother changed the home number. They didn't tell her. In Jamaica she didn't have an address. She just lived 'down the road'. She walked to the phone to call her son but couldn't get through. She wrote him letters, but they were intercepted by his dad. She kept writing, but eventually gave up. Pilgrim was living his life in England thinking she's dead. Whenever I see you I see you. From the age of eight he had to live with those kinds of things in his head. He lost touch.

Then at sixteen he had a call from his aunty. 'Your mother is dying,' she told him. She had cervical cancer. 'They tried to laser the thing, but they were like practising on her. Ended up burning out too much of her insides. So by the time she heals up she can't stand up or eat no more.'

He peels the sock back off his Browning 9mm, and lets the wooden stock lie flat in his open palm. If he was shot, what page would he be on in the paper, he wonders. A black-on-black teenage shooting isn't the hot news it used to be. Just another line of chalk for Trident to sort out. If he dies he will go and see his mum. So he doesn't care about the next shooter who comes for him. He can kill him and his friends. Inside he feels dead already.

Two days on, his hand still aches. He is already on an attempted murder charge and can barely hold the gun up to aim. He has a rep to keep up and needs money. He flicks through the numbers in his phone and dials his cousin, an old-school drug-dealer, and as his hand heals up he rides around with him. He finds the hood too crowded with other dealers so he expands into the West End even though it's controlled by the Yardies. He buys himself a used black cab, a Fairway TX1, two-door funeral. He takes a junkie, greases his hair up and slides a pair of plain-glass spectacles on his pock-marked face so he looks like a real taxi driver. He pays the guy in wraps. The Yardies stand a hundred yards away, smoking. They are hard, muscled thugs straight out of Trench Town with gleaming Nikes, a Glock shoved in their trackie bottoms. Pilgrim and his cousin park up in the West End, just before eight do their drop-offs and they go. Like clockwork. They leave the Yardies standing out there trying to make their million overnight. Pilgrim continues to make his P. He hears that Steps has been arrested. He carries on riding the taxi until the scars turn purple and knot together on his hand.

One night they are out in the back of the cab when Pilgrim's phone rings. It's an old friend, Drek.

'I've got this easy robbery,' Drek says. 'Come along. Do it with us.'

Pilgrim frowns and switches his phone to the other

ear. Last he heard, Drek is in the second year, studying aerodynamics at university. Now he has it in his head he's a big-time drug-dealer and is refusing to go back to uni. Well, thinks Pilgrim, good luck to him.

'I'm into something right now,' he says, stalling.

Ribz has disappeared off the radar. All the top boys are being rounded up. Sooner or later, I'm going to jail, he thinks. Despite himself he feels the call of the life.

'Come over tomorrow,' he says to Drek.

'Kentish Town, right?'

The next day, when Pilgrim opens the door, Drek is standing there with another guy. The newcomer is dressed in a baggy grey sweatshirt like a student. He wouldn't frighten an old lady with a £5 umbrella. Pilgrim scowls back and takes Drek aside.

'Don't bring people to my house, bruv.'

Drek looks blank, like Pilgrim's having delusions of grandeur, imagining he's on the FBI Most Wanted list. 'Who are you – the Fugitive?' he cracks.

'I don't know your friend here,' he gestures to the newcomer, who nervously gurns back at them. 'You and I could fall out tomorrow and this fool now knows where I live.'

'It's just Jimmy,' Drek shrugs.

The robbery sounds simple enough. It is a truck of designer clothes. They hold it up at gunpoint, take the cargo off in another car. That's it. For Pilgrim it seems pretty simple. The only problem is the match fitness of this crew – Drek and Jimmy. They are not like the real guys. He will have to watch them every inch of the way. One thing is for sure, though – this will be his last robbery. He's had it with this nonsense.

LONDON

A few days before, Drek and his pal pick Pilgrim up and drive him to Kingston. There they meet another guy, Obi. Pilgrim doesn't like Obi the moment he meets him. Obi smiles too much. He's laughing, making jokes. He's even worse than Jimmy.

'Why all the jokes?' Pilgrim scowls at him.

Obi shoots him a hunted look, eyes flicking from side to side. 'Nothing wrong with having a laugh and a joke,' he shrugs. He's like a school kid, praying he guessed the right answer, laughing because the whole thing scares the shit out of him. Pilgrim, the armed robber who hasn't smiled once, scares him most of all.

'This is a robbery here,' Pilgrim snaps, with professional pride. 'It's serious. As soon as I meet you, you're giggling. I don't want you joking around with me.'

He is so far into this thing now he cannot pull out. His only hope is to drill some sense into these fools. If only he had someone like Marlon with him on this. Marlon was two years older and took Pilgrim under his wing. He was prolific offender and he'd been going in prison and robbing banks from year eight and all that. Started off snatching women's handbags. It was fun. Quick money. Adrenalin. Some of them would chase, some of them wouldn't chase.

Sometimes you would get the jackpot of £50 and a mobile. You went and sold the credit cards to the African guys, you were all right for the week. Nigerian fraudsters – the uncles. Even better if there's a cheque book in the bag. They don't ask no questions. They all do their fraud and turn it into something else. Obviously more than the £100 they are giving you for the card. As a kid you don't really ask nothing. You've got £100, you can go and buy whatever you want.

He is very clear. 'Take the drivers' mobile phones away.'

They nod.

'Wear tights over your face.'

They nod again.

'We need a van to shift the stuff from the truck.'

They nod. The group breaks up.

When the day comes Pilgrim waits on the corner. It's early evening and on either side of him school kids tear past. One has a white skull mask on. Their shirts are untucked, heads thrown back in laughter. A few yards away a bus door opens with a loud hiss and the kids shove on. Pilgrim could step on and never look back. In minutes he'd be lost in the streets. A car horn goes off. He turns to see Jimmy behind the wheel. It's a Mitsubishi Colt, a small car with a boot big enough for a few Tesco bags. They are robbing a whole lorry. Pilgrim climbs in, slams the door.

'I told you to bring a van,' he says, turning to glare at Jimmy.

'We'll drive to the van,' Jimmy says.

Pilgrim stares ahead at the bus as its indicator blinks and it sways heavily out into the traffic.

'How are we going to fit a fucking lorry worth of goods in this small car?'

'The van's parked near uni.'

Fucking students, Pilgrim thinks, they think they're moving house. It's all going to take too long. A sullen silence hangs in the car as they edge through traffic towards the meet. They round a corner into a deserted industrial estate. The lorry is parked up ahead.

'When I get my thing out, pull the tights over your head and come out,' Pilgrim says. He glances round at Drek and Obi to check. They are wide-eyed like kids. As they draw near, the lorry looms up above the car like an iceberg. Pilgrim erupts out the car and marches over to the driver's door. The driver climbs down from his cab, tosses away his half-smoked cigarette and squints his craggy face at Pilgrim.

'Was it jeans you wanted?' the driver asks. He is under the impression he is going to make a quick sale on the side, before he delivers it to the depot. 'What size are you?'

'Thirty-six waist,' Pilgrim says. The driver leads him round the back as he hauls up the tarpaulin, muttering something about the labels. Pilgrim pulls his gun and presses the barrel into the back of his neck.

'You know what – I'm taking your van,' Pilgrim says. 'Get your friend out.'

He gets the second driver out of the lorry at gunpoint. Pilgrim signals for Obi and Drek to start unloading the cargo. He stands training the gun on the drivers as the others cram the goods into the tiny boot of the Mitsubishi. He moves round to the passenger side, keeping the gun up above the car's roof, yanks open the door, then dives in. Jimmy guns the engine and they roar off. The car rockets out of the estate, burns down a row of parked cars, still in first gear. They are pumped up.

'Throw them mobiles out,' Pilgrim yells, cranking down his window. Nothing happens. There's silence in the back. He wheels round, shoves his open palm in Obi's face. Drek and Obi look down at their knees, unable to catch his eye. Their faces are covered in such fine-denier tights that their features are clearly visible. They might as well be wearing cobwebs.

'What the fuck you wearing?' he shouts at them as the car lurches from side to side. 'You couldn't find anything thicker? My grandma could pick you out of a line-up without her glasses on.'

Pilgrim gestures at them to hand over the mobiles. Obi scowls out the window, screwing his face up.

'Don't tell me you forgot,' Pilgrim says in disbelief. He leans forward and sinks his head into his hands. Then he rubs his scalp feverishly, gripped by a spasm of rage. It's like his hair is alive with fleas.

'They called Five Oh already. For sure,' he says. Then he slams his hand down on the dashboard. They drive back to their uni to meet up with the van. Pilgrim looks at his watch. If he's not in and out of a place in five minutes he's going to jail. That's his rule. His watch says six minutes and counting. The others are too scared to speak up as the car pulls in. Pilgrim looks around at the university campus. Students mill around carrying lever-arch files, with sensible trainers and rucksacks. They are all white kids, wearing pastel colours from Gap, chewing gum and listening to their iPods.

'Where's the van, Jimmy?' Pilgrim asks.

'Let me phone him,' Jimmy replies nervously. The van driver hasn't been told he was going to be part of a robbery. By the time he comes back more minutes have gone past. The students stop chewing their gum, put their iPods on pause. It's growing dark but they still stare over at the three black boys, bundling designer clothes from a Mitsubishi Colt into a van. Before they've even finished

Pilgrim stops and listens for the sound he's been expecting. A siren wails from a block away. They give each other one final reproachful scowl, each one blaming the other, then scatter. Pilgrim is legging it down the street. The air is swarming with sirens now. The drivers must have been on their mobiles seconds after it happened. Ahead of him is a cul-de-sac, with no clear way out. He stops and looks around. Behind him he can see the pulsing light of the blues and twos, flashing against the walls of the houses. The street is bordered with wooden fences, topped with barbed wire into front gardens. Pilgrim refuses to go to jail. Not like this. Not with a bunch of amateurs in some bungled robbery.

He makes a split-second decision to go right, sprints at the fence, leaps up onto a green municipal bin and vaults up over it. His momentum is not enough to carry him clean over the top, so he grabs at the post to propel him. Barbed wire slices into his hand. His body keeps going, spinning over, feet first, twisting in the air. He hears the fence splinter, as he crashes heavily to the ground, scraping his shin. He's up again and running. Above him he can hear the powerful whir of rotor blades as the police chopper hovers into position. The white glare of its searchlight rakes the ground. Behind him dogs yawp, straining away from their handlers. Dogs are the thing Jamaicans fear the most, he remembers his father telling him. They are probably German shepherds, trained to chew off his gun hand. He cannot face jail. Not like this. The circle of white light swoops back and stays on him. The whole yard is lit up like a football stadium. Every rubbish sack, every line of graffiti dazzles and blinds him. Above him the rotor blades throb. Lights are going on inside houses. Windows are flung open as the whole neighbourhood is woken up. How long can he keep running? Has anyone outrun a police chopper? It's impossible. He has seconds left to come up with something, some ace up his sleeve. Fifty yards ahead of him on the road is a row of manhole covers. He runs over and bends down on one knee. From his pocket he takes the key to his flat, a Chubb, and levers it under the lid. With his good hand, he heaves up the metal slab. Then he eases himself stiffly into the darkness of the hole, his trainers feeling out the rungs.

At the bottom he lurches away down the tunnel. His hand, raised above him, feels ahead, his fingertips grazing on the sharp concrete. He runs blindly in the dark, listening to the echo of his feet hitting the water. Every twenty yards he stops, doubles over and heaves until it is an empty dry air heave. Then he carries on tumbling forward. He can't remember how long he is underground, how much distance he's covered in the dark stench. A tide of rage rises up and keeps him going.

Finally, his abs aching from the contractions, his fingers find a hole in the roof. He grasps around until they close on a metal rung embedded in the brick. Just below the street, he listens. No sound of traffic. He doesn't want to clamber into a busy road, lit by street lamps. With a final effort he eases up the deadweight of the manhole cover and hauls himself out.

After an hour of weaving through back streets, he finds himself outside an entryphone in Tottenham. He's stayed over at this girl's place a couple of times recently. She knows what he is. He's come to surprise her. Pilgrim is buzzed in and he tells her he has to lie low at her place. The cops will not think to look for a Hackney boy in enemy territory.

Early in the small hours police circle around his flat in Kentish Town and lie in wait for him. His housing benefit is stated as this address. The next day word reaches Pilgrim that the others have been arrested. The witnesses only report seeing three guys. Pilgrim stops using his cash card, and sends the girl out for supplies. He leaves no paper trail now. On the third day after the robbery he calls his father.

'The police are round here every day asking for you.'

Pilgrim can hear the strain in his father's voice. He had not anticipated how he would feel hearing him.

'Did you kill someone?' he asks.

Pilgrim sighs long and hard through his nose. 'No.'

'What did you do?'

He leans his head back and rubs the sleep out of his eyes. How long can he keep running? He remembers his father's face as he stood silhouetted at the door. He looked so old. He thinks about the stress on him of the life his son leads.

'I'm just going to go to prison,' he tells his father. 'Go and do my sentence.'

So that afternoon he walks through the front door of the station and turns himself in. The cops read him his rights. He sits in a bare room with a strip light, a mug of coffee and a tape recorder. A bald cop in a black Polartec fleece and jeans sits opposite him.

'The other three, Drek, Obi and Jimmy, are pleading duress,' the cop says. 'They will stand up in court and say you did all sorts of things to them to coerce them to carry out this robbery.'

Pilgrim gives a wry smile and shakes his head. He would expect as much.

'Let's talk about Elijah,' the cop says. They want Pilgrim to give up Elijah, the guy who had his Audi A3 blown up. They went into the Palace Pavilion to kill that boy for Elijah. Elijah is wanted for attempted murder.

'I'm not giving him up,' he tells the cops. 'I'll go to jail and do my sentence.'

Pilgrim goes to court, where he is tried as an adult and sentenced to six years for armed robbery. First, he is transferred to Portland Young Offenders Institute. On the cliffs of Portland Island in Dorset, Pilgrim finds himself amongst young teenagers. He hears rumours about the violence, the bullying, the brutal guards. As the door closes he thinks how he'll spend his twenty-first birthday in a place like this.

6: Prison

It's Pilgrim's first night in Aylesbury Prison. He was transferred there from Portland for stirring up trouble. From his bunk he stares at a small high window onto a walled yard. Through it comes the sound of one inmate goading his neighbour to kill himself. The taunts keep Pilgrim awake. They carry on hour after hour, relentless. A period of silence, then the bully's rage fires up again. The neighbour's cell is silent, as if he's already done himself in. In the morning, when the doors are cracked open, the bully swaggers out to survey his handiwork. He expects to find his victim snagged on his belt. But his neighbour stands, cradling a cup in both hands. His expression is calm, insolent. Then he lunges forward and flings the cup's contents at the bully's face. It is a mixture of boiling water and sugar. The sugar sticks to the skin and intensifies the burns. It is a classic prison attack. The bully screams and thrashes around, his fingers fly up instinctively to his eyes. Pilgrim watches the encounter. He must keep his own eyes open. He learns a key lesson of prison. You have to stand up to the other guy or you are finished.

Aylesbury is full of seventeen- to twenty-one-year-old violent prisoners, banged up all day long. The boredom and pressure crush them. In the beginning Pilgrim starts marking off the days. But it seems like his time will never end, so he shuts himself down. He doesn't send out any visiting orders. Seeing family just upsets him. He doesn't phone home. The fastest time passes is when he works in the kitchen. Washing up from 8 a.m., not back on the wing until 9 p.m. Some kids turn to Prislam. They do it for friendship and protection. Prislam is a huge gang, with special food. Some are crazy and say they are going to kill all the drug-dealers. Once they kill them all they'll use their money for toilets in the mosque, because that is all it's good for. Pilgrim starts to learn about Islam, just so they will leave him alone.

When he turns twenty-one he is transferred to a man's prison, Swinfen Hall in Staffordshire. His heart sinks as it travels further away from London, into the country. So far Pilgrim's reputation on the streets has carried respect with the teenagers inside. Further from London it will mean nothing. His only allies are now the handful of guys with him in the van.

'Listen up,' he says hunching forward. 'There are six of us from London. If anything kicks off we must stick together.'

Sure enough as he enters the prison he finds young men from twenty-one to twenty-five serving four years to life, but no familiar faces. He gets lots of dirty looks as he walks down the hall. He is a newbie on his own in B wing, and dangerously isolated. Violence can flare up the instant someone steps in front of you in the food queue. If you don't stand up to him, the next day everyone else will do the same. He assesses the situation and realizes he needs a survival plan fast.

First he gathers intelligence. He scopes the prison out.

Nine wings in all. He spots an ageing Jamaican inmate who is chatty with everyone, picks his moment and approaches him.

'Which gang are you with?' the old guy asks.

'Love of Money.'

'Sounds like a bunch of London pussies to me,' comes the angry reply. 'In here you are nothing if you aren't from the second city.'

'Manchester?'

'Fuck Gunchester, no way. Birmingham. Runs all the drugs in the West Midlands, has the best clubs in the country. In here if you're not with the Johnson Crew or the Burger Bar Boys you're as good as dead.'

'Never heard of them. Don't pay attention to some country boys.'

As he moves amongst them he can feel the weight of menace on him. He needs to establish an alliance, even with one or two inmates. Loners are liable to be attacked or exploited. He is watchful for contacts. So from 8 a.m., when the prisoners are unlocked for the optional morning exercise, through the 9 a.m. prisoner activities, he finds out all he can.

'Johnson Crew and Burger Bar Boys have a beef going back years, man. Like ten years. BB used to be Johnson, then they broke away. Johnson run the doors of clubs, sell the drugs inside. Their turf is Aston, Erdington and Lozells.'

'And the others?'

'Since 2000 it's been mayhem. Over New Year's, Burger Boys shot up two teenage girls and the papers went mental. So the cops had to bang up all the serious guys.'

'Thanks. Sweet.'

Pilgrim spends all day listening for London accents. From 6 p.m. prisoners are allowed to associate with each other. They have showers, go to the library, make phone calls or mix freely with other prisoners on the wing. It is then that he makes his move. He approaches an inmate and says in a low voice. 'You from London?'

The guy eyes him suspiciously. With the place run by the vicious Birmingham gangs, it is not something he is readily going to admit to.

'I'm from East,' Pilgrim says. 'Hackney.'

'South,' the guy says quietly, looking from side to side. 'But keep it to yourself, bruv.'

'Are there others too?'

'Sure. From South. But they are afraid to speak up. We're outnumbered by Brummies. Every maggot in here sounds like Ozzy Osbourne.'

At 8 p.m. they are returned to their cells. Pilgrim needs a plan to pass the time. He decides to move all the London guys onto B wing, where he is. As he travels round he tells them to cause trouble and get themselves moved. So fights break out. On the snooker table it kicks off, someone comes out of nowhere with two balls in a sock. One by one the Londoners are all moved to Pilgrim's wing. Before the guards know what's happening it's too late.

On the way to the library another kid grabs his arm. 'Have a message from outside,' he whispers, staring ahead. 'From one of your soldiers.'

Pilgrim nods. It's good that his soldiers have not forgotten him. Pilgrim looked after these boys from school, turned them into brave men.

'Kid wants you dead,' the messenger tells him. 'Says he's going to ice you. First chance he gets.'

'Now these pussies are sending me death threats,' Pilgrim shrugs. 'When I lived next door they didn't threaten me over nothing. Youngers don't know their place.'

There were light-skinned ones who he wouldn't trust with his sister. In Jamaica a lighter skin gets you a better job and some people buy bleach for it. In his crew the light-skinned ones chase the women, but they are weak. They don't have enough soul in them. They attack girls. They don't hang around when a knife is pulled.

'You inside now, where real gangsters walk the yard,' the messenger says. 'They're the ones to worry about. Rub them up the wrong way, they come after you.'

'Look at me, bruv,' Pilgrim grins back at him. He puts a menacing lightness in his voice. 'Do I look scared to you? Let me know how many guys from South in here,' he says, then walks away.

He decides he needs a weapon. In his cell he stamps on his Bic razor to release the blades. He then takes his toothbrush and melts the end with a lighter so he can press the two blades in. Best move is to come up behind your target, reach around him and drag it across his face from his mouth.

Gradually Pilgrim gathers all the South London kids together and forms his own gang. He thinks he might even roll with some of the older ones when he comes out. But the Birmingham crew run the jail. And the guards have clocked what Pilgrim is up to. It is 5 a.m. and he is woken by keys scrunching in the lock. It bursts open and men pile in. His bed is surrounded. He looks up into their faces. They are all guards.

'Get ready to leave,' one snaps. 'You're being transferred.'

This is how it is. He's moved to a new jail. He arrives, builds up his crew. Fights and trouble start until they are moved around. His crew robs the drug-dealers, steals mobile phones. He has to keep it moving. So he tries to take over the jail. Then the guards transfer him. Time after time.

But all those months of jail make him think. All those hours staring at the ceiling a few inches above his bunk, listening to his cell mate take a shit a few feet away. Then out for a few minutes to walk the yard. All this time he wonders how he ended up spending his early twenties in this hell-hole.

'Fuck the police. They just racist,' his cell mate explains. It's a popular theory in here. 'The kids today know nothing about Jamaica. Slaves doing all the hard work getting sugar for cups of tea. Now still doing all the hard jobs, not being appreciated. Cops only stop and search black kids. You got saggy pants and a Nike suit on, you're straight on the gang database. Man, they criminalize you for being young. If there's another Toxteth, I'll be the first out there throwing a petrol bomb at the meat wagon.'

'Bullshit,' snaps Pilgrim. 'I hear the race card the whole time. As soon as you exceed expectations you don't hear it any more.'

'Yeah? How come there so many black guys in prison?'

'Because they are stupid. Only one in ten guys go to jail. You ask anyone why you in here, most times it's because you made a mistake. "Oh, this guy grassed me up." Well, why you hanging out with that kind of guy? Choose friends who'll keep their mouth shut. I'm in here because I did a robbery with a bunch of idiots.'

Pilgrim keeps his eyes open, always learning. There are different types.

There are rude boys who act like they're in a rap video, making sure everyone knows they are money-laundering, selling drugs. They are always bopping, walking like one of their legs is broken, slanted to one side. If you are a real gangster, you keep a low profile. There are gym boys who spend the whole time bulking up. They take steroids and become angry. He sees that those doing a long sentence to life are more relaxed, they walk slow. In remand prisons like Pentonville and Brixton they are more upbeat, because of the constant changeover. In Feltham all the young kids were excited. It's their badge of honour. Some were scared but they couldn't show it. High Down is so close to the women's prison, Downview, they share a car park. You can speak to the women through the window, but everyone can hear you.

Some guys educate themselves. They read about the history of slavery, Marcus Garvey and Malcolm X. Pilgrim doesn't go for that. Some police are cunts, but there is good and bad everywhere. No racist Five Oh made him pick up a gun and go looking for trouble. He thinks about why he ended up spending his youth inside and when things went wrong for him.

He first knew things were going bad in primary school, when he went to swimming lessons. He used to dread them. They took place at a notorious school called Hackney Downs. It was just like a prison and full of the worst kids in the area. When they arrived for swimming, older boys were waiting for them like a mob of football thugs. He and his friends edged forward nervously, huddling together. Pilgrim was struck hard in the head by a missile. White smoke engulfed him. His eyes were burning, streaming tears. He bent over in a coughing fit like he was going to throw up all over his shoes. His heart was pounding. He stumbled blindly into the swimming area. 'What the fuck was that?' he wheezed, trailing drool on the floor.

The teachers left them in the pool while they sat arguing in a tight circle, visibly shook. Then they gathered them together when they were leaving, to psych them up.

'They're using CS gas,' the teacher said, ashen-faced. 'When we leave, let's all rush out the door.'

That was his lesson for the day. He was ten. When he made it home safely he stood in the street between the unisex hairdresser and the shop with white goods stacked outside at 'guaranteed low prices'. He looked across at Stoke Newington police station. Local bad characters often drew up on their mopeds, went into the police station and signed on.

'All right, Pilgrim,' a voice called out.

Pilgrim turned and saw this guy waiting at the bus stop. He wore a dark green suit with a dark shirt tightly fitted over his lean, muscled body. Probably Versace. He looked half-Indian, half-black. His light, blue-tinted aviators were pushed up on the bridge of his nose. His hand had two large silver rings, and a thin gold chain draped inside his unbuttoned shirt. This guy liked jewellery, he was flashy. He was confident too but tightly coiled, as if he was holding himself back from the verge of violence.

'All right. Nice Aviators. Where you get them?'

'These here are Ray Ban 3025.'

The guy laughed. 'I'll get you a pair of Aviators. There's a guy I know. Do me a good deal. What kind you like?'

'No way! You'd get me them shades. What's in it for you?'

'Nothing. Helping out the kids, that's all. I'll get you mirror finish.'

Pilgrim couldn't believe it. This guy was flash. He had money. Those sunglasses must cost around £200.

'How old are you?'

When Pilgrim told him, he raised an eyebrow.

'You look older,' he said. Pilgrim liked that this guy treated him with respect. It wasn't what he was used to. 'When you leaving primary school?'

Pilgrim asked around and found out this was Solo. He didn't know if he was a drug-dealer.

'Solo? He's a real guy. A serious guy,' his friend told him. 'A guy that no one messes with.'

'Why's that?'

'Because if you do him something he will come back and do worse. He makes his money. He will shoot you or he will stab you.'

The Olders like Solo always waited outside the school gates, taking an interest, looking for new recruits. They lined up and took Pilgrim under their wing. Gave him new trainers or a fifty-quid note.

'Plenty more where that came from,' they'd say next day. Before long the kids were selling drugs for them. There were Olders who came over, stinking of weed. Pilgrim didn't smoke, so when they gave him weed, he'd sell it.

Gradually he got respect from the Olders because he made them P. They were always looking for energetic little kids to make them money, extend their little empire. Solo was the kind of guy, every time Pilgrim saw him he had the newest trainers on, the newest Armanis, newest Versace, Avirix. Whatever was out at the time. He always had a good guy's haircut, one level or short back and sides, and all the hot girls. Flash. Next time they met Pilgrim quizzed him about his clothes.

'It's not about the clothes. You as a person, you could have everything, but it's the way you wear what you've got,' Solo told him. 'So when you walk into a room people know you're there.'

'How do you mean?'

'Confidence,' Solo said, cupping his hands around his silver Zippo. 'If you haven't got confidence you are nothing in this world. And that's all it is. You can be as smart as you want, have as much O-levels, but if you haven't got confidence then you are nothing.'

He lit another cigarette from the burning tip and handed it to Pilgrim. He lowered his voice as if he was telling him something of import.

'Apart from having my wits about me, confidence is what has kept me alive. I have been in positions where a guy is trying to kill me and I know that he is scared of me so I'm going to attack him. Because of that I'm still alive today.'

It was better to be under the wing of an Older, for protection. Otherwise some guy five years older could beat the shit out of you just because he felt like it. It was good to beat up kids, get a rep for yourself as a violent guy. There were a lot of people around trying to make a name for themselves on the streets. The Pembury Boys were on the rise. There was Daniel Cummings, a hit man for the Hackney Boys. Years later he shot up a major gangster, Adrian Crawford from Tottenham Man Dem. Cut the car off with his Vectra then stood in the street, riddled the guy with bullets while his pregnant girlfriend crouched behind the boot. It was brazen, because that's how reps are made. They arrested Daniel next day with his body armour on, waiting for the payback. There were a lot of people round that area on the make. But Solo was a real guy and still is today. Always flash, always one step ahead. He was a good teacher and Pilgrim learnt moves from him that kept him alive.

There was another Older called Sweet, because he was baby-faced. He was boss of the Wood Green Boys. Like Solo, he was a serious guy on the streets. So Pilgrim was being looked after by two high-ranking lieutenants who had already earned their stripes.

Pilgrim looked at the other kids showing off their new phone, Jordans or pendant. That's all people talked about. Arguments over money raged in the house. There were no holidays, nothing to do, no new toys as a kid, nothing new to eat but supermarket own-brand tins, nothing on telly but Z-listers horsing around and ads of beautiful people toying with gleaming sexy stuff like it was porno. He felt a vast sea of rage inside about missing out on things other kids flaunted at school. The rage burned like acid inside him until he could stand it no longer.

Sweet taught him how to steal trainers and Avirex jackets from the West End.

'Go into one shop,' he said. 'Steal the left foot from Wood Green, right foot from West End. Or you go to West End, order three different trainers, confuse the people and run out the shop.'

He took him into the West End on the tube. Coming out at Oxford Circus was a whole new world to him. Pilgrim waited with Sweet at the bus stop and listened to him carefully.

'You go to that shop, left foot on display, take it and go.' Sweet went on, nodding towards a sports shop-front window, 'Go back to Wood Green, right foot on display, take it and go. Simple. That's it. Or you order the trainers in your size and steal one foot out the box. Or you try on both the trainers, leave your trainers in the shop and run out.'

That afternoon he went home with a brand-new pair of trainers. As he walked up to his house one of the Youngers wolf-whistled at him.

'How did you get those?' his father asked, peering over his glasses. 'When you're not working nowhere.'

'I bought them with my pocket money,' he shrugged. His father took off his glasses and stared at him.

'How the hell can you buy a pair of £100 trainers with £5 a week?'

The next time he came home with a new jacket. His father said nothing. He sipped his tea and cast a jaded look over the stitching and designer cut in silence. He raised an eyebrow to show that he knew this jacket did not come from TK-Maxx. But he stopped asking questions. Pilgrim was already a young bull. His father did not have the fight left in him to stop him. He tried to ground him, to lay down the enforcement. But Pilgrim just snuck out the house. At the end of the street Sweet would be waiting, ever reliable, taking an interest in the boy's development. Pilgrim started to stay away at night. He took his beats and came home on Sunday. After a while his father started phoning the police and saying he was missing. There were a lot of tricky kids out there, the police said, they were doing their best to keep an eye on them.

'Just phone us and let us know you're all right and what you're doing,' his father said. His skin was leathery and lined. 'We can't control you. You'll have to learn one day.'

By the time Pilgrim was fifteen, his stepbrother was turning seventeen. He was changing too. When Pilgrim went to see him in his room he had bags full of money, others with wraps of crack cocaine.

'You're bringing this shit into the house, bro?' Pilgrim whispered, amazed.

'What's it to you?' his brother sneered. 'Gangster lil brother.'

His brother had seemed such a nerdy boy with serious plans. His mum didn't want him around the other side of the estate. But he snuck out. He channelled all he had into his drug-dealing and made a lot of money. Anyone who messed with him knew Pilgrim was coming outside to defend him.

The secondary school Pilgrim went to was Hackney Downs. Loads of the pupils there went to prison or ended up on the streets. The council left Hackney Downs to rot for years, until they couldn't even be bothered to look under the stone. Staff never lasted, the kids didn't show up and the school buildings were crumbling. It was closed down in '95, all the staff were made redundant. Then two-hundred-odd troubled kids, who'd been expelled from other schools, with broken English, were dumped in another Hackney school. The council didn't care if there was a bloodbath. When the Hackney Downs kids arrived, it was like a nightmare. The fights were lethal. Pilgrim saw people getting stabbed, teachers being robbed of their phones, their bags.

Pilgrim was on the way to break with his friends, in year eight or year seven. They passed a classroom with the door open. They looked in and saw some of the Hackney Downs problem kids in there. Then he heard someone cry out.

'Stop it!'

It was a woman's voice. They peered round the door. This mob had a female teacher in with them. She was in her thirties. They had pinned her down. One had put their jacket over her head. They were touching her up, running hands over her breasts, her thighs.

'Get off!'

Pilgrim felt an ache of dread between his ribs. He and his friends were still young. They had seen a few things out on the streets, but it was the first time they had ever been exposed to anything like that. What they saw in that classroom stayed with them. Although they don't meet up that much because they are pretty much all in jail, if they do they will say: 'Do you remember that time in school we saw that teacher being attacked.'

Everyone remembers it. It haunts them. The kids didn't get in trouble.

When they mixed the two schools, there were fights

every day from three o'clock. It became part of the school timetable, so it even carried on to the new year. Pilgrim had about four three-o'clock appointments where someone booked him for a fighting. He rubbed someone up the wrong way and they'd say to him: 'Graveyard. Three o'clock.'

So for his whole day in the classroom, if he didn't think he was going to win the fight, he'd be looking at the clock, counting the hours. 'All my friends are going to be there.'

They'd already formed their little group with the Holly Street Boys. They didn't have to worry because no matter who it was in trouble, another one would jump in and they'd help each other out. No one ever lost a fight. That was what gangs were all about – protection, safety in numbers.

There was this one time a guy kept coming to school with no money and asking Pilgrim for drinks. Why should Pilgrim give him drinks so he can save his money at home? Pilgrim finished a big black Tango bottle, then he pissed in it. Everyone watched as this kid came running out of PE, all covered in sweat, and Pilgrim handed him the bottle. The kid glugged it down, then froze. He sprayed it back up over the grass. They were all in on it and started laughing. 'Graveyard. Three o'clock,' he said.

This kid had an older brother in the year above. They were both London Fields Boys. Pilgrim was Holly Street at the time. Even though they were in the same class, after school they couldn't be friends. So that made it worse, the whole Holly Street Boy versus Fields Boy angle. The graveyard wasn't the MGM Grand in Las Vegas, but it was bigged up like the Holyfield–Tyson fight. Pilgrim saw how Tyson gave in to his ghetto fury, buried his head in Holyfield's neck like Dracula and bit a chunk of his ear lobe off and spat it out. So a large crowd came to this fight after school. Every time Pilgrim punched the kid his older brother winced like he was having a heart attack. They could all see Pilgrim was really hurting him. He had blood over his face, a puffed-up eye and splotches on his shirt. After a while he was just cracking up and couldn't take it any more. The brother erupted out of the crowd and gripped Pilgrim in a headlock. He started furiously pounding him. Luckily one of Pilgrim's old friends was there, a Pembury Boy. Pilgrim wasn't a Pembury Boy any more but his pal jumped in all the same. That was the first time he got badly beaten up in school.

Pilgrim was a talented robber, so he changed gangs like a Premier League striker moving between Man United and AC Milan. He started in Pembury, then Holly Street. He guessed the best money was to be made from stealing from other drug-dealers. You steal from a regular citizen and they will go to the police, start some taxpayer-funded investigation on your ass. You steal from another Jamaican drug-dealer, what's he going to do?

By that time he'd started jumping over counters and that. Always out with the older guys, they started robbing with a gun. Some people did not want to give up their stuff, so he pushed the gun in their face. He had to decide if he was really going to go through with it. A group of friends from school would go out in the morning and rob shops. At night-time they went out and hijacked cars. They sold them to the African 'uncles' who dealt in exporting stolen cars and credit cards. Everyone has to specialize.

What bound them together was something deeper than the rush of crime. They all had similar problems at home. Their dad might not be there. They had to live with their gran. There was some shit going on. That was the bond that made them best friends. Pilgrim found it difficult at home. He was bugged by something his sister had confided in him. Once when they were alone at her place she said to him, 'Do you know why your mum left here to go and live in Jamaica?'

'No, why?'

'I'll tell you another time.'

Pilgrim shrugged. His own father, Leeroy, had been abandoned as a young kid. His mum had disappeared with a new man who had seven of his own kids. To survive in Jamaica, you had to have your wits about you. He was looking for his chance to escape. Leeroy was introduced to Pilgrim's mum on the phone. She was a single mum, travelling with a daughter, looking for a fresh start. She was running away from something in her past. They got on well on the phone, until she moved all her things from England to Jamaica and they got married. Pilgrim was born in Jamaica.

Not long after that Leeroy went to England for a holiday. He never came back. He went to track down his own mother and her other children, and eventually he married again. Pilgrim's mother found she was the one stuck in Jamaica.

White-hot rage forces things deep-buried to erupt to the surface. His mum was dying by now and Pilgrim was eaten up with anger. He had a flaming row with his stepmother, acting as mean and vicious as he could do. At the end she was shaking.

'I'm going to tell your dad when he comes home,' she yelled.

'Tell him!' Pilgrim roared back.

His dad came home. It was a humid, dank night. They faced each other across the table. At this time Pilgrim was as dangerous as he was going to be. He listened to his father ranting and raving. A hot ember burned in his solar plexus, just between his ribs. He felt the roar of blood in his temples. His fingers trembled.

'I don't like what you are saying to me,' he cut in. He sat there with his 9mm Browning shoved down the back of his trousers. 'I'm a bad man. You understand you need to watch your mouth, bruv.'

Pilgrim's dad had survived Jamaica as a kid on his own, which made him no angel. He had a few moves. But Pilgrim was a blooded warrior now. He had come of age and was rising up in the streets. Deep in the gang lifestyle, he could more than look after himself.

'There are people out on the streets who would be afraid for their lives if they talked to me the way you are talking to me now.'

It was a threat. To his own father. He rose from the table.

'I've brung you into this world,' his father said through gritted teeth. 'I'll take you out too.'

His father's chair lay twisted on the floor. In another room someone was whimpering. A beat. Then another.

'If you can't live by my rules only one man can be under this roof,' his father said. 'So you have to leave.'

Pilgrim knew in his heart he could not shoot his own father. No matter how blindly the rage beat in his head, his father was his blood. The only thing to do was to walk away. So he left the family home, banished. For a while he lived with his sister. One night, exhausted from his day's robbing and hustling out on the streets, he was woken by screaming. The sound came from the corridor. It was his sister, yelling into the telephone.

'So who was my real dad, then?'

Pilgrim raised himself up on his elbows, piecing the conversation together. As he listened he found out that his mother had been raped. By her own father. He made her pregnant and she'd given birth to his daughter.

'How can you tell me that?'

His sister was sobbing on the phone. She just kept repeating the same line.

Pilgrim was in shock. This was the whole reason why his mum left England to go to Jamaica to marry Pilgrim's dad, to escape from her abusive father. His sister's screaming continued.

'What the fuck are you talking about?'

Later on it got worse. Pilgrim's dad and sister did not get along. His sister claimed he was abusing her. Pilgrim's mother denied this. Pilgrim did not want to think about it. This was his own father and sister. He began to hear stories of girls on the estate. One goes round to play PlayStation with a boy but three of his friends step into the room and rape her. Or girls have to perform line-ups to a group of gang members and they film it on their camera-phones.

So he just blocked it all out. He blocked out lots of things. He went somewhere else in his head, like he just pretended he couldn't hear. He learnt how to do that from a kid. He could switch off and start thinking about making money. That is all he thought about. How to make money.

It didn't last long with his sister. Neither of them could be around people. Pilgrim was like a traveller, he had to keep moving. She wanted him out of her house. She told the housing department that she had medical and mental-health problems. She told them Pilgrim's dad had died.

They couldn't find him a house, but they did find him a room in an old people's home.

'It's bigger than the cupboard,' Pilgrim sighed looking around. He examined the bed. It was a white metal bed with a metal frame underneath, and thin six-inch mattress. The whole thing was screwed to the floor. He lay down on it. It was really uncomfortable and dug into his back. It was a prison bed.

He was living with old people now. He didn't tell them his real name. They all looked as if they were about to die.

'Ah, David, you're not going to have dinner?'

'No, I'm going to have a shower.'

'Come and have a chat with us.'

But he didn't want to eat mashed potato and green peas. 'I'll eat with you tomorrow.'

The guy next to Pilgrim would put the same record on every morning. It was a male singer, with a deep, throaty voice. He would croon a few lonely numbers. Pilgrim put his head around the door. His neighbour, white, English, dressed up smart with shiny shoes on, was dancing round the room, in some old-style routine, putting one foot to the side, bringing the other up close to it. Round and round the room he went.

Pilgrim chatted to him. He was from the East End, used to work on a fruit-and-veg stall in the market in Brick Lane. He said he grew up knowing the Krays and all that. He was involved in a few mixes, Pilgrim was sure of it. The way he looked up to the Krays made Pilgrim laugh. How can you look up to men like that? Pilgrim had never had an older-man figure that he respected, there was no one on the street he trusted, no general or boss he admired. He only got on with Solo because Solo treated him with respect.

'Don't burn your bridges, no one will want to come and visit you,' the old man told him. 'Live your life in the right way because sooner or later you're going to end up like me.'

He told Pilgrim that his family couldn't look after him any more. 'I don't want to be a burden to people.'

He knew that Pilgrim would sneak girls in there at night-time. 'I saw you last night,' he said with a wink. 'If you can't be good, be careful.'

In his cell he thinks back on all these memories. Finally he comes to rest on his father. Many of the other inmates are fatherless. Their dads walked out early in life. His father stuck with him. He thinks about the hell he put that man through, as a gangster child, living off the streets. It pains him.

He serves his six long years and finishes his time in Bullingdon Prison, in Oxford, a new prison with galleries. It is dangerously overcrowded with nine hundred inmates seething in there. Conditions are cramped in shared cells. The training is mundane. There's no space in the library. One prisoner can't take it any longer and escapes. Pilgrim is a Cat-B prisoner, one down from the most violent, Cat-A, Maximum Security.

Finally, he is let out on probation. He finds himself back on the streets of Hackney. It's 2005. Inside he promised himself he's going to change his lifestyle. Everyone is watching to see his next move. Two months before his release his stepbrother was stabbed up. It plays on his mind. He wears a pair of sunglasses and a leather jacket and moves with stealth through his old haunts, trying not to run into any old enemies.

'Yo, Pilgrim. When you get out?'

It is an old school friend, Jay. Jay is the most dangerous guy in Hackney right now. The Youngers with Jay scowl at him. Pilgrim cannot believe how young some of them are. They look like they are seven or eight years old. They say hello because he's still a feared guy. In the old days if a Younger crossed the line then you'd make a phone call to his boss and say sort out your Younger or I'm going to have to take him out. Now it's different.

'Just last week,' Pilgrim says.

'Respect to this man, Youngers,' Jay says grinning. He is wearing all the swagger and bling. 'He's a real tough guy. Best armed robber in Hackney. Just got out of Bullingdon.'

Jay takes a call on his mobile and wanders off, leaving Pilgrim with the Youngers.

'Yeah, Pilgrim,' one of the young guys says. 'I've heard your rep.'

'Who are you rolling with now?'

'Guys. I just got out. Might leave the streets.'

The others laugh. 'You'll miss it too much.'

'I won't lie to you, when you're out there living on road it's nice,' Pilgrim grins. He feels paternal now towards these kids. 'All these movies, when you watch them, you see what happens in the end if you don't quit before it's too late. You can live a nice life doing crime, don't let anyone tell you that you can't. If you do it in the right way. But it's knowing when to leave.'

The Youngers don't seem to be listening. They are too gassed up.

'It's nice out there on road,' one says. 'Renting out the cars brings the girls out. You get fame, money and respect, yeah.'

Jay finishes up and comes over. He takes Pilgrim to one side.

'How old are those little ones?' Pilgrim whispers.

'Them are Tinies. Eight or ten. You see that a lot now. They're less likely to be stopped by the police. Their gang leader is about fourteen.'

'Eight years old?'

'They go younger than that. Babies are getting involved. You know by the time you is fifteen you've been stabbed up so many times already you're like a veteran.'

Pilgrim cannot believe what he's hearing.

'We had a code back in the day,' he says. 'Never get little kids involved. Never attack a family member.'

'Things changed while you were away,' Jay says. 'The kids today, they'll go to your mum's house. Attack your mum on the street. March your sister down the street in her school uniform, rape her in a line-up. I talk to kids where people's mums have had shotgun shots come through their door and shoot someone else in the house.'

'There's no general keeping the Youngers under control?'

'From fourteen you can become a general now. Shoot three people in the leg, you're the boss. Every lil kid has a 9mm Baikal handgun now. Some Older told him to hold on to it way back when. He put it under his pillow, then that fool was sent to jail. What's the kid going to do? He holds that gun and feels like superman. These Baikals and Tokarevs are pouring in from Lithuania ready for Christmas.'

He flicks his cigarette ash at a newspaper stand with a headline about a 'baying mob' of gang members. Jay can't talk too long with Pilgrim. Pilgrim's still associated with Love of Money, not Jay's gang. But sometimes people who went to school have a mutual respect. Pilgrim is not with his friends and Jay's not with his. They can stop on the road and have a laugh and joke. But if Jay was together with his people and he caught Pilgrim on his own, he'd have to do what he has to do. That's the way it works.

Pilgrim nods to Jay and wanders off.

He feels uneasy in Hackney now. His enemies have scores to settle. They wait for their moment for revenge. Any day someone could be on his tail trying to kill him. Drop his guard and he's going to get shot.

He needs to put a bit of money away, though. He is already known as a robber man, so he trades on that and extorts people in the area. Eventually he has little choice but to meet with Wolf, who is now acting leader of his old crew. There are new younger faces there too, building a rep for themselves. One of them troubles him. It's an old enemy, a guy he tried to kill before he went inside. He waits until Wolf is alone.

'Why's that fucker a member?'

'Nah, it's cool, man. He makes money.'

Wolf doesn't care for the code any more either. He just wants all the good drug-dealers in the squad. With money you get guns, cars, anything you want. People now buy the drugs off Wolf direct, cutting out the middle man.

'Once a traitor always a traitor,' Pilgrim says.

'You used to rob drug-dealers like him,' Wolf says, raising his eyebrow. 'When you come out of prison people wonder if you still have the fight in you.'

Pilgrim knows this is a challenge. He needs to show he's still got the moves. So he stakes out the guy's flat. He sees him climb out of a gunmetal BMW compact. Pilgrim forces him at gunpoint to drive back to his flat and cleans him out of guns and cash. He hands them over to Wolf. Then he sells the BMW for £6k. It's quick money and he's made his point. Later Wolf calls him and tells him to get the car back. Pilgrim is surprised.

'The cops are out looking for the guy who nicked his car,' Wolf tells him. 'I warn you, get it back or Trojan is going to be onto you.'

Trojan means an armed police unit. Pilgrim hasn't been out long enough to risk it. He rings the buyer, tells her he needs his car back, but before he gets there the car is picked up on a tow-truck in the middle of the night. He thinks about Wolf. His dealer is still making him money, even though Wolf now has his guns and cash. It reminds him of a book, *The 48 Laws of Power*. The first rule was

'Never Outshine the Master'. He wonders if he can trust Wolf and the Love of Money crew any longer.

Not long afterwards Wolf rings him up. 'I want you to ice someone for £15,000,' he says. "No one you know."

'Sounds interesting. Let me call you in ten.'

Pilgrim hangs up and phones his friend, a known assassin from Tower Hamlets. He explains about the offer.

'How much do these hits go for?'

'Twenty-five if you don't know the person,' says the man. 'Fifteen if you do.'

'I don't know the person and this guy's offering me fifteen.'

'He's robbing you of £10k.'

Pilgrim calls Wolf later to find out more details on the hit. It's a businessman in the City. This time Wolf wants another £5,000 from the £15,000, as a commission for bringing him the hit. So he's taking fifteen out of the twenty-five and Pilgrim's the one doing all the work.

Pilgrim needs to distance himself from Wolf. But he is running out of people to trust. The life is closing in on him now. He needs to make some money but his bridges are all burning. He has to make a decision. Everyone is waiting for his next move.

7: Brown

Pilgrim picks up the phone.

'Do you do your thing in West London?'

'Yeah, I've done stuff West. What is it?'

'There's a new kid I want you to meet with,' says the voice. Pilgrim sits in his office in Hackney, behind his computer. On the wall are photos of some of the guys he rolled with on the streets, back in the day. One is dead. The other is in jail. Pilgrim is nearly twenty-five now. In the last few years he's been making contacts all over London, but mainly Lewisham and Southwark, where it's been really kicking off. Those two are much worse now than Hackney's ever been. He doesn't like to hang out in his old neighbourhood and lives elsewhere. There are too many enemies, old scores and victims here. He is constantly looking in his rear-view mirror, zipping in and out of the traffic in the motorway. If he meets old friends in the hood, he doesn't hang around with them too long. You can't trust nobody.

'Where?'

'In Southall. He's Somali. May have used guns from a young age. Now fourteen, on the way to being a successful enforcer.'

'OK. First check that he is OK for you to give me his number.'

'He's really difficult to find. Even worse to pin down to a meet. His street name is Troll.'

Pilgrim wears an ironed beige shirt that matches his T-shirt, a diamond stud in his ear and a silver pendant swinging round his neck on an elegant chain. He grabs a scrap of paper and scrawls on it 'Southall. Troll.'

•

The light is fading. Two young Asian men walk away from the white marble and granite Sikh temple, the gurdwara, past the graveyard. They head in the direction of the sprawling Havelock Estate, Southall. One of them strains as he carries a sports hold-all, sagging with heavy metal objects. They move in the shadow of a wooden garden fence, which bends back under the three rows of recently tightened razor wire. The Havelock rears up to meet them. Brutish three-storey blocks obscure a low sun. The men hesitate on the edges, hug their ribs and blink into the labyrinth of dark alleys. It is a no-go area for the cops. They step forward and are swallowed into a pitch black opening between sheer walls of concrete. Once inside, one scurries ahead, keen to make it out the other side without encountering anyone. Kam, a skinny twenty-year-old, squats down and runs his fingers over the masonry, feeling for something, until they curl into a small crack at his eye level. He crams his face against the hole and peers in. A vast unlit underground car park lies beyond the wall. Kam feels calm and a dull dreaminess falls over him. The space opens out before him like a sea cave. Fight it, he thinks, stay focused. He digs his uncut nails into the knuckles of the other hand. Alert again, he spots movement in the gloom. Three silhouetted figures appear, leaning on their bikes. They are idle, but predatory. Jas appears by his side and bends down to look.

'Those are the guys who robbed me two days ago,' he whispers in Punjabi and gives a jittery nod. 'Bricked me in the face.'

His nose is broken. The exertion of crouching makes Jas's leg muscle spasm. After two days without a fix he is clucking badly. His nose runs, his eyes water and his head rolls. Kam is skinny, but Jas is skeletal. At twenty-six the brown has burnt all the meat off his bones. A bloated, makeshift bandage is taped to the inside of his forearm.

'Somalis,' Kam says. 'They always pick on Asians.'

But he's not going to let Jas's fear of the Somalis stop them stealing from the car park.

'They are lethal,' Jas groans.

He has a tender lump behind his temple, from a few nights back when he slept amongst the gravestones in the Havelock Road cemetery. The Somali gangs own the Havelock. They keep young kids in their school uniform dealing for hours in the stairwell of the tower block. Those who refuse are taken to the park, stripped naked and lashed with a whip. Then they are given a cup of tea and taken back to their mothers. One boy on a nearby estate was thrown naked in a lift with a pit bull and sent to the fifteenth floor. When the doors finally opened another gang member stood there filming him.

At night Jas lies awake listening as the gang's taunts and cat-calls echo around the labyrinth. He is terrified. He owes one Somali dealer, Troll, credit. Troll is rumoured to be the most vicious kid on the Havelock. One other guy took drugs on credit from him: big mistake. He said he'd pay him in two days. For a week he managed to avoid Troll. But then the dealer sent his friends out to hunt him down. When they got hold of him they gave him a bone-cracking beating in an alley. He couldn't stand up. They told him to get the money in two hours. Jas is now harried and desperate. He must get some cash.

Once a week he goes out on the rob with Kam. He'd rather be watching the whirlpool of feeding pigeons or sitting outside the temple, but it's their turn to feed the others' habits. It is a constant daily grind to raise the cash. Another day empty-handed and he'll be beaten, or even cast out of the group. Kam is tiring of Jas. He's lazy and he doesn't trust him. It appears that the homeless Sikhs survive together, but they only serve one master – the brown. They would risk anything to sink into the warmth of its embrace. After two days Jas's eyes have a craven junkie hunger about them. He's out to scavenge off Kam, and snatch his wrap when he turns away for a match.

The two men squeeze through broken slats into the car park then bolt for cover behind a line of parked cars. Kam sets down the hold-all. The tyre iron and wheel jack weigh a ton and he is panting. He can hear the thud thud thud of his heart in his temple. If stopped by the cops, how will he hurl it away into a bush? The Havelock Somali gang will snap his shin bones with the tyre iron. He prods Jas hard. 'Follow me.'

They tear off to one side, keeping low to the ground. Every three cars Kam drops down to a squat, to let Jas catch up. They catch their breath behind the boot of an old

Ford. Jas checks on the gang's location. Still talking in low voices.

'They won't see us,' Kam whispers. 'The lighting's bad.'

'Yeah?' Jas gasps. He is ready to call it a day, but is still haunted by what Troll will do to him. 'How much do these tyres go for?'

'£60. The stores resell them for three fifty. Four hundred.'

'Let's do this one,' Jas wheezes, thumbing at the Ford they are leaning against. 'Sell them two tyres for £150.'

'Look at it,' Kam snaps, screwing his face up. The car is coated in dust, the chrome bumper flecked with rust. It's a relic. Probably no tax or MOT. 'You won't get five rupees for these old tyres with the tread worn off. They want brand new or up to two years old. BMW, Mercedes are what they're after.'

He cranes around the rear brake lights and squints through the cars. 'There's a silver Merc over there,' he whispers.

Jas bobs up like a meerkat and peers through the rear window of the Ford. He can't see shit. The Ford's exhaust pipe is making him gag. About three cars away from the Somalis he spots the silver Merc. Three cars away! It's a suicide mission. They are lean, muscled guys, local thugs. He fingers the bruised egg on his temple again. It feels like it might burst. It's time to quit and go and lift some chocolate bars or booze from Tesco. This is madness.

Kam works his way along like a crab, knees bent, finding fingerholds along the back bumpers and tail guards of the cars for balance. How can he contort like that, Jas wonders. His knees ache like an old man's. Only the craving goads him on, the promise that soon all the pain will ebb away like a hot bath. 'Now,' he says softly to himself. 'Go.'

Jas sucks a deep breath down hard into his ribcage then flings himself headlong after his friend. He feels like he is moving in slow motion. Finally he drops down behind the Merc and squeezes awkwardly into the gap next to Kam, who doesn't look round. Kam works fast. First he inspects the surface of the front-side left tyre. Then he unzips the hold-all and eases out the jack. Skilfully he slides it under the tyre, attaching the cranking lever.

'You do it,' he orders. Jas grunts, sits up and cranks the lever. He pauses as it emits a metallic clanking sound. 'Get on with it.'

He cranks again. The lever stiffens as it takes on the weight of the vehicle. Kam grows impatient. He digs his fingers into Jas's arm. 'Come on!'

Suddenly there's an explosion. A terrible screaming erupts in their ears. For a moment Jas paddles at the air, as if he's being attacked by a swarm of screeching bats. Kam's shocked face, appears in front of him, lit up in yellow flashes. Then it vanishes. An icy dread comes over Jas – a car alarm.

'Who the fuck is that!'

It's the Somalis. They quickly encircle the Merc like a military unit.

'You hijacking our cars?'

'Fucking car thieves!'

Kam hurtles down the alleyway, shoulder scraping the walls, and charges headlong into the dark. He can sense at least one Somali behind him on his mountain bike, braking and weaving like a unicyclist. Jas, forgotten, abandoned, has no plan of escape. He crawls under a nearby car, trembling, his teeth gritted. Gunshots ring out. He keeps crawling, hauling himself spiderlike under the next car. He lies there, shivering, gripping folds of his stomach to stop it rumbling.

'Motherfucker!'

'One guy's still in here!'

'Fuck him up!'

Two Somalis loop around on their bikes, legs locked on the pedals. One holds out his weapon hand and trains it along the line of cars. They must hunt this intruder down. They are the front line. This is their hood. He must be flushed out and made an example of. They prick up their ears, listening for a sharp breath, a whimper from their prey. Jas lies still, paralysed with terror, a hole burning in his gut. He closes his eyes and prays to his guru. He will renounce heroin and return to his family.

'Yo! Check this out!'

Their attention turns to the bag of tools. 'They're after the tyres,' one says. 'Gotta be junkies.'

One tests the heft of the tyre iron and swipes the air with it. Soon the outrider rolls back, out of breath. He lost Kam somewhere in the labyrinth.

Jas lies still in the dark as the cold seeps through his extremities. It feels like half an hour before they call off the search and continue chatting. Jas crawls to the end of the line, and slinks out of the car park. He darts through the estate, looking over his shoulder. His bearings are skewed by fear but after a few wrong turns he finds himself in a narrow concrete gorge. At the end is a blue door. He runs up to it and ducks to the right into a tiny alcove. He huddles there, in the dark, out of breath.

At eye level is a square opening in the wall where people hurl their rubbish sacks. Jas leans inside the darkness of the vent. A slash of light seeps under a padlocked metal door on the far side. The sweet, dank honk of rubbish punches up into his nose.

Jas vaults his knee onto the lower sill of the vent and hauls himself over. Steel cylindrical municipal bins hem him in. This cell holds a whole block's worth of waste. Jas eases the bins against the vent to screen him. He makes out Kam's silhouette inside his sleeping bag on the concrete floor space behind. They greet each other in whispers, as Jas sits and stiffly unlaces army-style boots.

'Those guys didn't see our faces?' asks Jas.

'No,' Kam says. His long fingernails are caked with black dirt, and he picks an insect out of his hair. 'There are fifteen of us, remember. Spread over six bin rooms.'

'All Punjabi?'

'One Pakistani.' Then he adds, 'They won't know who it was. Might be someone coming in from outside.'

This does not reassure Jas. Troll is still out there, waiting. Southall has been home to Punjabi Sikhs for three generations, with cheap housing close to the airport. But Jas's group, about a hundred strong, are homeless junkies, outcasts. Even the temple can refuse him entry. The fact that the Glassy Junction pub takes rupees and you don't need a word of English to live in King Street for ten years will not help him if soldiers from local gangs like Murder Dem Pussies or Grit Set hunt him down, shank him for late payment.

His nose streams over his top lip in an itchy trickle. His shoulder muscle stays painfully tense and as he moves his toes grip the ground as if he might fall off. All night long the car park and dark pools of the communal spaces will be alive with the screech and holler of drug-dealers, who belt out tinny music from their mobile phones. One mother pleaded with the neighbourhood police and collapsed sobbing on the floor, saying she couldn't take the intimidation any more. The cops reminded her that she was the same resident who refused to step up to sign a crack-house closure for them. Jas lies down next to Kam by the wheels of the bin.

'I met a guy at the gurdwara,' Jas says. 'He's living in a disused NHS nursery. On Hamborough Road. They have light and water.'

Kam doesn't want to listen to Jas's moaning right now. He wants to sleep while the brown is working. 'You're only thinking about it because you haven't fixed up,' Kam says.

He needs the brown to help him sleep, to block out all the shit entering his head. Kam injects £30 worth of heroin a day so he can wrap himself in cotton wool. Nothing will bother him now until dawn when he will address once again how to sustain his three-wrap habit. He thinks of the three years he ploughed fields in a farm in Italy. He was clean then. Two years ago he came over, worked for six or seven months as a building-site labourer. But the work dried up in the recession, and he had nowhere to live. He met other homeless guys from the Punjab and the older ones got him on to it as a way to combat the cold. He has friends that are working who give him money. There are Sikh dealers as well as Somali. Kam tells himself he will give up the drugs and get another job, if he can find support. It is cold in winter and they will have to stop up the gap under the door, but rats will still burrow in. He closes his eyes and thinks how green the grass is in Jalandhar after heavy rain.

'It could be worse,' Kam says. 'Another group of guys from Nawashahar and Ludhiana live in a derelict pub on the other side of Broadway, the Northcote Arms. One has gangrene in his leg. He won't get it treated. He thinks that if he loses his leg he'll get permanent leave to remain in UK.'

He chuckles quietly about this, not really knowing why it is funny. Those guys are better off on the street. The Northcote is wet, has a leaking roof. It reeks so badly of disease. Some of them have livid red pimples that keep itching. They are everywhere, in the web of their fingers and toes, in their elbows and in the folds of their balls. It is scabies. It will work through all of them, like the cold and flu. Over two years a few of them have been found dead. Kam brightens as he comes across a hard lump in his pocket. It's the Nokia phone he stole that afternoon.

'Look.' Kam waves a small white light from the mobile from side to side. 'Got to be good for a tenner on South Road.'

The Afghan Sikh hawkers will buy a phone from a clearly homeless junkie with pinned eyes. They know they only have to pay £10 or £20 for a quick sale and can resell for £100. The addicts can shoplift for clothes, a small stereo, TV. Most thieving is mobile phones, the newer Nokia ones. Everything is about surviving day to day, hand to mouth. A £30-a-day habit is £210 a week, £910 a month.

'Can I see it?' Jas asks slyly, his fingers reaching out for it, his eyes burning. Kam scowls at him and quickly buries the trophy deep inside his sleeping bag. There is no way he's going to let him swipe it so he can stop clucking. He rolls over with his back to Jas.

The craving keeps Jas awake in the dark. He wishes he hadn't had his weekly call with his parents. He felt crushing shame as his mother told him his father was running in from working in the fields to speak to him. As he waited in the cut-price booth on King Street, he saw a rotund, chortling Sikh in the next booth. His belly was wobbling like jelly as he laughed. His Beamer was parked outside. He wore Skype headphones over his turban, a clean open-neck shirt and neat beard. He was laughing at the computer screen, where two women, in bright saris, were sitting on the end of a bed laughing with him. It was some family in-joke they were teasing him with. His whole body was shaking, knocking his iron kara against the desk. Jas told his parents he couldn't access Skype. He didn't want them to see the gaunt, sunken-eyed condition he was in.

His father came on, panting from the dash.

'I was spraying with a hose in the wheat,' he apologized.

'When you spray pesticides you must wear protective clothing,' Jas warned him.

'The pests are too clever,' his father laughed. 'They're evolving too fast for these new pesticides. I don't know why I keep paying all this money. The soil is bad now. Diseased, waterlogged.'

Jas tried to cheer his father up by telling him he was looking hard for a job. He thinks of his father's hands calloused from toiling on the field, steadily poisoned by pesticides. His father who worked hard to save up to provide Jas with a better life. Two years ago he paid for Jas to travel on a student visa to study business management at North West London College. Jas couldn't find enough work in his twenty hours a week quota and quickly used up his dad's money on rent. His landlord chucked him out after three months, when he couldn't pay, and he found himself amongst the homeless Punjabi guys on the streets of Southall.

'The friends I am staying with are kind,' Jas lied. 'Very kind, good people.'

His father purred with approval.

'In Sikhism our guru teaches us that we will become like the people we spend our time with,' he said.

How true, Jas thought. He was the only homeless guy not on heroin when he came to Southall. When you hang around with other men it's human nature that the one who is not on heroin soon will be. Especially if it's snowing outside. He could never mention to his father the bin room, the drugs, the rats, the daily grind of stealing.

Now, shuddering in the dark of the rubbish cell, he can't block out the burning guilt he feels. So he grits his teeth and thinks hard how to steal the phone off Kam. This is all that matters.

The irony of it all is that yesterday he scored a wrap. He carefully rested the brown powder on his knee, in the folded aluminium foil. He could not wait to light it, see it start to run, to burn down to a beetle, go the colour of Coca-Cola. If there is too much Mannitol in it, it turns a reddy-brown colour and won't fix you up. That red means the dealer's stung you. He's bumped you. You've basically bought shit. Some people buy Mannitol and gouch out, but that's silly. Sometimes it's not very pure, it can be cut to fuck with bicarbonate of soda. They get it straight when it comes in then the dealers stamp on it. They put the Mannitol in to make it run, otherwise pure heroin would sit there on the six-inch square of foil and frazzle.

He reached around to his left for a match. No matchbox.

Jas has had friends go over on heroin. Or they have been on script to get off smack. They take a tablet, Naltrexone, which blocks opiates getting into the system, but with twelve tablets in a box, who's going to keep taking until the end? Methadone is no good either. The government would love to have all the junkies parked on methadone because it's so cheap. Hitler invented it so he could send his troops into battle on suicide missions.

'You got a match?' he asked Kam.

Southall is the cheapest place in the UK to buy class-A drugs. He's had friends die on him because the heroin in Southall is too strong. All he needs is £10 to buy a 0.3 gram wrap of brown or brandy. 0.6g is £20, but you can be scammed and find it's only really 0.4g. You can get 'one of each', a mixed bag of whisky and brandy, crack and smack for £20. £10 of crack is enough for two or three pipe smokes. This gives a short fifteen-minute high and then you smoke the heroin for your come-down for the rest of the day.

'There at your foot,' Kam said. 'Can you see it?' His knee dipped a fraction and the foil sailed to the floor. He flung his hand out too late, pawing at the air as the powder vanished in a fine cloud of dust. For a junkie it was like locking yourself out of the house. Stupid. He threw his head back and howled a strangled cry of despair. And now twenty-four hours have passed without anything in his system. Kam has gone quiet now. This could be his moment to make a move.

'Kam?' he says, testing him. He can hear Kam lightly snoring. He edges beside him to check he has gouched out. To double-check, Jas clicks his finger in front of Kam's face. Then he gently eases his hand into the opening of the sleeping bag and burrows down in search of the mobile. He guesses that Kam has wedged it between his thighs. His arm slides in up to his elbow and his hand tracks across his stomach, tapping for signs of the hard casing.

Kam grunts and rolls over.

Jas rolls with him, then eases his arm out and lies back again. You rob someone too many times and you become an outcast, Jas thinks. It will be a long, hard night.

In the morning, before six, they get up. One of their number goes off to work. Kam cannot take any chances with Jas clucking so badly. They head to the temple at seven thirty for breakfast.

The gurdwara rises like a marble and granite fortress. The gilded dome roof soars high up above, as if floating in the clouds. Tourists bar the pavement, aiming their cameras up in awe. Gurdwara Sri Guru Singh Sahba is the biggest Sikh temple in Europe and cost £17 million to .5build. Jas's eyes roam hungrily over the expensive Nikon lenses and shiny leather man-bags, then he and Kam pad slowly up the gleaming white marble steps and into the first hallway.

Jas half-expects one of the attendants to step forward and block their way. If they are highly intoxicated they are refused entry. If they smell of alcohol they have their food brought to them outside. They stop by the door, unlace their shoes and put them in the rack of wooden foot lockers.

'This place takes half a million a month in donations,' says Kam.

'How come?' asks Jas.

'One-day prayer. Three-day prayer. They pay in donations to have prayers said in the glass booths upstairs.'

They take orange cloths from a large bin and carefully tie them around their heads, then they walk through the marbled halls into a great hall. It is vast and can seat three thousand people. Long thin strips of carpets stretch away before them to the tables where the langar is served. Men and women sit on the carpets eating. They take metal trays with partitions and queue. Older, turbaned Sikhs wordlessly spoon out traditional Indian chapatti and dal lentils, spiced potatoes, then sweet semolina and yoghurt. Tea and water are served in brown plastic mugs. The guys serving the food are volunteers.

Jas and Kam are too ashamed to go upstairs to pray on the first floor. A good Sikh must wash, wear clean underpants and stay pure of mind. Cleanliness is a strong tenet of Sikhism. Jas and Kam are dirty and smell bad, with class-A drugs teeming through their blood. They take their food to a dark corner, behind a pillar, and wolf it down facing the wall. At a nearby wall, eating on his own, Jas spots a thief friend.

'I'm going to go see Vijay,' Jas says, moving off. 'Try my luck at Tesco later.' Vijay glances at him as he comes over, carries on eating. He is the most prolific thief in Southall. He has a huge black beard and wayward thick hair, like a pirate captain. Vijay and Jas were like brothers, but they fell out over stealing. One time Vijay carried ten ladies' coats out of TK-Maxx over his arm. He just walked out with the alarm going, but security collared a different guy. The truth was that the security guard just felt sorry for his Sikh brother, and turned a blind eye.

'What is the plan?' Jas asks. 'I'm clucking like crazy.'

'Let's go for bottles of booze from Tesco,' Vijay says, stroking his beard.

'How many?'

'£500 worth.'

Jas looks sceptical. Vijay is angry that Jas doubts him.

'Last time the head of security actually asked me how I did it and suggested I advise Tesco. It highlighted some kind of loophole in their system. But the truth was very simple.' He holds up his hand for Jas to inspect. 'See, Vijay has incredibly strong nails. I prised all the security tags off. No one else can do it.'

'So this time they'll see you coming a mile off.'

'This time is different. We use three guys.'

'Three? How come?'

'One guy comes in with a backpack. He stands in front of the security camera and a second guy blatantly puts bottles of booze in the backpack. The camera is seeing everything. This alerts security. Then you go round the corner where a third guy is waiting with a trolley and empty Tesco bags. You unload the booze into the bags. Then both the trolley and the decoy head out the door simultaneously. Security collars the guy with the backpack.'

These ideas are sound. They agree to meet later and Vijay leaves the temple.

'What's the plan?' Kam asks as he comes over. Jas wonders if Kam was awake when he tried to steal the phone. Did he feel his hand go in?

'Tesco,' Jas says, munching his chapatti. He decides not to reveal Vijay's tactics to Kam. 'They have these big chocolate bars. I can sell them for 50p in the shops on Broadway.'

'That's twenty bars,' Kam says unimpressed.

'No problem.'

Jas wonders if he could do a stint of dealing to sort himself out. He remembers a fifteen-day run, when he was dealing for the Somalis. They paid him £40 a day. He sold thirty-six wraps and made them £360. But they all have knives. They are bored, uneducated, creaming the money off benefits so they don't need to work. They all smoke skunk. On the fifteenth day they robbed him.

A lone figure is watching them, like a sentinel.

From behind a table the man stares fixedly across as he raises a glass of water. He wears his turban like a crown, a proud ambassador for his faith. He has a clean, neatly trimmed beard, his dagger, iron kara bracelet, all his five Ks. Dark forces are working, weakening our people, he thinks as he looks at these hunched, wretched guys. How did these men from the Punjab, in their early twenties, full of promise, end up like this, sleeping rough, addicted to strong drugs?

The watcher remembers when he grew up in the 1990s in Southall College he never saw a Sikh taking drugs. He became aware that there were steadily more alcohol shops, as they slowly became more like the English, a nation of drinkers. He strides over and greets Jas and Kam. He hasn't seen them for a few weeks.

'How are you guys?' he asks.

'Fine. Hi, Hardeep.'

They remember his name.

'Where are you sleeping now?'

'In a bin room on the Havelock.'

Hardeep tries to close his nostrils to the smell they give off. Kam's head lolls forward drowsily. In all the time he has moved amongst the homeless, he has never seen a junkie or a homeless alcoholic in a turban, because a proper, practising Sikh would not let himself sink that far. The new generation of young Sikhs are different. There was one old guy, Singh, who was living in a disused garage. He said he was working, but he lost his job, the landlord chucked him out. They gave him a month's rent, enough to get his feet back on the ground. But it is easier to get someone off heroin than off Special Brew or the strong stuff.

'You must be brave,' Hardeep tells Kam, looking him fixedly in the eye. 'Our guru teaches us to be brave and remain in high spirits, as under God's will one day you will have the glow of freedom.' He gestures across the atrium of the gurdwara to a portrait on the wall. Kam eyes swim over the counter where they serve food, then focuses on a huge portrait of one of the Sikh saints, Sant Jarnail

Bindawarra. 'Remember how Jarnail fought for us and taught us to stand up to oppression.'

Hardeep looks for recognition in Kam's eyes but only sees his eyelids glistening and hooded.

'India promised us independence, but in the constitution they say we are still Hindus. They invaded our holiest place, murdered young and old Sikhs. And nothing about it in the Indian media.'

'Yeah, right,' Kam begins. 'A downward spiral.'

'Dad always said the Punjab was the richest place in India,' Jas chips in. 'Now the pesticides have poisoned the soil. No jobs for young people.'

Hardeep nods sadly. These boys must have had a dream that coming to England would make everything better. He is trying to help these kids back on their feet, but the old boys who run the temple have got their heads buried in the sand. They help out the women first. The older generation see junkies as shameful, they don't have time for them. Jas and Kam are too fearful to return to their parents in the Punjab and tell them they fucked up. He knows of a guy who shamed his parents by smoking drugs at fourteen in his bedroom and was banished to a life on the streets of Southall. The disgraced family returned to the Punjab, rather than live with the stigma of a drug-user under their roof. When he was young, boys smoked cigarettes, then in 1994–95 he started hearing stories on the grapevine of people at his school who smoked cannabis. Now, Southall and the Punjab have a massive drugs issue.

The problems have brought in Muslim and Sikh gangs like Holy Smokes, Tuti Nuns. There was the nail bomb that blew up the pub on Lady Margaret Road. No one said anything, but that was drug-related. Then they had a concert with Dizzee Rascal in protest against gun crime and something kicked off in the Tudor Rose. A guy fired through the wood of the partitions, killing two young men. The Tudor Rose is boarded up now. But young guys are making money with drugs. He has seen thirty photos on the cops' wall of gang members.

'Why don't you go and pick them up?' he asked the cops.

'Red tape,' they replied.

Government is saying they are illegal. If they don't come off drugs they'll have their benefits cut. Hardeep will continue to help them from a humanitarian point of view, whether they are legal or not.

'You remember Dick Whittington?' Kam says dreamily. 'Came to London because he heard the streets were paved with gold. But when he got here, he was just left to the rats. Then a magical cat came and killed all the rats and saved him.'

Hardeep frowns. He looks across at Jas and Kam. They are such young men, barely twenty. Where is this story going? He nods to both of them as if understanding that this is an in-joke.

'So,' Kam says finally. 'Where is the fucking cat?'

Jas starts to giggle idiotically, his head lolling forward. Hardeep sighs through his nose. It's time to go. They are talking nonsense. He extends his hand to them warmly. 'We will try to help you,' he says again. 'I will go and pray for you both.'

He moves away and walks up the marble staircase past

the soaring stained-glass window. The light floods through orange saffron banners that flutter over a pitcher of the holy water amrit. In the water stands a double-edged sword. During prayers it will be run again and again, over and over, through the water, cutting the prayer into it to make the water holy. Outside the prayer hall Hardeep bows with his hands cupped and takes a glistening ball of sweet brown rice. He drifts towards the altar where a holy man waves a feathered rod from side to side. If only the homeless guys could see this, but they are too ashamed to come upstairs.

Jas and Kam leave the temple and wander into town. Kam disappears into a shop on King Street with the phone to claim his tenner. They will head off towards the dealers so he can score. Jas stays outside. He feels confident about his Tesco plan. Then on the other side he sees Vijay. He is surrounded by four uniform, who are turfing out his pockets. Vijay looks stubborn, but wretched.

'Then what happened?' one of the uniform ask him loudly, for the whole street to hear. There are two young female police. They hold clipboards and stare at Vijay, sucking their teeth.

'How did it end up in your pocket?' another one asks drily.

Jas keeps on walking, scouring around for some other junkies, to see what they are up to. All the junkies know each other, know each other's story. When Kam catches him they see a white guy, Tony, whose pale blue eyes are pinned. Tony was in care in Gloucester. He is twenty-four and has an on-off girlfriend in Hammersmith who makes software. He always dreams of being a father, but they lost a child through a late miscarriage, then another child was born but died soon afterwards of leukaemia. Tony is articulate, soft-spoken and gentle even. But the brown has addled his mind, and as he talks details become blurred in his head. His girlfriend says that if he gives up the drugs she will set him up in his own limo business, which he used to run back in the day. But does she even exist? No one knows for sure. All Jas knows is that every junkie has a plan to give up. For Tony, if he can make it to Perivale, he has a room he can stay in for £19 a week, where he could do the three days. But there is only one bus driver who will let him ride the 607 to Uxbridge for free if there are no inspectors around. So he waits for him.

The pair pass older white-whiskered Sikhs in dark-blue turbans, and shopfronts with garish saris in pink and purple with gold sequins. Bangra music, the smell of spices. A young Asian guy in cornrows, short wispy beard, shuffles along, jeans hanging down below his buttocks to reveal grey underpants. There's a discount jewellers with gold trinkets next door to the huge silver lettering of TULIP hair and beauty. Kam walks along staring wall-eyed up to the sky, his mouth hanging open.

At the corner of Havelock Road a group of junkies are transfixed by a gathering of pigeons. One guy stands, arms outstretched, imagining that he has herded them skilfully into this tightly packed circle, as the pigeons clamber over each other's backs. A handsome Pakistani man in his early thirties bows to Kam. He has the beginnings of a thick beard and is chatting to pretty girls as he leafs drowsily through some paintings. He sells them to restaurants, not because it is a career but because it yields just enough money to score some brown. Kam knows his story too, how he went to grammar school in Slough and university, specialized in IT, but when he became divorced he started taking heroin. He blames his whole descent on his wife, how she took their daughter away from him. He lives with his family and has promised them he does not take drugs. They must be blind if they can't see it. For now he's only a man on the way down. In about six months he'll be with them in the bin rooms.

A dozen restless Somali teenagers have set up their stall selling drugs at the entrance of the park, yards away from the Tudor House mansion, the medieval, black-cross-beamed facade that holds the community centre. One stands guard beside a tall granite war memorial, which bears the words: 'In grateful thanks for those who gave their young lives for their country.' Jas waits here looking uneasy. As Kam draws near to the dealers a high-powered camera, hidden in a street lamp behind tinted glass, whirs to life. It zooms in on him, tracking his progress up the Green, and relays a grainy image onto a TV screen, which flickers on the face of a police officer, who sits in the dark of a cupboard-sized room peering up at a bank of six screens. He's on the first floor of Southall police station. A uniform police officer eases a control stick to stay on Kam.

'IC4 male, five foot ten, suspected user, in dark-blue track suit approaching plot,' he says.

The screens show CCTV footage from around the borough. The officer tugs at his collar. It's hot and airless in the booth, but he doesn't let his gaze waver. He relishes his role, as the central Observation Point, or OP, in an unfolding surveillance operation. He thought he picked up a murmur of excitement in the morning briefing, as the operation was detailed over a PowerPoint display. The targets of this initial phase are users like Kam and Jas. His description of Kam is relayed to three unmarked police cars and other vehicles containing uniformed officers, staked out in strategic positions around the plot the dealers are occupying. Plainclothes will use the details to pick up the tail on foot. They'll follow them for a couple of blocks, then uniform will close in, stop and search him, then on finding the wrap arrest him for possession. The more users they arrest, the stronger the case against the dealers, or so the theory goes. OP rolls his neck. He wants to play his part, which he decides is to provide them with running commentary, like a DJ. He notices how Kam's heavy tramp lightens as he draws closer to buying his mid-morning.

'He's got a spring in his step,' OP says. OP's words crackle into the covert earpieces of three detectives – two women and a man – who sit and listen in a battered Mondeo, tucked away in a line of cars on a nearby industrial estate two blocks away.

'Fuck,' winces the female detective in the back seat. Howling static pierces her eardrum.

Kam notices how friendly the dealers seem with each other. He's seen this before. How they hug each other, pound fists, grab each other's forearms in embrace. Some dawdle on mountain bikes. There is a short, stocky kid there, who has grey trousers round his hips and black trainers. He turns to alert Jas.

It's Troll.

8: Enforcer

Jas freezes. The loose cluster of dealers scowl him up, heads cocked for trouble. Troll is talking to a friend, who balances on the pedals of his mountain bike, legs locked. His view of Jas is obscured by a heavy-duty golf umbrella, branded Ricoh, which dwarfs him, a giant toadstool. If he glances over his shoulder he will see a drug debtor, giving him the finger for four days straight. Jas knows what happens to guys like that. He has heard the stories of the beatings, the bats, the hammers. Troll has a brutal reputation and fourteen prior convictions; under the childish exterior he is a ruthless fighter, a little man of steel. He's fourteen but word is he's already killed a man. Without waiting for Kam, Jas twists stiffly away in the flow of the crowd and disappears down an alley, leaving his friend alone amongst the dealers and Troll and under the hovering eye of Southall police.

'Let me go on the back,' Troll says to the friend on the bike. For a moment he seems just like any other kid asking for a backy. He doesn't have the high forehead and soft, elegant features of some Somali boys. He is sullen, squat, dark-skinned with thick curly hair. Already a dead weight presses his head down beneath his shoulders. When he talks it is hard to hear. He never smiles. This plays well amongst the Tinies and Youngers, who mistake it for menace. Only his mother sees the shy teenager who never shouted at her until two weeks ago, when he snapped at her for money to buy cigarettes. His clothes are drab. He doesn't show off any colour-coded swagger and bling like other wannabe gangsters.

He is in year ten, the fourth year of secondary school, but his English is still at primary level. Other sparky Asian thirteen-year-olds groan and headbutt the desk during his slow, stumbling answers. But they only taunt him once. In the break he hunts them down, unleashing a fury of violence. Five kids are too scared to come to school. One teacher beckons Troll up to the front with a curling finger. Troll recognizes an insult reserved for dogs in Somalia and feels he is despised. He rears up and glowers at the man.

'Do not mess with me,' he whispers.

Troll's mother continues to clean the house, feed him, pick him up at three thirty, unaware she is supposed to also take part in school meetings, help with his homework and communicate regularly about her son's progress.

Formal warnings arrive for her from the school. She hands them to Troll to translate. They detail how violent he is, how other children are afraid to go to school. If his fighting continues the school will permanently exclude him. He reads to her aloud: 'Your son is the best student in class. We have not seen such a good boy for a long time. He is a joy to teach.' She claps her hands in glee.

For months she remains unaware that he has been removed from class and now sits with two other trouble-makers in a confined, airless room where the radiator rages. He is alienated. They bring in a speech therapist and psychologist. But out in the corridors and playground, he still uses violence to solve any problem. Finally, they tell him it is to be his last day, that he cannot come back.

The kids file out of school. Troll barges past, flat-footed, surly. He scans the waiting cars. He sees one kid brandish a painted face mask. Another touts a new MP3 player. They smile at their parents, who ask them about their day, then walk them to the car jangling keys. Troll observes it all blankly. There is no family waiting for him. But lounging out the window, in designer shirts and chunky silver rings, are the next best thing – the Olders.

Troll's eyes come to rest on Ali, a Somali Older. Ali leans on his black VW Golf, which at £16k is an affordable solid getaway for the gangster who can only hire an Audi A3. He wears a long white cotton djellaba. He wears it not because Saudi-style clothing has displaced the Somali macawii sarong, or because his mum wants him to dress like a good Muslim boy, but because the predominantly white police are less likely to stop and search him dressed in a djellaba than in his Nike Jordan black basketball hoody. Grime music booms out of the open window. He nods at Troll, who stamps angrily towards him, his flat-footed little soldier, his ATM, his man of steel. Ali is relieved to see Troll is still a loner, without any visible mentors or friends amongst the staff or pupils.

But one pretty Asian girl waves to Troll. She knows he's into phones so she shows him the aluminium armour case on her new Nokia N97. He seems wrong-footed that she is friendly to him. Most girls can't be bothered with his limited English. Then she waves and is gone, skipping off to her girlfriends.

'Who's that?' Ali asks, frowning.

'She's in my class.'

The Older opens his eyes wide.

'Who's interested in girls, man? Girls are just for set-ups. MOB. Money over bitches.'

'Her name's Geeta.'

'Whatever. Watch yourself, Younger. Pretty girls are the bait. You listening to what I'm saying here? She'll have glitter and shit on her eyelids and bangs in her hair. She'll ask you to come with her for a walk in the park. Just you and her. When you get there it'll be an ambush. There'll be like ten guys there with bats and shanks and shit. You will lose your life. Coz you were thinking with this.' Ali grabs his crotch through the djellaba.

Troll frowns at him. He doubts Geeta is like that, but he says nothing. The Older can see he's unconvinced. The car stereo thuds out into the street: Tinie Tempah's 'Frisky'.

'You remember that Shakilus kid in the paper, stabbed up in South London, in Thornton Heath. He was lured into an ambush by this honey-trap girl. She took him off some place on the bus. All the time yeah she was texting the other gang, he's coming, he's coming. So when he got there a whole pack of them stabbed him up. Fucked him up so bad they killed him.'

Troll scuffs the ground with his foot, looks down the street. Geeta is at the corner already. Strands of hair blow messily over her face. She clamps her hand to her mouth and shrieks as they pore over a girlfriend's text. Troll heard that a Somali Older transferred out of Feltham fell in love with a Pakistani girl and decided to leave the streets for her. Her father said he wasn't good enough for her because he wasn't educated. So he signed up for a course and paid up front in cash with £6,000 of his drug money. Just think – all that hard-earned P down the drain, just for some girl.

'We use girls,' the Older says quietly, following his gaze. 'When some dealer is flossing and making good money, we send a girl in to scope him out, get up close to him, find out where he keeps his cash. We promise her a cut. Then we go round and take this guy's door out, mash up his place. Take his money.'

'Yeah?'

'Right. If he's fool enough to let her into his house, tell her where the treasure's buried, man he deserves to be robbed.'

They sound stone cold, these girls, Troll thinks. Best for him to steer clear of Geeta.

'Who needs a girl around anyways?' Troll shrugs. 'MOB, right?'

'Right,' Ali sighs. At last his message is getting through. 'Better just make your P and be a millionaire.'

Ali started Troll selling drugs for him. The kids start young, in their school uniform in the stairwell of the tower block. The Olders keep them there on an all-day shift, round the clock, to rope them in. After a week or so they arrange for someone to rob them, so they have to pay back the debt. Then they're hooked in for good. If the mother goes to the police they will come after her. Sometimes she is raped. When Troll earns his drug money he wraps each £100 in a rubber band and hides it in a metal trunk, accessed only by a hole in his bedroom wall. He brought his clothes over in it from Somalia. The trunk's nearly full now. When he's an Older he will know what to spend it on. In Mogadishu, his family did not have anyone abroad sending money home, which made them vulnerable. Everything was up for grabs. A car, a horse, a bag of food.

When Troll was eight a jeep pulled up alongside him and his little brother. The roof of the jeep had been sawn off to mount a machine gun. A man in military fatigues pushed his sunglasses back onto his head and squinted at the boy.

'Where's your father?' he asked, lighting a cigarette. He didn't wait for an answer. He knew he was away.

'You must be the big man in the family now,' said the man as he scrutinized Troll's clothes. 'And provide for your mother.'

He would pay him if he just carried guns around for him, he said. At first he was given a whip to carry. Then he was given a Russian AK-47 assault rifle. There was no school, except for a private school in the centre of Mogadishu. The civil war had spelt the end of school for every kid. Now he would find his own training amongst men. They paid him £20 a week, which seemed like good money. They forced him and other kids to volunteer.

Troll sat in the back of the jeep, as it bucked over the potholes, heading out of Mogadishu. The white one-storey buildings of the city receded into the distance. Soon there was just open countryside and thin, wiry trees stripped of leaves. The camp was two plastic sheets, made like tents. A pile of dry thorns was burning. Their trainer was a lighter-skinned man from the Caucasus, with scars on one side of his face and chipped teeth. He spoke to the boys in Arabic and English. He showed them how to take out the magazine, check the firing mechanism, dismantle and put together their rifle.

'Now do it blindfold,' he said. They laid the pieces carefully out on the sand in front of them. As Troll held the gun up the man came and kicked his legs hard so that he spread the weight and was more stable. But when he looked down the cross-hairs his hands trembled and the skyline waved up and down.

'Lie on the ground on your stomach,' the trainer snapped. 'With your legs apart and hold it steady that way.'

The man pointed out a row of metal objects that glinted in the sun about twenty yards in front of them. Troll squeezed the trigger and felt the butt slam into his shoulder. He closed one eye and squinted into the sight. The objects began to go zing as he hit them. It was hot, and when they finished he was coated in a layer of fine dust from his chin down.

They drove back and he was stationed at a crossroads by the market to check for people when they came off the bus. Men wearing trousers of Western length or smoking cigarettes were singled out and lashed. Any man talking to a girl not his daughter or wife was taken away.

Two militia climbed on the bus when it stopped and marched off a teenage boy, several years older than Troll. The boy's feet dragged in two long winding tracks in the sand.

'Follow us,' the men signalled to Troll. They tore the boy's shirt off and tied his hands round a tree. Then they handed Troll the whip. Troll stared at the boy's arched back, his ribs and the bumps of his vertebrae pressing on the skin. The whip cut into the skin with a sharp crack, like a dry branch snapping. Afterwards they put the boy's shirt on and they gave him a cigarette. It hung on his lower lip with the drool of saliva, then dropped into the sand.

'You're a real little soldier,' the men told him. They were pleased. He was still not sure what the boy did wrong, but it was something to do with wearing the wrong clothes.

One day they took him out to a farm and told him to point his rifle at people who lived there.

'They need to believe you will pull the trigger,' they told him. 'If they don't fear you, you have no power over them.'

He saw how grown warriors let him walk away with their animals, their land, their houses, everything. His mother used part of his weekly earnings to buy a small bag of salt, rice, spaghetti, canned meat and vegetables. He bought himself a single cigarette. He became the man of the house.

'I hope you are not in trouble,' his mother said.

Somalia was disintegrating into further chaos. But the men saw how brave he was and they told him he would have to fight alongside them. They went into the centre of Mogadishu, where the buildings were crumbling, the walls marked with bullet holes.

'If you see someone carrying a gun, shoot him first,' they said. 'Or he will kill you.'

So they sat behind a low wall, listening to gunfire, then running for cover. He tripped, and grazed his palms on thorny scrub so the sand and dust got under the folds of the cut. He looked round to see what tripped him and saw a dead body. He remembered his training and kept on watching and shooting.

'I'm tired,' he told the men.

'Take this,' they said and gave him white pills and a bunch of khat leaves to chew. 'It will turn you into a hyena-man at night. You will be able to fight like fury.' Afterwards he felt alert and no longer needed to eat. His mind could focus on fighting. They wanted him to fight for forty-eight hours without a break. He felt so confident, like he'd really had taken on the special night-time senses of the hyena-man.

One day when he was eight he took part in a gun battle in a ruined street. A man in sandals and a macawii ran towards him firing. Troll shot him. He saw him go down and not get up. Troll took his rifle and ran away. He could hear the others running after him, but he was faster and lighter. That night he did not speak to his mother, but just lay in his room shivering. Outside he saw the silhouette of thin black trees against the streaks of red sky.

'Can we leave?' he asked his mother the next morning.

Everyone was trying to leave. Going to Kenya, Ethiopia, Holland, Germany, England, America. Europe was like a fortress to keep out Somalis. But his mother kept trying, asking around.

Finally she found she could apply for asylum in the UK if she pretended they were Ethiopian. She told him that a better life was waiting for him, that they would live in London only until Somalia calmed down.

'Every Somalian dreams of the day they will return to their country,' she told him proudly.

He carried all his clothes and possessions with him in the small metal trunk. When they arrived in London they found themselves on the Golflinks Estate in Hayes, near

Heathrow Airport. It was a dump but at least not a shanty town, and there were no blown-up buildings. It had graffiti, broken windows and was alive at night with the sounds of fights and even gunfire. It was 2005. Troll was ten years old.

At his new school Troll was taunted by classmates with copies of the *Daily Mail*, which had frequent anti-Somali stories: 'Foreign aid worker kidnapped by pirates', or 'Benefit scrounger gets five-bedroom house', or 'Somali gang kill WPC on way to daughter's birthday'. Somalis were singled out as trouble-makers.

He quickly learnt that to survive on this block meant affiliation with the local gang. Kids were mugged to test their mettle. As a Younger he had to earn his spurs. Some older kids jumped on him in the stairwell, but he fought back viciously.

The Olders were always waiting on the wall for Troll after school, just as the kids flooded out on the bell. They'd beckon him over and lean on car bonnets and chat to him. Ali was also from his clan, the Hawiye tribe in southern Somalia and Mogadishu. Like Troll he was born in a mess, in a lawless area.

His mother carried on as if she was back home. 'You know you have a Somali mother when she tells you to turn off the telly and read the Koran, change out of your school uniform into a djellaba and pray five times a day,' Ali joked. 'We're looking for a Younger like you to make P,' he told Troll. 'You are man of the house. We're always looking for a good soldier to step up for the Grit Set.'

It was like Mogadishu all over again.

The Grit Set was the local gang. Their rivals were the MDP, or Murder Dem Pussies, known for breeding fighting dogs.

'What are MDP like?' Troll asked.

'Fucking lethal, man. They're stabbing people up all over the borough, yeah.'

'For real?'

'In April they shanked that kid Kizzle in Hammersmith. Bright kid, yeah, with like ten GCSEs. Out with his chick, Cookie, down Hammersmith Broadway Shopping Centre. Some local kid like taunted him. So he can't let that slide, even if his girl is telling him to walk away, leave it alone. Goes around the corner, bang, straight into the ambush. Nine guys from MDP. Knives, hammers, whatever. They set the pit bulls on him, stabbed him up. Killed him, basically. Then they all leg it. All gassed up, laughing, totally psyched. Ambulance crew see right away they can't do nothing. Stabbed in the heart.'

'They come this way?'

'Yeah. They headed up to Windmill Park in September. Five months after Kizzle. Stabbed up some guy because some fifteen-year-old kid had his mobile nicked.'

He tells the story. A pack of about twenty MDP kids piled into the 207 bus and chased a twenty-two-year-old Somalian student, Yasin, all over the Windmill with broken bottles, sticks and knives. 'You Grit Set. You Grit Set,' they yelled. Stabbed him three times in the head. Yasin fell into a coma and died a week later. He wasn't even in Grit Set.

'So where were they from?' Troll asked.

'All over, man. Southall, Willesden, Acton, Shepherds

Bush and west Ealing. All over West.' One of the group was a twelve-year-old kid. The ringleader, an Older, was nineteen.

By the time he is twelve, Troll is already an active gang member. He's decided early on to take his chances with these Hawiye kids. They promise him new trainers and £120 a day. The dealers explain the rules to him.

'Take four wraps at a time. When you run out you cross the road to the Cambuulo restaurant and take four more.'

It's there that the stash is kept. Their operation is based on knowledge of Crown Prosecution Service guidelines – being caught with twenty rocks of crack cocaine is enough to secure a conviction for peewit (possession with intent to supply), which could send you away for up to two and a half. Cambuulo had a crack-house closure served on it a few years ago but it has started up again.

Troll quickly becomes known to the police for street dealing, another kid out to prove how hard he is repping his ends.

By now he's seen so many weapons he realizes he has to protect himself. He's been robbing people at gunpoint since he was eight. He is a good shot. He finds some Somalis wear their ASBO like a badge of honour. He knows that to be feared earns him respect and a good rep. There had been a code before where you never went after a family member, where a Younger knew his place. That was gone now. By attacking a sister or mother you got more leverage. Proved you were the hardest guy on the estate. There were hot-heads who chewed too much khat, who would stab some-one for a dirty look. He had seen in Somalia how a man could chew khat, then still go out to work or go to the cinema. But here the older men could not stop, they were mashed the whole time. Some were wide-eyed, jabbering nonsense. An Older would beat up any Younger they found, so you had to be protected by another Older.

At fourteen he's clocked up a large number of convictions. He wants to graduate from street dealing. Shotting is a mug's game. Small money and high chance of being arrested. He recruits his own little crew of two others. He makes £100 a day now and has access to a big block of cannabis, like a kilo. He has an Asian friend who can get £3,000 worth of stuff in about ten minutes. He's half Pakistani, half Afghan. The other Olders are a mix of Sikh, Asian, Somali.

Everyone in the area knows Troll's rep now. If they come to fight him, they know he has money and weapons. He has access to a Mac-10. A small pistol will cost him £850. A clean 9mm is £1,500. He will bring dogs. He has two pit bulls in another house he can use.

The Olders hear of his growing rep as a kid who has no fear, who has killed already. A former child soldier is prized amongst so many wannabes. They keep asking him one question: 'What's your price? Would you do it for a grand?'

Sometimes they say more. This is a lot more than the warlord was offering. They turn up the pressure on him. A Sikh guy has raped an Older's girlfriend. They need to avenge her honour.

'If you damage him we'll give you money,' the Olders tell him.

It's a rainy, cold evening when the car pulls up next

to Troll and two other Youngers, thirteen- to fourteen-year-olds, good fighters. In the back of the car, the girlfriend sits, shrunken, arms folded, barely lifting her eyes from her knees. They cruise around Lancaster Road until it slows down and the girlfriend IDs a man on the street. He is a Sikh guy of twenty-five, walking head down, hands in pockets against the rain. Troll tells them to park up round the corner. He piles out with the others. They club the guy from behind and pin him to the ground. They keep on beating him. Troll lands more and more blows on him. At first he fights back, his arms flailing, clawing at the air like a man who is falling. Then his movements slow. Finally he is floppy. They keep on hitting him, kicking him. Again and again until he doesn't move at all. Then, panting, with flecks of blood all over his hood, Troll gives the word. Suddenly he feels scared that the man isn't moving. He runs off with his boys. Across the street people see it happen and call the cops. But they are black boys wearing hoodies. It is night-time. Nothing happens. As he walks home, he tries to drown it out and flicks his MP3 player to Kiss FM. Travie McCoy's song 'Billionaire' comes on.

For the next few weeks his mother is on his case. She insists that Troll finds another school and shouts at him until he agrees to meet one of her few friends in the Somali community – Jama. Jama is his only hope of finding an education.

Troll finds him in a tiny cubbyhole office, down an alley off the Western Road, just opposite the bus stop where his friends deal drugs. Jama is fifty years old and he looks like an intellectual, with a light beard, glasses, a jacket and tie over his white cotton djellaba. He left Somalia ten years ago and has been studying at university in Italy and the UK. He trained to be a social worker and now teaches English and skills to the Somali community in Southall. Upstairs is a room of computers. At £2,500 a month the rent is crippling him.

'We'll try to find you a school,' Jama tells Troll. His voice is gentle, kind. First he approaches Ealing Council but soon hits a wall. With Troll permanently excluded from one school, and a string convictions, no headteacher wants him. Jama picks up hostility to Somalis from the people he contacts in the council and job centre. The older ethnic communities see them as trouble. But how can they treat Somalis like this when they've been through the same issues once themselves? Jama's seen a long line of street kids like Troll. Every two weeks he visits brighter, more articulate eighteen-year-old Somalis in Feltham Young Offenders Institute. He has eight children of his own.

As Jama strides to school to pick up his kids, he sees Troll skulking around with dealers at the bus stop or in Rec Park. He wonders how he can possibly save the whole community of his people single-handed. Inside he rubs his forehead with his finger and thumb. He is gaunt and tired from a month of fasting. With eyes closed he listens for news of when he can eat again. As he talks to his colleague about Troll he starts to shake with frustration.

'So many children taken into care, given to non-Somalis,' he says. His colleague is a jolly, white-moustached teacher in a tweed jacket, slacks and polished brogues, like an old-fashioned gentleman. He also fled Somalia, in a small boat across high seas. 'The system is not prepared for Troll. After five years with the warlords how could he sit in a class with ordinary kids who have never known war? It is no surprise if he ends up on the streets. Troll is accustomed to hold a gun to people's heads and see them beg for their lives.'

Jama knows how vicious Somalis can be. They are trained warriors. One evening as he leaves the mosque at 11 p.m. he sees a car deliberately knock a man down outside Cambuulo restaurant. The car then backs up and runs over the man again and again until he is a limp rag doll. Soon afterwards the Somalis attack Cambuulo with automatic weapons, smashing the glass and everything. The Somali gangs are becoming so powerful, Jama thinks, they are taking over London.

Finally Jama has to give up on Troll. The kid's future on the streets means either jail or death if he stays. He recommends to Troll's mother that the boy is sent back to the north of Somalia. It is more stable there, well away from Mogadishu and the clutches of al-Shabaab and the warlords. They already sent one teenage gang member back and he became a religious teacher. Another one got married.

Troll doesn't like this plan. He's building up a good rep on the streets, his trunk is filling up with money.

'My mum is planning to get help from social services to have me sent back to Somalia,' he tells Ali. 'If I'm sent back I'll live with relatives.'

'To the north you'll be OK. Or Kenya. But if you're in Mogadishu you're fucked, man. If al-Shabaab see you walking along in jeans and T-shirt, they'll just hack your legs off.'

Troll's main fear is not his mother, but the cops.

Another conviction and they might deport him. The police are closing in. Safer Neighbourhood cops know the grip the Somalis have on the Havelock Estate and the local CID team of plainclothes detectives are tightening the noose. For several days now they have carefully recorded Jas, Kam and the other junkies buying drugs off the Somali teenagers on CCTV. One Pakistani user stops in front of the dealers, rubs his jaw then asks for one of each. The dealers hand him a wrap of heroin and another wrap with two rocks of crack. He passes over the £20 that he made selling paintings over the last two days. Then he is gone. As he walks down the street, the CCTV hidden high up in a street lamp swivels to follow him.

'Tall IC4 male leaving a known dealer,' says OP in his narrow, unlit room, hunched over a bank of CCTV screens. He describes every detail he sees into the operation's central microphone. 'Wearing a brown dishdash. It looks like he's hiding it in his ear. Walking southbound.'

This time the description is picked up by plainclothes detectives, dressed in hoodies, jeans and trainers, sitting in a battered car. One female trainee closes her DC exam manual. They've been chatting for hours, waiting for something to happen. Greg, a good-looking, hollow-eyed detective, tracks his finger along a page of the London A–Z. An experienced street cop, five years a DC, he tugs on a baseball cap and jumps out of the car. One of the others shoves open the back door and follows him a few paces behind. Working in pairs, they have to pick up the tail on the junkie on foot for a few blocks.

'Suspect is walking past the betting shop, with a bit of purpose in his walk,' OP continues. 'In front of him are two single guys in white T-shirts. They are going to cross the road.'

Greg brings his hand up close to his mouth. Under his fleece he wears a covert harness. A flesh-coloured lead runs up the inside of the arm, with a button to press when he speaks. Microphones are buried inside the lapels linked to the earpieces. 'Which one am I following?' he snaps into his wrist.

His partner takes over the tail, staying a discreet distance behind the user. She presses the button on her wrist to come on the airwaves, but nothing happens. She keeps pressing but the other cops only hear a series of muffled beeps. OP is blocking her as he hogs the airwaves with his commentary. Five minutes later she yanks open the car door and flings down her tangled radio.

'Why didn't he shut up?' she groans.

A few blocks away, two uniform officers recognize the suspect user from his description and step forward to intercept him.

'Routine stop-and-search,' they tell him, so he won't tip off Troll and the dealers. Finding the wrap on him, they read him his rights and sling him in the meat wagon. Greg is still nervous that word will get out and blow their cover.

'The wheels are going to come off this so fast,' he mutters in the car, shaking his head. 'This has been cobbled together just to placate the community.'

At the start of the morning briefing the drained, jaded unit had listened to details of the local imam's complaint about an escalation in gunfire and shootings on the streets. CID had put together a 'buy-and-bust' operation to go after the Somali street dealers at the bottom of the chain. Mr Big will remain untouched at the top of the drug hierarchy. Greg knows who he is, which five-bedroom house he lives in. A Pakistani businessman, he even hugs an embarrassed Jama in the local mosque and calls him 'uncle'. But this operation won't touch him. Street dealing will disappear underground for a while and create some good publicity. It's short-term, though. The war on drugs has been going on for thirty years.

Greg suggests that they put a camera in the apartment opposite the Cambuulo where the stash is kept.

Jama watches the police trying their best. But he knows it is relentless. He can spot the undercover cops as they drag people into cars on arrests. The cops look sick, haggard, with long, lank hair, almost like they've been sleeping rough.

As it grows dark, the Southall surveillance operation wraps up. There have been four arrests and Southall station doesn't have the custody rooms to hold them. The prisoners are bussed across town to a police station with more holding cells. It takes the CID team several weeks to secure warrants to raid ten premises where they suspect the drugs are hidden. The team meet at dawn.

'This guy considers himself untouchable on the estate,' the lead detective says disdainfully, as they draw up in a convoy. 'There's a samurai sword on the wall as you go in. And a pit bull.'

Four vehicles head off in convoy. One of them is a van containing the cops in helmets, riot gear and flameproof overalls. This team are from the Borough Support Unit, a specialized group of extremely fit police who deal in breaking down doors and gaining rapid entry. Two of them are trained medics. A chill dawn is starting to break as BSU flatten themselves against the walls of a council house. They crouch like sprinters, lined up in front of the door. Their breathing is heavy inside the visors. They have seconds now to gain entry. A jemmy is worked into a crack in the door and opens it a fraction. The metal teeth of a high-power hydraulic clamp slide in. One man cranks the pump furiously with his foot. A huge guy grips the handles of the bright red ramming block, poised to swing. At the sound of a crack he swings again with his whole weight. It smashes into the door frame, splintering it off its hinges. The others power past him, thundering up the stairs.

'POLICE!' they yell.

A vicious dog can be heard barking loudly behind the closed kitchen door. A specially trained officer moves forward. He is soft-spoken and grey-haired in a navy fleece and glasses. He slips in and closes the door behind him. The fighting dog hurls itself at him. He lets it lock its jaws around his protective arm-covering and skilfully slips a lasso around its neck and tugs it tight. Then he retreats to the end of a long metal pole. Halfway through the morning's warrants the cops stand by the van taking stock. One heaves off his helmet and rubs his face, exhausted from pounding up the stairs. They are disappointed. One suspect evades arrest by staying with his girlfriend. A second suspect isn't at home. Was there some problem with the intel?

On a chill, drizzling Tuesday following the dawn raids, Jama is inside teaching Somali mothers some faltering English phrases. He hasn't seen or heard from Troll for weeks. Troll's mother reports that her son sometimes stays out all night, returning days later. She worries he's sinking out of her reach, further into the underworld. As he walks through the streets he passes the Pakistani user who was arrested in the recent police operation already back on Southall High Street selling paintings to restaurants. A few hundred yards on he passes Jas and a group of junkies. As usual they are staring at a circle of huddled pigeons. It's slow today but Jas has until late afternoon before he starts to cluck. He hears that the dealers went to ground for a while after the police crackdown, but he has their mobile numbers. You can always find them if you want them.

Pilgrim steps out of the train onto Southall platform. Today there is no distinctive diamond stud in his ear or silver pendant round his neck. He is dressed in anonymous dark clothing. His three mobile phones lie in his wardrobe at home; instead he carries a cheap pay-as-you-go black Nokia 1661. A high-speed train roars through the next-door platform like a nuclear missile. It whips up a grit storm of litter, so passengers twist away, only peering down the rail when it's long gone. Pilgrim uses the distraction to rummage in his gym bag, checking the contents.

He spoke to Troll yesterday to confirm the meet. He arrives early to scope the place out, check where the back exit leads, which tables are away from the window. He does this out of habit. But it's different now. He's working for Five Oh.

He's never seen Troll before but he knows the kid already. He knows nothing of his story but can easily sense the rush and adrenalin this kid gets from the streets. Pilgrim knows what it's like to be a feared fourteen-year-old thug. He met another dangerous fourteen-year-old last week in Lewisham, who wants to be a general. The week before he was in Southwark with a kid who fired a shotgun through someone's letterbox. The same story, total chaos. Most times it is too late to save them, they are in too deep, so he just tells them his story. It gives them something to think about, before they are swallowed up by the darkness.

Pilgrim pulls the collar of his jacket round his chin. He slips stealthily through the crowded streets, meeting no one's eye. As the wind slants the rain some retreat under the awnings of a shop selling bright beaded saris. Pilgrim puts his head down and keeps on moving. He doesn't want to let the kid down.

GLASGOW

9: Seventy-One

'Whatever you do, don't tell anybody,' the detective chief superintendent says, looking right at Karyn McCluskey. They're alone in his office, door closed. She looks right back, with pale-blue eyes, through a nut-brown fringe. All in black but for a silk scarf tight around the neck.

'That explains why you left the social early. You said you were in training for the triathlon.'

'I'm still training. I can't drink. I'm such a cheap date. Renowned for it.'

God, he thinks, she's hardcore, McCluskey, still running up the Malvern Hills at dawn. He only appointed her Head of Intelligence for West Mercia Police six weeks ago and now she's pregnant. Overseeing a force of two thousand officers and a few still think women's role is to make tea.

'It won't show for months,' she shrugs. And that's an end to it.

'Are you not coming back to Scotland?' the baby's father sighs to her on the phone when he hears the news.

'No, I've just got here,' she replies.

He would have loved her to return to Glasgow and raise the wean with him. He's a joiner, they've known each other since they were three. But few men can match the drive Karyn took from her dad. A sixth dan in judo, a black belt in the Olympic team, he lost his job when steam trains finished and just retrained at the University of Stirling as a biology teacher. She believes she can do anything. Plenty of Glaswegian men never even make it into the centre, let alone leave the city itself. They stand in the doorway of their local having a sneaky cig and suddenly they're fifty. But she's already worked in Tanzania, Northern Ireland and now Lancashire. She's very happy in West Mercia and stays for several years. It would take something very special to make her leave.

When the offer eventually comes it's too big a challenge to ignore. To head up intelligence in Scotland's largest police force, Strathclyde: eight thousand officers and a chance to train up the whole department.

Her first few days are a load of introductions, get-to-know-you chats with tea and biscuits. A cop interrupts one and puts his head around her door. Something about his cropped grey hair and the deep bags cut under his eyes makes her think he's a detective.

'We need an analyst,' he says. 'There's been a murder in Barrowfield.'

'Any more detail?' she asks.

'It's a teenager. Gang fight. He'll not be far away.'

That didn't take long, Karyn thinks, she's barely unpacked her box. A few hours later another cop appears, younger, dead keen. 'There's been a murder. In Shettleston. Drug-related.'

It is starting to feel like something out of *Taggart*. Soon there are six murder rooms going at one time. The whole of West Mercia has a few murders a year, Glasgow has seventy-one. It is the most violent city in Europe. The murders are driven by the gang culture on Glasgow's remote schemes: the kids out in the vast, bleak '50s housing estates such as Easterhouse. Gang members are local white youths. A typical murder involves a sixteen-year-old having a drink to steady his nerves, walking less than half a mile from his flat and being killed in a one-on-one arranged knife fight with some kids who live round the corner. It's all about territory. All through the bitter winter these undernourished guys club each other to death to guard a couple of graffitied streets and a patch of wasteground. Anyone who strays outside their area risks attack from a rival gang.

Karyn is completely stunned. Half the job is just keeping up with the bodies coming in.

'Seventy-one murders a year,' she says as she pours the boiling water into a line of mugs for her staff. 'That's appalling.'

A stocky, forty-something cop waits his turn next to her in his Kevlar stab vest. 'That's lower than it's been for years,' he says, taking the kettle off her. He gives her that look, the one with the raised eyebrow. She knows it well. It says I'm not going to have some intelligence-gatherer, no matter how senior, knocking our hard work. Especially not a woman. 'We've got a 98 per cent detection rate.'

He's one of the old-fashioned cops who like to call analysts civilians, because they're not real police. All he does is put fire in her belly. Seventy-one murders is still atrocious. They might be great at solving them, but they don't seem to be able to prevent any. She puts the word out to a few people that she is keen to get a real handle on this gang violence. An older analyst, Margaret, with a wispy ginger bob and Pringle's cardie, calls her into a darkened room.

'Take a look at this.' On Margaret's computer, images flicker. Karyn soon realizes it is grainy CCTV footage. Nothing has prepared her for the scenes she witnesses. She is watching a full-scale gang fight, a regular occurrence on Friday nights when kids from the outer schemes meet up in Glasgow's city centre, or on bridges over the River Clyde. Battles are fought with hatchets and scaffolding poles picked up from building sites, or samurai swords and machetes, kept in pride of place above the mantelpiece. On the screen a wave of boys charge across Sauchiehall Street, Glasgow's main street, slashing their rivals outside a busy shopping mall and running back. One victim slumps behind a car. Five guys stand over him. Machete blows rain down on him. Karyn watches grimly. It looks like they're trying to hack his head off.

'Look at these guys,' Margaret says quietly, tapping the side of the screen. Karyn's eyes move from the attack to the pavement just beside. Older shoppers are ambling by with Tesco bags, chatting on their way home. 'Like a Sunday afternoon stroll.'

Karyn cranes forward in her seat as the camera zooms in on a lone kid in a baseball cap. He holds a knife. Someone runs past and he slashes him across the chest. The kid looks down at the blood on his knife then shakes his fist in the air with excitement. He is blooded, he's earned his spurs. Karyn takes it all in.

'The victim was stabbed in the upper torso,' Margaret explains to her. 'He's not involved in the fight. Not even a gang member. Just an innocent passer-by. He dies at the scene.'

'And what about the kid?'

'David,' Margaret says. 'He's used the knife earlier that same night to rob someone of their baseball cap. He gets seven years for culpable homicide.'

Karyn sits and says nothing.

'It wasn't a difficult murder to solve,' continues Margaret, 'given the CCTV footage, DNA and witnesses.'

'Not difficult to solve,' Karyn says finally. 'But difficult to prevent.'

'Aye.' Margaret shrugs. She glances at the wall clock.

'I want to know everything about that kid's life,' Karyn says. 'Family background. His whole story from when he was a wean.'

Margaret nods and leaves. Some days later she appears in Karyn's office and puts down a buff folder. She pulls a chair across and plants it firmly next to Karyn's, flicking quickly through her findings.

'He lives in the fourteenth most deprived ward in Scotland, with loads of gangs, all territorial, all engaging in recreational violence with knives, golf clubs, bricks, bottles, whatever is handy. David's involved with one of the gangs. At twelve he's been charged twice with breach of the peace, considered without parental control. At thirteen charged with housebreaking, assault, shoplifting and theft. Between fourteen and fifteen he's stealing cars, drinking more, solvent abuse.'

'In other words he's a Ned,' Karyn says drily. 'That's how the tabloids would put it. A Vicious Thug, a Hooligan, a Yob, Scum, Feral. Another out-of-control kid with no respect.'

'Aye.'

'Go on.'

'He's born in the early '80s. His mum's an alcoholic and lives on income support. He has a sister. When he's three he moves with his mum because of domestic abuse. The following year he and his mum move again to the ninth most deprived ward, because of continuing harassment from his mum's ex-partner. Three years later they move yet again, David is seven. By the time he is eight, his mum can't cope and David moves in with his granny through the week. Living in that house are three adult uncles who have about a hundred and twenty previous convictions between them, mostly for drugs and violence. A year later David's family are re-housed again because the ex-partner reappears. Over the next three years the family move home a further three times due to local authority plans for demolition and regeneration.'

'What about school?'

'All this time he's at school. When he starts secondary school in the early '90s, he is puny in stature, undernourished compared to other boys in his year. He has started to get involved with the gangs. At thirteen he's skipping school and commits two breaches of the peace so social workers become involved. He's terrorizing other wee kids and becomes excluded. He breaks into houses, has a home-supervision order and is referred three times for assault, shoplifting, theft and breach of the peace. He is drinking. When he is fifteen. His family tell social services to get stuffed. Later that year he is charged with theft of cars. The next year he graduates to assault, assault and robbery, attempted murder and murder.'

'No one picks up any of the warning signs?' Karyn asks.

'When he's sentenced to seven years for culpable homicide, the judge said in his post-trial report, "There did not seem to be any indication in the background or supporting evidence suggesting that David is anything other than a pretty ordinary teenager. He seems to have a decent and supportive family".'

'How did he get on in prison?'

'When he's nineteen his mum dies of a heroin overdose. His sister is in care. He's caught with two other prisoners dealing drugs. The following year he is released on licence back into the same house in the same street. His release report says: "Scottish Ministers note that on release David can look forward to strong support from his grandmother and his wider family in Glasgow and his employment prospects look favourable".'

Aye, plenty of heavy characters in organized crime in the East End would be dying to employ a convicted killer, Karyn thinks. They'd be queuing up. She writes down the name of the estate where David lives. Easterhouse. A remote scheme in the north-east of Glasgow.

Karyn is intrigued and disturbed by how common David's story is. She needs more figures.

'Find out how many gangs there are. How many members. What age are they.'

One evening Karyn is putting her coat on, rushing out to pick up Rowan from school, when another large buff folder thuds onto her desk. It sits on the passenger seat as she pulls up at her parents' in Grangemouth. Her mum reads Rowan 'The Daughter of the Skies', a fairy tale, as Karyn kicks off her shoes and retires to her room with the file. It reveals that there are a hundred and seventy gangs with three and a half thousand gang members aged from around eleven to twenty-three. That night she lies awake and David's CCTV image flashes through her mind. Is there a growing army of three thousand violent kids out on the streets? Through the cold window pane she can see the orange light of oil towers and gas flares from the BP refinery on the horizon. When could someone have stepped in and turned things around for David? Was there a moment when you could have sat him down and tried to change his behaviour? When his mum died, or earlier when he first came to the attention of law enforcement? Or would it have been better to help his mum when she was pregnant and for the first few years of David's life?

She is still troubled next day as she goes to the senior CID meeting. There are about fifty men around a huge table. She's the only woman. This is the biggest gang in Glasgow, she thinks. At the head sits Graeme Pearson, the deputy chief constable. He is well presented and wears a deep-lined frown. He looks to her like a politician.

'Gentlemen and lady,' he begins, opening the meeting. She fields a couple of looks.

Afterwards they mill around chatting. Pearson is gruff but he's a no-nonsense cop, a workaholic and a battler who entered CID at twenty-one. He witnessed his first slashing in a chip shop aged twelve. Next she finds herself with a thick-set uniform police, with salt-and-pepper hair, his thick black eyebrows knitted into one in the middle.

He's talking about gang fights. Instinctively she starts to lobby him with ideas.

'What about campus officers in schools?' she says. 'Good male role models. People will feel safer. Truancy'll drop.'

'Who's going to pay for that?'

'The schools pay half.'

'Oh, really? They don't have to arrest anyone. Our share is one less cop who's out there on the beat chasing the guy with the samurai sword.'

'You have to prevent the violence before it happens,' she insists, chopping the air with her hand. 'By the time he's got the samurai sword it's too late.'

She starts in on David's story, how he skips school and hangs out with his pals in a gang. As she talks, he raises his finger signalling for her to make way for him. She ignores it until he looms over her. The moment she finishes he launches into a rant about budgets.

'You're telling me to take cops off the streets when I've got guys out there who can barely manage their workload now. Any solution has got to be based around hard enforcement.'

He's raising his voice so much that heads turn. Other conversations peter out. Karyn feels the weight of eyes on them.

'I don't normally choose to have a battle of wits with an armed man,' Karyn says, 'but for you I'll make an exception.'

There's a beat. He glances about sweatily. Then he starts laughing. Others grin and relax. The tension evaporates. I need to make some allies, she thinks as she steps into the lift. I need a senior cop with some braid on his shoulder who will back me up. The old-school cops only listen to braid. They aren't used to a woman like her who's so hard-wired, so absolutely single-minded. Her sisters are the same. One lives in Daytona and flies a Learjet for a multi-millionaire called Randy. The other's in Northern Ireland, an Oxford-educated research scientist who specializes in diabetes. So career-focused they've not had any weans.

Evidence is what she's after, if she's going to convince people.

'Karyn? There's been a drug murder.' She looks up from her desk. There's a senior detective there, with a neatly trimmed white goatee.

'How do you know it's drug-related?'

He strolls jauntily into the office, looks around, hand in pocket. He's got a glint in his eye.

'Burnt-out car miles from the scene. Victim known dealer. Two head shots.' She punches an extension in and finds him an analyst. He summons one of his team for a briefing.

'John Carnochan,' he says extending his hand. 'Deputy Head of CID. Interested by what you said about campus officers.'

Now is not the moment to get back into a discussion on budgets so she keeps it chatty.

'Why did you become a detective, John?' she asks.

'I remember one night standing at two or three in the morning soaking wet as a uniform cop, I had two years' service in Lanarkshire at the time, and the CID drove past in a car. And I thought, I'm bloody having some of that.'

They laugh again. She likes him. Her eyes fall on David's file. There's a Post-it on it with one word: 'Easter-house'.

'Ever worked in Easterhouse?'

'I was in Easterhouse in uniform. It was great. 1986. It was just after the riots in Barlinnie.'

'See many gang fights?'

'It was normal.' He sits on the edge of her desk, warming up, bit of a story-teller. 'You had a brown-paper-bag day. A brown-paper-bag day was a Saturday or a Sunday. When you came in the day shift, there'd be brown-paper bags containing blood-stained clothing all the way up the stairs, you know, with production labels hanging out. Someone would say: "Don't touch that! That's mine. I haven't fixed that!" Then you'd get to the waiting room and there'd be two people lying sleeping and there'd be witnesses who were too drunk so they'd be keeping them sober so they could interview them in the morning.'

It's always when they're drunk, Karyn thinks. Must be the bravado.

'In the night shift you didn't get a lot done. It was a triage thing, it was a fire-service thing, you attended and did what you could. If there was a serious assault or an attempted murder you'd get down to the hospital, possession of clothing, try and get a statement from the complainant, if they told you to piss off you'd get them to sign your notebook, so you could have a note in the morning saying, this is what we've done, this is what needs to be done, that's who it was. It was really just managing the workload.'

'That's what the other guy said,' Karyn offers, 'managing the workload.'

After that she chats with John when she can. They are yin and yang but he is well liked, enlightened. He's been there thirty-six years. People stop what they are doing and listen to John. What's more he has braid on his shoulder. They are still working hard, her department, CID, all of them. But at the end of the year she drops a newspaper on John's desk, jabs at a line with her finger. 'Read that,' she says. 'New report out by the Scottish Executive.'

John picks up the paper and shakes it open. '"Glasgow had the highest murder rate in 2003 of any city in Western Europe",' he reads.

2004 begins and there is no let-up in the bodies. There are eighteen murders in three months. In March there is one so violent it that shocks the whole department. Kriss Donald, a fifteen-year-old, is dragged into a car from the streets of Pollokshields by a gang. They drive him two hundred miles to Dundee and back, on their mobiles all the time trying to line up a house to take him to. They drive him back to Glasgow, to Clyde Walkway, near Celtic football ground. Then they hold him down and stab him thirteen times, injuring a lung and his kidneys. He's still alive. As he lies groaning on the ground they douse him with petrol and set fire to him. The person who finds his charred corpse thinks it is an animal.

Karyn puts down the file, shakes her head and says to John, 'Can you imagine what that poor kid went through? He wasn't even in a gang. Just lived in the wrong area.' She gets up and paces the room. 'What are we actually doing here? Nothing's changed in thirty years. We're great at detection, but we've never varied our murder rate.'

A month later, in April, a forty-six-year-old drug baron is found slumped at the wheel of his silver Merc in a cul-de-sac in Springboig. Shot in the head. But still there are gangs going at it on Friday nights with hatchets and claw hammers.

'I've got a hunch that the murder rate is actually higher than we think,' Karyn tells John. She taps a report from Cardiff. It proves that many victims of violence there who stagger into A&E don't even report the crime. They are too scared of reprisals. Or they're gang members who don't want the cops to know. 'I bet it's the same here.'

'You'll need evidence,' John grins, ever the detective.

So Karyn phones up the surgery at the Accident & Emergency Unit of the Glasgow Royal Infirmary. 'I want to come in and speak to you about violence.'

'What about violence?'

'I don't know. Not until we get into it.'

She meets a consultant called Michael Sheridan, an earthy Glaswegian.

'What you hear about is the murder rate,' Michael says. 'But we see the attempted murders.'

'How many?'

'In a year? About three hundred.'

Karyn is shocked. This is far above the official stats. 'What about slashings?'

'We have a serious facial injury every six hours. Predominantly gang-related.'

As fate would have it, Michael is in the middle of his own study. This could be a strong piece of evidence, she thinks. As Karyn suspects, most people are too terrified to involve the cops: Michael estimates that as much as 70 per cent of violent crime is not even reported. It makes a bloody joke of the rise and fall in the crime stats.

Over the next few evenings, as Rowan sits patiently in her office, Karyn compiles Michael's final research into a report. She stands over John while he reads through it. He whistles and shakes his head. 'Only 30 per cent of our violence is reported?'

Karyn is keen to know when they can present their findings to the chief constable and the force executive. All those grey-haired men with braid on their shoulders. She fiddles with the beads around her neck, a habit she has when she is agitated.

'You'll have to hold fire for a day,' John says. 'We're going to London. We've been summoned to the Home Office for a round-table.'

It's a three-line whip. They fly down that day. At the Home Office they find themselves in a small room with about twenty people: John Reid, the Home Secretary, is at the head. He seems older than he appears on telly and smaller in the chair. His staff lower a cup of tea and a biscuit in front of him.

'University of Stirling,' Karyn whispers to John beside her, sliding her eyes in Reid's direction. 'Same as my father.'

The meeting is formal, with piles of hard-copy materials. Reid is flanked by men in crumpled grey suits. 'His Spad,' John nudges her back, eyeing one of them, a younger, harder-faced nerdy type who talks about political risks. Karyn's face looks blank. 'Special adviser.'

'Four young men have been murdered in Peckham over the weekend,' Reid begins gravely. He outlines the details, the national concern about youth violence. An elegant black woman in her forties speaks up, slightly theatrical in her manner. She introduces herself as Decima Francis.

'This has been bubbling for some time,' she says. 'After Damilola was killed we completed analysis in Southwark. We've had this mob violence, huge numbers, with girls too, attacking just one kid. Ten on one. But we're moving away from that now into guns. In Birmingham you have the cross-border issue coming in. A girl I spoke to was too scared to cross the road to visit her mum in hospital as she thought she'd be beaten up or killed.' Decima is angry. Karyn is impressed with her passion. 'I worked in Boston for years and it's following what's happening in the States. The kids are getting younger and younger now. It's coming from America. Now we're just picking up the rubbish. Musicians calling women bitches and whores. I'm from St Kitts and when we got American TV it changed the country in five years. Gangs started fighting, families broke up, shootings. Young people are buying into gang culture because it's sexy, dangerous, invincible, daring. But England is about class, poise, language, etiquette. We've lost that. We've lost the use of language. Everyone has become so cowardly.'

Decima works with excluded young black men who were involved in gang crime. She has stood onstage at the MOBO Awards and bellowed out to an auditorium of black musicians to stop calling her a bitch and a whore.

'This is about the failure of young black men,' Decima continues, fixing her eyes directly on the people round the table. 'When I came back from America in 1995, I saw these young black people hanging around on the street. It was like: what are they doing there? Why are they there? Because there were so many of them. They said they were excluded from school. This is England. Who thought of anything so stupid? You just cannot exclude young children from their society. That is where they spend most of their life; that is where they build their history; that is where they have their friends. If you do it to adults, within six months they are depressed. What do you think happens to children? The way that the young people dress and behave and the words they use that are not British, they are not Caribbean and they are not African,' Decima said. 'We do not say "nigger", we do not use those words at all. What I have seen is that as that word, which has come to Britain out of the music, has become part of the way that our young people speak, the young people now treat each other in the same way as the Ku Klux Klan in the Deep South, and the way that we kill each other as young people is exactly the same callous, brutal and inhuman way, with total disregard for anybody and anything. They will shoot in the morning, outside a school, outside a fish and chip shop, in McDonald's, in front of parents and children, and they are using that word. Before we used it we never had this kind of killing – not by children on children – and they are the only ones using it, so we must be very mindful. If the Asians' or if the white people's young people produced music like that, you would stop it in a heartbeat, you would stop it immediately.'

Karyn looks at her as she pounds the table with her fist. Why are people not angry like this in Scotland? she thinks.

Why doesn't Scotland have this kind of voice, a Scottish Decima Francis? Scotland is dispossessed.

'What is missing is that we have forgotten what it is to be British,' Decima goes on. 'It is not OK to be British any more. It is not OK to be proud. It is not OK to say, "Clean the streets. Clean your windows. Make the place look nice. Do not throw your rubbish on the floor. Get up for old women and young children. Behave like adults and behave well. This is a civilized country." We are not doing it any more, and we need to start again.'

Next up is the Reverend Nims Obunge from the Peace Alliance. He is articulate, energetic and in a smart suit. He also pounds the table with his fist and talks about how we are abandoning a whole generation of young black men to the streets. Karyn decides it's time to step in.

'This is not about young black men,' she interrupts. 'It's about young men.'

Decima and Nims and John Reid all turn to look at her. They've picked up on her Glaswegian accent, she thinks.

'Because in Glasgow the men we deal with are all young white men. All the victims are young white men. All the offenders are young white men.'

This stirs them. She has their attention now.

'In London, Manchester, Birmingham, there are large numbers of ethnic minorities in gangs. OK. Aye, and race is an aggravating factor in terms of deprivation and a whole range of things, but our murder rate is just as high. Don't get me wrong, this is not a competition to see whose murder rate is higher, because any is too many.'

John Reid scribbles a note on his pad. She carries on.

'In Glasgow it's been going on for much, much longer

and this isn't about race, it's about masculinity. The Glasgow hard man. It's very easy to think that's the way it's always been so you'll never be able to fix it.'

They all nod. The discussion carries on. Reid is lively and engaging. The consummate politician. Occasionally his civil servants chip in. They speak very cleverly, but underneath are most committed to not doing anything new. At the end Reid greets Karyn and John warmly as fellow Scots, drops some political gossip at Gordon Brown's expense, then moves on. Decima Francis comes over.

'I know Glasgow,' she says. 'I worked in the Tron Theatre when it opened in 1981.' She grabs Karyn's arm. 'You're right, it's the same kind of attitude. With the poor, there is a tendency to ignore them. It's them. It's the poor.'

On the plane back, John is animated. 'What did you think?' he asks.

'Decima Francis. Nims Obunge. They were spectacular,' Karyn says, pouring a pot of cream into her coffee. 'I looked round the table of people and I realized this is what Scotland doesn't have. They had a voice down there. In London they are right next to the Home Office.'

'They are still angry,' John says, shaking his head. 'Angry at young people getting murdered. And we aren't.'

'That says something about Scots that is very different from down south.'

Karyn leans over and squints at John.

'We're summoned down to London for a round-table because four kids get killed in Peckham. But this weekend in Glasgow we had five people murdered. There was no round-table here. No one even mentioned it.'

They both let this sink in. Five murders and no one is sending a team up to Glasgow.

'Remember Philip Lawrence? A headmaster was stabbed outside a school and everyone said they had had enough. Or Damilola Taylor? They were turning-points down south. But the other day I was looking at a cutting about a woman in the East End of Glasgow. A young boy who was sixteen had been stabbed, she came out and cradled his head while he bled to death in the gutter. I thought people would read that story and think, we've had enough. But nothing happened. You know what, I couldn't believe it. This poor grandma, who didn't know this young guy, went out and cradled his head whilst he died. And nobody gave a hoot. He's murdered, and so what?'

She pulls her beads off over her head and smacks them down in her lap.

'I remember seeing some footage of a young cop in Ayre, talking about a boy who gets stabbed through the heart, through the chest with a screwdriver, so much so that it goes right through to his other side and he's lying on the ground bleeding to death saying, "I don't want to die, where's my mum." The cop actually cries on the film and we edited it out. But can I tell you. I can barely witness that. Let me tell you if you are not absolutely bloody angry that that can happen.'

'Aye,' John nods. 'There was a murder the other day. An old woman got murdered and it got detected very quickly and they were interviewing people in the street and they interviewed two Glasgow guys in their forties. They were OK. They were saying, "It's ridiculous, you know. People can't even sleep in their beds, it's absolutely outrageous and an old woman like that, people taking liberties." They were great, two of them. Then we spoke to a couple of young guys in shell suits, seventeen or eighteen. Could hardly string a sentence together. You didn't know what they were saying. They didn't know what they were saying. Mumbling.'

They sit in silence for a beat.

'So something's happened,' John says. 'It hasn't always been like this.'

'It's since the '80s, you think?'

'Aye. We haven't always been this drunk. Something's happened in the past two or three decades and it's about de-skilling of communities, taking the bloody very jus of the community out and leaving nothing left. They cannot cope. Hopeless. Hopeless men.'

Karyn laughs.

'You like that.'

'Hopeless men. I get that.'

Tiny scattered fragments of light from a city appear far below.

'Lots of these young guys are nae innocents,' Karyn says. 'Sometimes they get themselves in situations that they shouldn't be in. They drink too much, they take risks and a whole range of things. But nobody's got the right to take away their life. Nobody.'

Once back in headquarters they decide to take it to the top, to set up a meeting with the chief constable, William

Rae. Karyn clenches her fist and gives John a light punch on the shoulder. He's turned out to be the ally that she has waited for.

After a few days he appears at her door.

'Willie is an absolute gentleman,' John says. 'He'll see us. He's an articulate and thoughtful man.'

Karyn has never seen so much braid in one room. They make their case as forcefully as possible. Rae has in front of him Karyn's report with the evidence to back up their claim. Towards the end she says, 'You have to understand, what our report is saying is that only 30 per cent of your violence is reported to you. So when you're saying the murder rate's gone up 2 per cent or down 3 per cent it's not really making that much difference.'

There is a pause while he considers this. He is a relaxed leader, preferring to let others take the spotlight. He asks them about their work.

'At the moment all we're doing is stabilizing the patient, if you like. We're actually quite good at that. We have over 90 per cent detection rate for murder. It's straightforward. But we catch the feckless and the stupid, is who we catch. These gangs have been round for forty, fifty years. Attitudes haven't changed. So we know that we need to do some things differently. Some of it's about enforcement but other stuff is about making partners step up to the plate.'

Karyn tells him about the A&E Department, the intelligence analysis her staff have done of the gangs.

'The motto of the police is to protect, to guard and to watch,' she says. 'To protect you have to prevent as well.

So we need to do something earlier. Earlier than enforcement.'

Rae nods thoughtfully. He turns to John.

'Do you know where you're going on this? I mean, have you got . . . a map?'

John stares at him in silence. Tricky question. A lot of the things they have been thinking about are intuitive, just ideas they came up with because the current ones weren't working. But he is a detective and detectives are always good at thinking on their feet.

'No,' he says. 'But we've got a compass.'

'I like that. I like that.'

Rae peers carefully over the senior male faces around the table, looking for the right detective superintendent to delegate the work to. His eyes return to John and Karyn.

'Well, you two seem to have a good idea, why don't you do it?'

Karyn raises her eyebrows and glances at John. They expect Rae to delegate the idea or provide some resources, but they don't expect him to give them a free rein like that. Jesus, Karyn thinks, we're actually going to have to see this thing through.

They thunder down the stairwell and out the glass doors. Karyn wheels round to John and shoots him a look that says, What now.

'Partners,' he says simply. 'We need to build a coalition of the willing.'

Rae is no slouch either. Whenever he bumps into someone he says, you need to call John and Karyn, they're looking at violence in a new way. Early on they secure a meeting with a senior person from the Prison Service, at Polmont Young Offenders Institute. All the young gang members end up here, and Karyn herself used to work in here years ago. It used to be a wee, scummy prison, she thinks, absolutely hideous. Karyn slings her bag through the X-ray machine and takes a ticket for her keys and mobile phone. She and John shoulder-barge through a turnstile of thick stainless-steel bars. It's still a pretty horrible place: the blocks are really narrow, very old.

They sit with the senior contact in an airless meeting room.

'We opened a brand-new hall in '03,' the guys says. 'Which has finally ended the practice of slopping-out in Polmont.'

'And I know they're still packed in two to a cell made for one. Still locked up all day,' Karyn says. 'Scotland's got one of the highest jail populations in Europe. Bar-L, Greenock, Polmont. They're all packed. Eight thousand four hundred prisoners. You've got over six hundred young guys in here. It's not working. We've tried it for forty, fifty years. We've tried to bang them up. It's not working. We have to do something else as well as that.'

The guy frowns as he listens. He hasn't finished telling them about the new hall. He sucks his teeth, like he's got a bad taste in his mouth.

'We still have to bang them up, don't get me wrong,' Karyn continues. 'I'm the very woman to try to put some of these people away. But we want do to violence reduction. We want to do something really quite different. To try to break the cycle between the generations – so you don't see grandfathers, fathers and sons in there.'

He nods at this. Stand in the yard with the screws and they can reel off the sons of inmates or ex-inmates passing through the system. He listens, but at the end holds up his hand.

'It won't work,' he says, shaking his head.

'Why's that?' Karyn asks.

He looks at her as if the answer is obvious. 'It's too big,' he sighs. 'Don't bother.'

Then he shoves his chair back and in a blink they are being passed their mobiles and keys. Out through the turnstile into fresh air. Karyn strides away from the high walls, fuming. John has to double-step to keep up. He's livid too.

'Too big, don't bother?' John says in disbelief, throwing his arms wide.

'We'll give up our violence reduction,' Karyn snaps. 'You hold him, I'll hit him.'

'He's institutionally paralysed. He'll just let it carry on.'

'Aye, it's just scummy people in a certain part of town and that's what they'll always do.'

Soon they find this guy is not the only one. John pulls some strings to get them in a room with a high-ranking civil servant. He wears a dark navy suit. His middle-aged spread is carefully hidden by what looks like a brand-new tie from Buchanan Galleries. He also wears a permanent grin, one that widens the more John lobbies him. He keeps saying: 'You're absolutely right, John,' and John finds it annoys him. He knows that behind all the charm he's planning to do nothing.

'You've been doing the same thing for ever now,' John snaps at him. 'When are we going to see some learning on this?'

'Six months probably,' he smiles back. 'Maybe longer.'

Afterwards in the car park John shakes his head at Karyn. 'Those superagreeables really annoy me.' She nods.

'Six months, maybe longer,' he exclaims, frustrated. 'Two years, maybe? Or five years? Any chance that this is going to coincide with your retirement? Now there's a notion.'

They are both growing deeply angry at how resistant people are to change. Karyn doesn't sleep well. She feels short-tempered next morning as she drops Rowan off at Adelaide's Baptist Nursery, dead convenient, right across the road from police headquarters in Pitt Street. They wait in the horizontal rain for it to open at eight. Then she has to peg it up the hill for the morning meeting – also at eight – and sneak in at five past.

'I've asked them to change it for a year,' she moans later to Margaret, shaking drops from her mac. 'Meetings can move. Meetings are just meetings. I can't leave a toddler at the gates.'

'What did they say?' Margaret asks.

'No. You're either there or you're not. I'm the only woman.'

'I don't know how you cope on your own.'

'I'll stop going. If they want my input, they can come and find me.'

Margaret nods, impressed how Karyn does not take no for an answer, does not accept it when people say to her it can't be done. Anything can be done, if it's the right thing: you will always be able to find people that can come and help you. Margaret sidles out the door, thumbing at her desk apologetically. Karyn is lost in a murder report.

'Margaret,' she says, not looking up. 'You're in Shettle-ston Road at 10 p.m. on Friday night. Who's more likely to stab you, a guy who carries a knife or a guy who has to go home and get one?'

'The guy carrying.'

Karyn nods slyly at her, like she's already locked into one of her hunches. Karyn darts out of her office, marches through the swing doors to another room. Uniform officers in black short sleeves are plodding through statements on the computers. She taps the shoulder of one she's met.

'What happens when a guy is caught with a knife in the street?'

'The cop says can you check out this guy, what's he got. No, he's not on PNC and he's got no history. All we'd do is take the knife off him, report him at the scene and let him go.'

'Take the knife, let him go,' Karyn nods, taking it in. 'It's not exactly visible justice.'

Karyn calls her team together in a hurried meeting. Her new hunch is that you are more likely to be murdered by someone who has carried a knife in the past. There are a lot of pending cases waiting to go to court. They need to lobby for a new system. From now on a guy caught with a knife gets taken back to the cells, he'll be DNA'd, finger-printed and held in custody for the next day in court. Swift visible justice.

They battle this one through right to the end. It isn't easy. They succeed in changing the Lord Advocate's guidelines of custody. But she still can't sell it to the cops.

She picks up grumblings about the extra workload for them.

Sometimes things happen that make it much easier to get a message through.

Just after dawn one cold October morning, Thomas Waddell, nineteen years old, finishes his all-night car-wash in Maryhill Road and gets on the number 40 bus. He makes a couple of lewd remarks to girls, brags to the driver about a conquest, then falls asleep. Around seven thirty he gets off the bus and walks the rest of the way along the River Kelvin canal walkway. Coming the other way is a woman power-walking, in a red cotton top, jeans and trainers. Farah Noor Adams, a youth worker at the local Citizens' Advice Bureau, has just taken her eight-year-old daughter to school. She is thirty-four, a petite Pakistani girl with long black hair. She notices Waddell, a gaunt, agitated figure, following her. She phones 999. But her calls don't get through. He closes on her. She tries again but still no answer. Then suddenly wiry hands grab her from behind and pull her to the ground. He drags her into undergrowth beneath the shadow of a viaduct. There he hits her in the face with a brick and rapes her. She pleads for her life, but he strangles her. The attack lasts half an hour. It is in broad daylight.

Two workmen discover her. The police put up a cordon and take DNA samples from her body and clothing. They run the DNA through the system and nothing comes back. Waddell has no previous convictions. He's a clean skin. After a week the cops are despondent, they think they aren't going to get him. The local community is deeply shocked. The papers pick it up and run photos of the victim, cranking up the pressure on the detective super in charge of the investigation, Kenny Watters. He issues a statement saying: 'We have received a disappointing response from members of the public since our appeal. We have still not received any further sightings of Farah after she dropped her daughter off at school.'

It looks like Waddell is going to get away with it. He doesn't even live in the area. But recently collected DNA has not been put through the system. Ten days beforehand Waddell was stopped and caught with a knife. In the old system he would have been let go, but he was taken to the station, where they took his DNA, fingerprinted him and reported him for court. A week later, when they run the DNA again, he comes up.

Karyn and John watch the news of Waddell's arrest on the telly.

'It's the best thing we did,' she says to John. 'I don't know how many murders that prevents, but it must be a good thing.'

'You can sell it to the cops so it's not a bad thing.'

'It's a start.'

She looks at him, her eyes narrowing. 'If we can fix this in Glasgow, we can fix it anywhere.'

She knows that the kids out in the East End schemes are still staging gang fights on Friday and Saturday night. She needs somehow to get inside that culture. Somehow she has to fully understand who these kids are and why they are fighting.

She slings her coat over her shoulder and waits by the

lift. The doors scrape open to reveal the uniform officer with thick black eyebrows who she argued with in the early days. She squeezes in next to him.

'We wouldn't have caught him if it wasn't for your lot,' he says, punching the button. The lift rattles on down.

10: Saturday

It is Robbie's thirteenth birthday. His mother hands him a present wrapped in a brown-paper bag. He balances it on his upturned palms, feeling how heavy it is. He peels the paper back to reveal a scored handle, then a thick blade. It's a machete.

'We can't protect you,' his mother shrugs. 'You have to protect yourself.'

Saturday comes to Easterhouse. The most dangerous day of the week. Parents hold their breath now until Monday. Robbie squints out of his rain-slaked window. All he can see is the black outline of barren hills and featureless rows of houses. His eye rests on the dark patches of wasteground, far away from any infrared CCTV cameras. Over this jagged, stony ground the pitch battles will ebb and flow. He sees himself edging into the fray, holding up his machete. The others charge at him out of the darkness. He's not fast enough. A swipe at the back of his head. He stumbles. Closes his eyes, feels sick. If there was a way out of this tonight he'd take it. He cranes left so he can see the bus stop. Everyone would see him get on. If he lived in Gorbals or Cowcaddens he could walk to the centre. But these schemes in the North-East are bloody miles away. He'd be skelped on the top floor of the 38 bus or the X19. They throw bricks through the windows. They wait for him at the bus stop, get on with paying customers, attack him and shove through the fire exit at the back.

Cops in B Division assemble at HQ in Shettleston Road. They zip up their stab vests, check the fast cuffs. They file out the back, to the waiting vans, past a huge bin full of weapons they have confiscated. Hatchets, swords, fireman's axes, pickaxe poles, claw hammers, machetes. Their orders are to scour patches of wasteground for gang fights, all over Easterhouse, Baillieston and Shettleston. They patrol up and down flashpoints like the Edinburgh Road. Running from the cops is all part of the buzz for the kids, who vault over fences, race in the dark through parks and trees. But B Division are super-fit. One PC has been doing a seventeen-mile round-trip cycle from Airdrie to the city centre after his dad had a bypass. They shift along the seats. The van's engine fires up.

In Easterhouse it starts during the day with the younger kids, who sit on the top of the hill throwing stones towards their rivals on the hill opposite. Between the hills lie several hundred yards of playing fields, shared by the two local schools, Rogerfield and Sinclairs. It forms the perfect battleground. Seven-year-olds warm up to the main event. One with a shaven head runs down onto the pitch, hurls a stone never meant to hit anyone. He stands his ground. His frozen fingers stab furiously at the air as he baits them.

'Go home and play with your toys!' the taunt comes back.

It echoes amongst the thin trees. The kid watches as a rival in a white shell suit lumbers down the hill towards him. He blurts out one final yell, then bolts the length of the pitch without looking round until he scurries onto his summit, panting. This game of chase hints at what's to come.

Robbie grinds out the joint stub and fans the smoke out the window. They nod. It's time. In a tight group of five his pals head out down bleak winding roads of dirty yellow houses and grey roofs. Robbie lives in Drummy territory. They never call it low Lochend. It's Drummy. Always has been. A cluster of houses, a couple of streets. He doesn't have to go far before he crosses the border into Den Toi territory, a stone's throw away by Rogerfield Primary School. There he risks being attacked. If he pops down the Westerhouse Road for a bag of Skittles he's in Aggro territory.

Earlier that morning he went for a haircut and took eight of his pals. Only two of them got a haircut. But if he'd been alone he'd have got a right good beating. If he heads north to the sports centre, the Auchinlea Road can sometimes be barred by the Garthamlock gang, the Jet, singing, 'With a bottle and a brick and a corporation stick. We are the Jetto!'

So they never leave Drummy streets. Never make it to the centre of Glasgow. He'll live and die in a square mile.

'Fuck the rest.'

They start to psych themselves up for the fight, as they walk past boarded-up windows and a Spar barricaded behind metal grilles.

'We are number one.'

'Fuck the Provvy.'

'Grasses,' one snaps, jerking his head at a wall of graffiti that reads 'Keiran Friel on protection. Like father like son'. The wall belongs to Keiran's seventy-seven-year-old granny. Robbie scoots off to check the bushes where they planked the weapons. Still there. You can buy a lock-knife in the fishing shop in Shettleston or a golf club in town. Axes and claw hammers down the DIY. Hatchets from the building site. Samurai swords hang in pride of place over the mantelpiece. Or use a wee kitchie.

They spent ages working out how to upload photos of themselves giving the finger and drinking Buckie. But some kid in Aggro has made a flash website with top-ten gang photos. They change as people vote for them. Everyone's talking about him and his poncy software. Flash bastard.

They head up the hill. Robbie shivers at the thought of what's to come. He feels dizzy, desperate for a drink. His heart sinks when he finds only young 'uns round the fire.

'Where are the troops?'

Soon older teenagers arrive, more seasoned gang fighters, lean fast runners with wiry frames. One in a G-star Raw T-shirt is just out for serious assault and permanent disfigurement.

'How was Polmont?'

'A heavy canter. Like a holiday.'

He brings a big bag of carry out, the sign that it's all going to end badly. Three litres of Frosty Jack for three quid will do it. Mad Dog 2020. A half-drunk bottle of Buckie is thrust in Robbie's hand. He takes a swig. It's sweet like a Coke. Slips down easily. The glass bottle comes in handy for a missile too. The caffeine in it will keep him pumped up. He feels less scared now, steeled for the fight.

'Fuck the Den Toi,' he yells out. He's into it now. His dad ran with a gang. They've been around for ever, since Easterhouse was built in the '50s. The Drummy, the Provvy, Aggro, Den Toi and the Bal Toi.

•

John and Karyn sit in a car in the rain outside Shandwick Shopping Centre, eating cheeseburgers. They've just met a local community worker.

'Can I tell you, the gangs that cause the most problems are not the Bal Toi,' John says. 'The gangs that cause the most problems are Health, Social Work, Education, Police, Local Government, National Government, because they fight over turf just the same as everyone else. That's our budget, no our budget, we can't spend that, that's got nothing to do with us. Happens the whole time.'

Karyn is about to post the last mouthful, but hesitates. 'You worked here in uniform, didn't you?' she remembers.

He nods. 'Once there was an Orange parade here.' He waves his hand out the window. 'There was a bit of trouble going round, so the super in charge had decided he would cut it short. We ended up in Cairnbrook Road, which runs between two high schools – St Leonards is still there, but Lochend Secondary was like a non-denominational school. We parked there. Ahead of us was a group of really unhappy people. Usually young guys. There were bottles and bricks. It was really a stand-off. I remember the super-intendent walked forward and a band member walked forward as well. He was saying, "Let the guys from the band get in the buses and go." It was fine. Then from the back of the crowd this bottle came winging over, I can still hear the noise it made – foo foo foo as it flew through the air. Someone said: "Watch the bottle!" and the superintendent said: "Watch yourself!" and he actually pushed the band member, and he pushed him into it. It couldn't happen better if he'd lined him up and it'd come down in the middle of his head.'

They both laugh. John churns the ignition.

'It was called a donnybrook at Cairnbrook. A donnybrook is a fight.'

She looks to heaven. She knows what a donnybrook is. The car eases away towards the M8, back to the city centre.

●

Behind them darkness falls on Cairnbrook Road. The kids huddle to talk tactics, like it's a football game. It doesn't pay to be so out of your heid on alcohol that you skew your balance. To survive you have to stay on your feet. If you stumble they'll swarm all over you before you can get to try again. Trick is to get in a frenzy of blows that rain down on the other prick while he's down.

These ten-year-olds can run like the wind. And it doesn't matter if you're skelped in the back of the head by a ten-year-old with a hatchet or a twenty-year-old: you'll still get eight stitches. Robbie sees Drew standing on the edge prodding the flames with a stick. Something's on his mind. He goes over.

'Got a machete for me birthday,' he says.

'Mad,' Drew says. 'Who gave it you?'

'Me mum.'

Drew squints up at him. It's hard to read the look. Then goes back to prodding the fire.

'Reminds me of a wee story,' he says. 'Of Mick and his son.'

Robbie squats next to him. Drew's good at stories. There's a guy in the East End called Mick, real East End character. He was well known for armed robbery with a shotgun, always well planned and extremely violent. He was fearless. The smallest sleight was met with fury. The cops and screws would only tackle him if there were at least three of them.

Mick stabbed his father when he was seven. He grew up in borstals, care homes and prison. He ran with the gangs as a youth and had a temper he could not control. The only staple in his and his wife's life was heavy drinking. He beat her and she fought back.

Last time he comes out of prison he's fifty-two. Looks about seventy. Only in for five months' custodial, for charge of an offensive weapon. The drink has left him half-mad. It's Christmas. He's been evicted. All the homeless accommodation barred him for his rages. It's a bitter night, minus ten outside. Mick shuffles through the snow-drifts to a dovecote where he lies down to sleep with the pigeons. His social worker gives him a flask of hot tea every morning and rings around for a spare bed. It is the coldest part of the year. Don't take food back to the dove-cote, he warns him, you'll attract rats. Mick takes food back. That night the rats come. They bite him so badly in the night, he is hospitalized.

'You said he had a son?'

Mick feels all torn up about his son. Paul. He's nineteen.

He was given a whole load of free coke by a dealer, until he was hooked. Now he's in debt to the dealer to the tune of £4,000. So he turns to his dad. In the East End of Glasgow, Mick tells him, there's only one way of making money, and hands him his shotgun. So Paul uses it to hold up a security man. He takes the cash off him, goes round the corner and slings it in the dealer's face without counting. It's £40,000.

Robbie thinks about this. Paul's dad gave him his gun.

They squat there looking at the flames. Then Drew looks around for drink, but the bag's empty. 'Where's Caprice with the carry out?'

Caprice is a scheme-hopper. She can move between Drummy and Den Toi. She goes with Chris from the Den Toi. They know each other from the local secondary school, Lochend. Chris badmouths Drew to her. She's not clear how the grievance starts. There is something about Drew that Chris doesn't like. Probably because he is Drummy. Chris says Drew's a dummy, have you heard about him, he's this, he's that. Then she catches Chris texting another girl to hook up and she has a fight with him. He bites her arm. She wants to get back at him. So she hangs out in Drummy and goes with Drew and carries all the stories Chris tells her about him. Chris says this about you, she tells Drew. She exaggerates and makes things up. Chris says this about your mum and dad. He's going to do this to you. It gets bandied around Facebook and Bebo. Texted to everyone. That stirs things up. It doesn't need to be about a lassie. It's a Drummy and Den Toi thing.

She's lucky. Her mum and dad work full-time. Her older brother is dead protective of her until he's caught fighting on CCTV and gets the jail. Then she starts getting in with the wrong crowd and becomes the loudmouth instigator. Caprice hates school because she wants to hang about in the scheme with all the boys who dodge school. They'll be up at the chip shop fighting. There is a wee patch of grass by the road. The boys run back and forth and she and the girls shout, sing, egg them on.

Tonight she goes out early to avoid the cops and buys a three-litre bottle of Frosty Jack cider. It tastes of chemicals. Caprice can go to the post office in Wellhouse which is full of booze or Jaspers in Provanhill which sells to the wee ones and doesn't ask for a passport. Instead she goes to an off sales with a sign in the window: 'Buy a bottle of vodka and get free bread.' She walks quickly, not wanting to run into anyone she knows. 'Just getting carry out for my mum,' she says if challenged.

It is cold. Her fingers are biting. She queues to buy a burger roll. Two schoolgirls with short ties sing along to a tinny radio. One has her head hung down, the other looks at Caprice with her lip curled in a half-sneer. Behind her on the wall is a poster of an old lady opening her door a crack. 'Drug-dealers don't care where the money comes from.' Next to it is one for home insurance at 50p a week. Two girls from the chemist in pale green doctor's overalls stand, arms folded, shivering.

She pays for the burger roll and leaves. She avoids the Centaur pub in case she bumps into her grandfather coming out. Sixty now, he was a plater in the shipyards and smashed both his pinkies between the metal plates. Now they curl inwards permanently and he cheerfully rests his pint on them. He sits at the bar while a welder shows him his two mobile phones.

'Welder two phones,' he snaps. 'Shove it up your arse. I hate a welder.'

Unknown to him, his teenage grand-daughter takes the carry out to the top of the hill.

She gives Drew first swig. He tells her about his day. He sleeps late, watches daytime TV, goes round to a friend's house to play Saints Row II. He'd like to play football but the pitches are private property, so he has to scale a towering wire fence to play and almost tears his ankle jumping down the other side. Some guys fly pigeons but that's not for him. He starts thinking of himself as a ned and he might as well stick to his wee neddy ways. The gang fights are the adrenalin rush. They wait for them all week. Drew tries to psych himself up to go and find the sword he's planked. Caprice eggs him on to give Chris a really good beating. He remembers the taunts online. The things Chris said about his ma. His face flushes red. He takes another swig.

The rain is horizontal now. There's some sleet in there too. His fingers sting and are white at the knuckle. He digs in the ground and brings out the sword. It's eight or nine o'clock and pitch black except for the fires burning on top of the hills. The orange flames blow sideways and sizzle in the rain. They won't last long. Drew has drunk enough now to give someone a battering. He nods to his wee brother.

'When you're older you're going to be one of the boys and chase the Den Toi. You protect our scheme.'

His brother knows what this means. He has to sit this one out. Drew ruffles his hair. They can hear Chris and the Den Toi yelling taunts about Drew. Drew stands on the brow of the hill and feels the rain on his face. Behind him Caprice and the girls goad him on.

'No other team can chase you, Drew,' she yells into the wind. 'They're shitebags. They think they're mad but they only batter junkies.'

Drew checks he has his mates on each flank, then five of them charge down the hill. He can hear them just behind him. The hillside is muddy. He lurches to one side as his foot skitters, then rights himself with a jolt. That was close. Whatever happens he mustn't slip. If he does he'll be finished. Drew runs out onto the wide space of the pitch. It's so dark and wet he doesn't know who is who. He can't be sure it's his mate is behind him. Someone storms past him swiping the air. He grips his sword and swings it towards the charging form. It connects with someone's shoulder and they roar out in pain. Fuck knows who it was. You just skelp the person closest to you. The number of times they've battered each other. Aye, he's seen that loads of times.

Drew is panting now, out of breath already. He wheels about this way and that, his hand frozen around the hilt of the sword. Where will the attack come from? All he can see is shadows of bricks, sticks flying. They chime as they bang on the metal goalpost just by him. Then he hears the thud of feet on hard ground. Sounds closer. He makes out weapons jabbed up into the sky. Dark figures are hurtling towards him across open ground.

He scuttles away with heavy, muddy feet. He can hear

them behind him, grunting taunts. The faster ones are gaining on him. It happens so fast it feels like a planned ambush. He strains to pull clear but there are too many of them.

'Shite!'

He should have been more careful. Above him he can just see the orange of the Drummy fire. He must be back at the foot of the hill. There's a scythe of a blunt object behind his head. He leaps forward, pulling his frame out of range. A few more strides to the top and he'll be safely back amongst his pals. It's scary but exciting. He feels a rush.

But the hill is steep and slippy now. His trackie suit clings to him. He lunges forward for the next stride, but his foot skids away at a mad angle. His ankle buckles and he pitches forward, throwing out his wrists to break his fall. Hard ground races up towards him and snaps his head back. In a daze he shoves the wet earth away, scrabbling back to his feet. The mob close around him. He is sluggish with terror. He hears the swoop of a blade. A crushing pain flattens him. Cold mud fills his eyes and nose. His fingers claw the rocks. The shadows swarm in.

'Stab him.'

'Stamp on his head.'

The air is alive, a fury of belt buckles, golf clubs, knives.

As the attackers disappear, Drew is left twisted and broken on the ground. Every bit of his body hurts. He's torn and slashed. But he's still so pumped up from fighting, with alcohol and caffeine in his veins, that he's not sure of the severity of his injuries.

He lies there for ages, terrified they'll come back. Several hands grab him and drag him roughly up the hill.

Voices jabbering. Is one of these idiots going to call him an ambo? He cries out for his mum. Dark waters close over him.

When he comes round a siren is screaming. He's on a trolley, under a blanket. An oxygen mask is clamped over his face. The adrenalin works to keep him alive, shutting down the blood flow to parts of his body he doesn't need to keep going. He is a healthy young kid, fast as a greyhound on the open moor. He can compensate for losing a lot of blood.

The speed they're going, must be the Edinburgh Road to the centre. He is leaving Easterhouse, he thinks blearily. At the north point of the ring road the ambulance sharks so sharply left into the A&E entrance he nearly rolls off the trolley. They clatter him down and wheel him through the doors. One of the doctors cuts his clothes off him and asks about his breathing. Drew is too out of it to say anything. The doctor shoves his jaw up and they suction blood noisily out of his mouth. He thuds his fingers onto Drew's bare chest, listening. The doctor bends over his face and flashes a white light straight into his eye.

'Drew?'

The nurse cradles his head as she holds the mask to his mouth. She hooks up bags of fluids. Tubes trail down to his arm.

'What happened, Drew?'

'Got battered,' Drew croaks.

The faces blur and fade. They mumble something to him. He asks if his mum is there.

'When he is reasonably stable I'll have a more detailed look at him and pick up the facial injuries. You'll need to page a specialist in maximal facial.'

Christine is in her bed asleep when her bleeper goes off. She scrabbles round for it and turns it off.

'You asleep?' she whispers to her husband.

'Not any more,' he groans, and rolls over.

He's a dentist and it's a real bone of contention when her bleeper wakes him up in the night. The damage is done now. She gets out of bed and in the hallway calls the hospital.

'Young lad come in from Easterhouse,' the doctor from Accident & Emergency says, giving her an account of Drew's injuries. Christine listens and nods.

'I'd better come in,' she says.

She gets phoned about a whole lot of very different things, some of which are more straightforward than others. Some nights she stays in the hospital. She dresses quickly and tiptoes over two sleeping dogs. She scrapes the ice off the windscreen, churns the ignition and pulls out into the road. She drives faster at this time of night as there's not much traffic. It only takes her twenty minutes.

She first sees Drew on a bed draped in a green gown. The nurse crams the oxygen down on his face. Christine can tell immediately he's in pretty bad shape.

Right from the get-go Christine has seen victims of trauma like him, young men with a difficult background, from deprived areas of town. They come in with big open wounds on their face made with knives, or blows to the head from a baseball bat or a machete. Their injuries are significant, not life-threatening but bad in terms of the disfigurement. No plastic surgeon can magic away scars like that. A typical Friday or Saturday night for Christine is to walk in and find a young guy like Drew, sitting down, his face covered in blood, his back with tattoos and older, smaller stab scars. It happens all over Glasgow. When she worked in Lanarkshire people usually came from Coatbridge, the rougher end of town. They smelt of alcohol but were not so intoxicated that they didn't know what they were doing. These lads don't drink to get drunk.

She remembers one who is admitted in the middle of the night. He has a massive slash wound across his face, running from the corner of his mouth to his ear, far worse than a vertical one because it does not fit into any of the face's natural wrinkle lines. A mouth-to-ear scar is never going to fade away, she thinks, as she stitches him up under local anaesthetic and pops him in a bed. He's a bit drunk when he comes in and so she keeps him there for a bit longer.

She goes on the ward round the next day and back again to see him just before visiting.

'I thought I'd better come and speak to you now because you're sober and you've got this big scar on your face,' she says. 'We've had to put in quite a lot of stitches. I just want to let you know that you are probably going to be left with a scar for life with that, because it's in a bad place. You know we couldn't make it disappear, so I just want you to be aware of that before you leave hospital.'

He glances up from his bed. He's about sixteen.

'Don't worry about it, hen,' he says. 'It's not a problem.'

Christine looks at him in surprise.

'It would be a big problem for me. That was why I was coming to speak to you.'

Soon afterwards four or five of his pals troop in to visit him. They all have a facial scar. So he fits in better. Years from now any girl he meets or people in the street will look at his face and think he's bit of a hard man, he's been involved in violence.

Christine can see that Drew has injuries from blunt trauma as well. There's a lot of baseball bats sold in Glasgow but not many balls, that's the old saying. She runs through the possibilities in her head. From the neck up it tends to be broken cheekbones, broken lower jaw, smashed-in teeth, broken nose. Sometimes if a wee boy has had a right good beating he will have a combination of these injuries, what's called a mid-face fracture where the bones of his face can be disarticulated from the bones of his skull. His face will all be in pieces like a chocolate Easter egg smashed against a table. Not life-threatening but difficult to fix. A broken jaw will probably keep him out for a few weeks. It will be very uncomfortable, difficult to eat and he'll lose a lot of weight; his lower lip and chin will go numb. For a long time later when he bites into food it won't feel right, the teeth won't fit together. Sometimes the blows from the baseball bat or golf club break up the cheekbone and damage the eye socket so badly there is nothing to hold up the eye. The eyeball drops down slightly. He looks squinty. He has double vision and finds it very difficult to drive, to ride a bike or play snooker. If he gets a really good whack in the eye he'll get a haemorrhage behind the socket and the optic nerve will get squashed. He will go blind in that eye. The golf clubs they use in gang fights are usually woods. They have longer shafts so you can build up more force. The skin can burst open like a tomato.

Christine cradles Drew's head carefully and tilts it forward. She peers under the oxygen mask. There is something else now, a bruise forming in a wavy marking on his face. She traces it with her finger: it suggests the imprint of a shoe. Someone's stamped on Drew's head. She can picture it.

'Drew, when did this happen?'

'Last night,' he groans. 'On pitches in the scheme.'

She's pleased with his responsiveness. He's not confused, which means no haemorrhage, brain damage or stroke. A stamp can result in that and a fractured skull.

The nursing staff look haggard, their shirts purple and blue. They work hard to resuscitate a cardiac arrest, then stop to record the time of death. One walks away, pulling down the face mask, then into a side room to tell the family. A gasp of grief. A baby is jiggled by a family friend. People drift by, shattered by what they have witnessed.

Christine leans Drew forward and checks his back. There are some older, smaller scars and fresh bruising.

'You've been in before, haven't you?' she asks.

'Aye.'

Drew has a nasty facial laceration but as far as she can make out the bone is intact underneath. A machete would leave a bigger cut with the jaw in little pieces. They'd rebuild the jaw with small plates and a big reconstruction plate, a heavy duty piece of metal put in where the bone fragments are. The patient loses a few teeth, can't smile and has a droopy lower face, as the facial nerve gets damaged.

'Follow my finger with your eye.'

The worst things Christine sees are lost eyes, bits of nose or ear bitten off. She thought ears only got sliced off in *Reservoir Dogs*, until she saw it. Drew is stable enough so she sutures his gash tightly.

'I'll pop in to see you tomorrow,' she says. She cannot find any next of kin for Drew. She tells the nurse to track someone down, heads home.

The room is blurred. A strip light burns into him. Drew blinks. His mouth is dry as sand. A woman's head looms over him, not the blonde earlier, this one has pale-blue eyes, a dark-brown fringe. She's like a nurse, but doesn't have the uniform. All in black with thick black beads around her neck.

'I'm Karyn,' she says quietly. Then the pain returns, rising until his whole body and face ache so much it feels like his head might explode.

'It's not working out too well for you, is it?' she asks quietly.

•

The cafe in the Centre for Contemporary Arts is packed. It's in a courtyard, under a glass atrium. Dead trendy, with home-made scones, muffins and cakes, smoked-haddock fishcakes and organic fruit teas.

'I got a Spoodle for Rowan,' Karyn says. 'She's allergic to some dogs.'

Karyn knows Christine's a dog-lover. They met because she stalked her. Karyn wrote to lots of people asking for help and Christine was one of the first to reply. Showed her the CCTV of the gang fight, told her David's story. Christine's passionate about her work too and despairing about the boys like Drew who keep slashing each other for no good reason. As they leave, Karyn gives her directions to a school she's visiting: Christine has volunteered to go too.

A few weeks later she sits in front of a classroom in the schemes. The kids are fourteen years of age, so small they seem undernourished. The wee boys are quite a lively bunch.

'You can't carry a knife because it is illegal and you'd go to prison,' Christine says.

The boys think about this long and hard.

'Could we put two snooker balls in a sock and carry that about?' one asks. 'As that's not officially a weapon.'

'If you put all that energy into thinking then there's no telling what you could do.' Christine smiles. 'What do you want to do when you grow up and leave school?'

'Don't know, don't really have any ideas.'

'You could train to be a doctor. Or a dentist or a nurse.'

'Oh, I could never do that.'

'How do you keep yourself safe where you live?' Christine asks.

There is a nice wee girl there, well presented and everything. Bright eyes, wide open with interest.

'The close that I live in, in the stairwell in the flats, the guard down there is always selling drugs and threatening us when we go past,' she says. 'And he stabbed my brother.'

At the end Christine asks the kids what they think they have learned. The wee girl puts her hand up.

'You just have to be your own person.'

Christine nods. 'Aye. That's right.'

She gathers her things and moves off to leave. She looks back at the girl, frames her face as she waves. How long will she manage to be her own person when she's got all this stuff closing in on her? The memory upsets her as she drives back. If I could just take you home, she thinks.

'I like my wee young offenders, I do,' Karyn says to Christine. She's brought her to Polmont now to talk to guys like Drew.

'Have any of you experienced domestic violence?'

They all put their hands up.

'Has anyone got a dad in the family?'

All hands stay down.

'Have you been stabbed?'

They all put their hands up again.

One of the guys is nineteen. He pulls his shirt up. She counts about seven stab wounds.

'What would your mother have said?' Karyn asks.

He leans forward in his chair and she can see his eyes closely. They are like two black holes.

'My mother kicked me out the house when I was fourteen,' he says. 'She doesn't even know where I stay.'

11: Striker

Cathy knocks on the door of a mansion house with a crumbling yellow exterior in Dennistoun, in the East End of Glasgow. She is tall in her skinny black cords, with her thick red hair piled up. She is let in and goes upstairs. In a single room is a man, late thirties, dressed in white sports clothes. He looks a bit like the footballer Paul Scholes, if Scholes had been ravaged by addiction and led a punishing life in Glasgow's East End. His head sways gently.

'Hello, Kenny,' she says.

Drowsily, Kenny clears clothes off a chair for her. There's little in the room. Leaning against the skirting are a couple of crime thriller DVDs and biographies of Alex Ferguson and Wayne Rooney. A pair of cheap trainers lie beside them. He is pleased to see Cathy. She's the best thing that's happened to him in a long time. She first went to see him at Bar-L when he was in for a domestic assault. She recommended him for probation and straightened him out for five months. Kenny's eyes are wide open and expectant. A toddler's eyes. He speaks slowly as if every sentence is another piece of a puzzle.

'I'm sick of this place,' he says. 'It was supposed to be sixteen weeks. I've been here for twenty.'

'Believe me, there are far worse,' Cathy reassures him quietly.

She's seen places like one wet house and hostel, notorious in the East End. It's hideous. From the outside it looks like the Great Eastern Hotel used to look: inside it's just a mass of rooms that stink. Violence. Drugs. The staff there don't really do anything to stop the goings on. They should sack a lot of them. Supplying drugs, selling drugs, selling of stolen goods. The number of deaths. Most people are on the verge of death. Cathy has got another client down in a wet hostel in Dalmarnock. You can see young guys there with limbs missing. Some will see the end of their days out there. Then there are places like Fordneuk or Kirkhaven where the staff are absolutely brilliant. The inmates are still drinking but they are doing it in a nicer environment.

Hope House is probably the biggest hostel, with around a hundred beds, down on the Clyde. It's just open drug-dealing at the front door. It's opposite the Sheriff's Court. At the office they call it No Hope House. On the streets Cathy can see dealing everywhere. When she walks to the bus stop every day to go home at quarter to five a guy is by the estate agents on the corner selling heroin. The police must know. The other day a colleague walked by Hope House just after lunch and an obviously drunk girl ran around the corner into a little lane, pulled her trousers down and started peeing. The colleague looked around him and realized they were all on heroin and oblivious to someone standing peeing against a wall outside the office at two o'clock in the afternoon in front of everyone or your granny.

'How are you, Kenny?' she asks, careful to speak slowly and in calm voice. He's been thinking about the past again.

He lived in the East End, in Parkhead with his mum,

dad, three brothers and sister. Parkhead is so near to the Celtic football ground he could hear the roar of the crowd. He was the oldest. At primary school Kenny was a good football player. His family was fine. He'd leave the house at seven o'clock before school started. He was playing for the school team. He was special on the pitch, tore the defence apart with a cheeky grin. He won a wee cup when he was nine years old. He dreamed of following Alex Ferguson into professional football. Fergie'd put a lightning bolt under St Mirren, taking them from the bottom of the second division to be champions, top of the league in '77. If Fergie, a plater's son who lived in a tenement on Govan Road, could become a striker for Queens Park aged sixteen, then Kenny could join the young Parkhead team.

The day he won the cup he raced home excited to tell his father. His dad set off at five in the morning for the building site and appeared on the doorstep at six each night. Kenny flung the door back.

'Dad! We won a wee cup at school. For the footie.'

His dad was hunched from the hard, physical work at Parkhead forge. That evening his lower lip hung slack with drool and he wheezed like a dog, his breath stale and sickly with the smell of McEwan's Export. He barrelled inside, his eyes dulled with rage, and shoved Kenny's mother against the sink. Her hand snuck quickly into his pocket and brought out a clutch of coins.

'You think a tin of macaroni and a bag of chips is enough for five kids?' she hissed.

Then the prick punched her. Kenny froze. He kept punching her until her head went floppy, hair stuck to her face. She slumped over the stove, groaning. Kenny flew into his dad's back to shove him off. His father easily crowded the skinny nine-year-old into the corner, gave him a man's doing. Kenny' nostrils filled with the smell of cigarettes, sweat and dust. His father wiped his rimy mouth with the back of his shirt, then chopped Kenny's legs from under him with hard-capped working boots. He had a giant's back from hammering rivets all day. He put his whole body weight into snapping punches into the boy's face.

'You're Davy Ross's boy,' he wheezed.

The beatings carried on from that day. The only break was when he collapsed into an armchair and fell asleep. Once his mother tried to pull him off Kenny but he shouldered her right across the room and through the tenement window. Kenny was always too terrified to go back into the house. He ran away and shivered in the freezing close at night. The cold bit into his thin frame. Sometimes his pals put him up, but they lived with their parents so most times he slept in huts or disused buildings. It went on until he was thirteen. His ma would find him and drag him back inside the house, stand him by the warm stove until he stopped shivering. She was brand new.

Cathy nods as she listens. Out of force of habit she makes connections in her head with other clients and cases. She runs a domestic-violence group for ten guys from the East End. As boys they saw their mums beaten. Some tried to protect her and got assaulted. Later in life their demons were unleashed by drink and drugs. They beat their wives. The women suffer thirty assaults before they pick up the phone to the cops. Then the men complain to Cathy: 'She got me the jail.'

Some men are far more dangerous than others. There's the ones who shove, push and humiliate every day, the habitual abusers. But the more sinister ones get on fine for years until a violent rage explodes out of nowhere. A slap or a hair pull is followed up with a punch. The torn fist reaches out and grabs a household ornament. Fingers scrabble for a bottle or a kitchen knife. Then a door is ripped off its hinges. Their women live in terror of their lives.

Many of Cathy's male clients have been quite badly physically abused as children. One man last week explained to her that compared to his childhood his assault on his wife did not constitute violence. His father had used all sorts of objects: big bits of wood, belts, anything that came to hand. He had a fractured skull, fractured legs, broken arms, he'd broken everything. It started when he was six. His father had been convicted and spent some time in custody. It must have been brutal in those days to have that kind of prosecution.

Another recent client was arrested after chasing his ex-partner in a car. She ran through the streets as he careered in front of her trying to run her down. Cathy looked into his background and discovered that when he was ten he went into the family home in Drumchapel and found his mother stabbed thirty-six times. She was killed by two teenage boys. He didn't receive any support at the time. He just had to bury it inside. He's in his forties now. He's had a couple of relationships, no violence towards the children, sees them on a regular basis and has good support. It may well be that this situation has crept up and bitten him in the arse. That's a horrific experience for any ten-year-old, to see their mother die like that.

Kenny cradles a warm mug of tea in his fingers. His eyes flit past Cathy to the corridor.

He remembers one night as a boy. It's winter. He approaches the house from the unlit street and a light is on in the kitchen. His mother is talking to someone. No sign of his father. She's with a forty-year-old man, balding, well fed. Kenny creeps in the door and peers into the kitchen. His mother looks up. She shudders like he's a ghost. Something is very wrong.

'What is it, Mum?' he asks.

'I've got to take you into care,' she says. 'You're running away from the house.'

His last walk with her is to the Edinburgh Road. She takes out a few cigarettes and closes his fingers around them.

'Stash them away,' she says. 'It's only for three weeks.'

He knows she is lying and that she's seeing him off for good. He is scared, not knowing what will happen to him now. She walks away and doesn't look round. He is taken through dimly lit corridors. The boys he passes look lost. Some sit in the corner, holding their knees, rocking back and forwards. Terrified.

'Do you want to play snooker?' Kenny asks one.

The boy just stares into space. Kenny thinks about his two younger brothers and sister playing together in the warm living room, with his mum. Why is he in here while they stay home?

Then he's taken to see a psychiatrist.

'Here, have an apple,' he says, holding out his hand. Kenny frowns at it.

'It's a snooker ball.'

'Just testing your focus.'

He's now among kids whose parents did not want them in the house any more. They are beyond parental control. Some have stolen cars, committed violent assaults or been running with the gangs. For the next fifteen years he keeps bumping into them: at the approved school, in the prisons. There are no kids from his part of Parkhead, so he has to be able to fight. The place stinks of polish. He stares out into the yard where a hard, rough-looking crew from Barrowfield are playing football.

'I'm going to play a bit of footie,' he says to a boy next to him.

'You're too young. They'll skelp you.'

They scowl at him as he runs amongst them. But his footwork is so fast, they notice how he can control the ball. One thickset thug fancies himself. Kenny skims the ball off him and flits through against the wire mesh. The lad is livid. Next time Kenny has the ball this lad bears down on him like a rhino, ready to bust his nose open with his heid. Kenny waits with a twinkle in his eye. Then he nutmegs him. The other boys roar at his cheek. Next day the thug sneaks up behind Kenny and smacks the side of his head with a dumb-bell, nearly breaking his jaw. He knows that he'll have to fight back. So he gathers lads around him and next time stands his ground.

'We're going to transfer you to a secure unit,' one of the staff tells Kenny, after the fights increase. 'But not until you're sixteen.'

So that night, when all the staff can be heard hollering at the Old Firm game, he crawls across the roof and takes a running leap onto the top of the wire mesh. He knows they won't discover him gone until the game is over. So he keeps jogging through the night to Glasgow Central Station on Gordon Street. An overweight man in a Pringle jumper walks through with his wife and daughter and Kenny falls in right behind them, his head bowed. He makes it to Blackpool and wanders through the bright lights of the Golden Mile, amongst families who head out there for a holiday during the Glasgow fair.

In 1989, when Kenny turned seventeen, Glasgow was suddenly flooded with drugs. He started taking jellies, a prescription drug: Wyeth made good ones. They made him feel invisible. To feed his habit he shoplifted, broke into houses and robbed. Glasgow Council sandblasted the old tenement blocks to remove the black soot. People talked with fear about Aids. He even threatened a shopkeeper with a bloody syringe, but hated himself afterwards. Sent to Glenochil Prison in Stirling, he walked past a long line of inmates queuing for methadone. They slugged back a fat measure of green syrup that would have killed a sober man, then back on the wing spat it up and shared it out. There were familiar faces from the approved school in there. He twisted and groaned on the bed of granite.

'On heroin the bed's like a marshmallow,' came a voice from the bunk below.

So he tried it. He came out to find Gorbals, Barrowfield and Possil were heaving with street drugs. Looking like a coat hanger with clothes on, he would go up to Killearn Street in Possil at 9 a.m. to stand in the freezing cold. Other addicts were dotted around. The window would twitch and there'd be a scuffle to get to the front. He'd put twenty quid through the letter box, and fight his way out. Everyone for himself. Sometimes if he only had £10 he'd signal to go round the back to the bins and there'd be a fight.

The worst day is Sunday. It's cold turkey. He cleans the flat from top to bottom because of the energy. When someone dies or overdoses in Parkhead he wonders who is selling him the good stuff.

Kenny only has one old pal, John. One night they're walking through Tollcross Park, just south of Shettleston. It is a cloudless night and a white frost clings to the branches. An old car wheezes past. In the headlights a cluster of dark figures rear up in front of them. Shouts fill the air. They lunge at Kenny and he goes down. He glances over to see the glint of steel and the steam of breath in the moonlight. John is stabbed seventeen times. He doesn't make it. For months afterwards Kenny's head is pounded with black thoughts that chew on him like crows. The only friends he has are other junkies and cons. One night he takes seventeen jellies to block the thoughts out. Then he cooks up a £20 wrap on top. Halfway down the syringe he overdoses. In Glasgow Royal Infirmary they struggle to resuscitate him: he stops breathing for two minutes. Then three. With oxygen cut off his brain starts to die. Kenny just lies there as the clock keeps ticking. When they finally bring him around he has not been breathing for four minutes and thirty-three seconds.

'I was a walking miracle,' Kenny grins. 'Ended up in the papers.'

•

'I can't believe it.' Cathy glances over a pile of case files to listen to a female colleague who's down from Stirling to work in their office. 'I've just started interviewing East End clients. I think I must have got it wrong because someone said they were drinking four bottles of Buckfast and taking a hundred and fifty Valium a day.'

Cathy nods. She hasn't got it wrong. The quantities of alcohol in particular are absolutely unbelievable. One man drank forty-five pints in part of one day. Three bags in Glasgow is nothing, nothing. Three bags of heroin. It's just nothing. She sees her clients getting more and more creative. They start injecting themselves with alcohol because otherwise it doesn't get to the brain fast enough. They'll just fill the syringe with vodka and inject it into a vein.

Cathy and her colleagues take the new girl out to lunch in Coia's Cafe, a bustling, family-run Italian restaurant that's been in Duke Street for decades. It's a bit pricey for the East End but Alberto's service is fantastic, with Frank Sinatra crooning and fresh seafood pasta.

'I remember my first day at work,' Cathy beams at her. 'Fifteen of us went down to Tennents Bar in the West End and this guy came in with carry out, started trying to interest us in his stolen goods.'

It's always been like a close-knit family with her colleagues, they never forget a birthday and when she was ill they gave her a huge card and basket of toiletries from the Body Shop. They are always supportive and talk about clients over a bottle of wine in each other's flats. If she's had a really tough case or a death, she'll need a night out. The line managers come too, which is unheard of in other departments.

They'll all go down O'Neills in Merchant Square, a big, safe pub with local touring bands, and have a good dance, let their hair down. The younger ones slag Paul like crazy about liking the Stones, Leonard Cohen or Dylan, because there's a twenty-year age gap across the board. Then they hit Arta bar for a boisterous late-night Catalan session on their embroidered red sofas. Cathy is usually in the hardcore element who stagger on to Gala Riverboat Casino, which is open until five. It's full of drunk girls and sleazy underworld types. They take your photo as you go in, but at least give you free soft drinks if it gets messy. The Christmas party is always at Oran Mor, a quaking cultural complex with bars and a club inside a converted Kelvinside church, with a huge neon halo around the steeple.

During the day the rewards come rarely and when they do they are small – finding a bed in a homeless hostel, having a wee cheque from a charity. A real achievement is to find someone a flat or a job. All her colleagues are compassionate, they came into social work with good values, to improve the quality of people's lives.

After lunch at Coia's she goes in and sits with her men's group from the East End, careful to keep her voice calm and slow, like a satnav. In the first exercise she asks them to name and identify emotions, but it's incredibly hard for them. A man in the East End of Glasgow isn't allowed to cry his whole life except at the birth of a child. The only emotions allowed are anger and happiness, anything else is weakness. So when she starts to explain what shame is, what it feels like, it's as if she's teaching them Swahili. But the others who've been there longer are able to give hints to the new arrivals and Cathy is rewarded with their shaky, incremental progress.

By the final week, when they describe the events that led up to their offence, the change is phenomenal. She finds their new level of awareness poignant. As they file out, different men, she feels it is all worthwhile if they no longer try to solve every problem through violence. The real test will come one Saturday night, as they wait at the bus stop in the rain with soggy chips and some clumsy kid knocks into them. She tidies the group's paperwork in an orange file and grabs her coat.

●

It's 1996 and 'Wonderwall' by Oasis blares out from the twenty-fourth storey of Kenny's tower block in Shettleston, wrapped in dirty fog. He turns to the lassie beside him, runs his fingers through her dark hair and feeds on her pale-blue eyes.

'Maybe you're going to be the one who saves me,' he whispers.

He's grown up with her in Parkhead. Being with her

keeps him stable. He's down to just a little speed every day. She's pregnant and they are so excited. It feels like a new beginning for Kenny, to become a father at twenty-five. She barely takes a quarter every two days. Nearly nothing. Her bump is a thin wee one. He feels calm resting his ear against her stomach, thinking about the small life inside.

He wakes in the small hours to find her leaning against the door frame, trembling. The contractions come fast. In the maternity ward she clenches her teeth with each wave of pain. She grips Kenny's hand, crushing his fingers. Her blood pressure is high as she goes into labour. The monitor's numbers fall as her heartbeat drops. Then it stops completely. The swing doors fly back and machines clatter in on stands. Her grip slackens. Shoulders with gowns crowd round her, shouting to each other. Kenny calls out to her. Then her heart starts again. It's too risky to delay labour so they use forceps. The obstetrician takes out twin curved blades to clamp onto the wean's head. Then her heart stops again. Kenny watches her slip away into a coma. Her body shakes so hard the bed rattles. Flecks of froth bubble at the edges of her mouth and her pale-blue eyes roll back into her head. He wails so hard they tell him to control himself. Then his son appears, wet and slithery with blood. He sobs to meet his child. With strong hands his partner's sisters take the baby away. Her coma lasts for four days. Kenny sits in the corridor of the hospital as her family rages at him.

'Yous scummy junkie,' they seethe. 'Yous done this.'

Her sister takes the wean home with her. They keep Kenny's name off the birth certificate. They ban him from seeing his partner or son ever again. He feels like his heart is breaking.

If he could find one good, kind friend he might stand a chance. But round every street corner is a gaunt junkie beckoning at him with a bony finger. Let's club together and split a bag, he croaks with a gumless grin, there's a chance of a one-off caper to make us a thousand quid. Whenever he stands at the bar in the Barras or Gallowgate, glancing up at the football over his pint, there's always a pair of small black eyes boring into him from the corner. They never blink. Suddenly they're inches from his face. We were on the same wing together in Barlinnie, they say. Or Kilmarnock or Glenochil. Before long a message is delivered to him. You know that guy who you had that run-in with, who hit you with a snooker cue? He's in a pub down the road in Shettleston. Take my car. I've got an open razor under the seat. We'll be there and back in half an hour. And he can't say no. No man in the East End of Glasgow walks away from that.

Then one day his ex-partner comes looking for him. She allows him to take the boy to school. Then swimming. To the carnival and the shops. That chance to be a father lifts him up.

Now he sits opposite Cathy in the probation hostel in Dennistoun. He waits for them to find him another place in Parkhead or Springboig. Cathy is good to talk to, she keeps him going. He's a third of the way through Alex Ferguson's biography. Fergie worked as an apprentice toolworker in the Clyde shipyards. He wonders if, maybe, if that prick hadn't been his dad he might have played as an amateur for Parkhead. He escorts Cathy to the front door.

'My pal Michael. He used to sleep in skips fourteen years ago. But now he's happy, he's got a girl. She's brand new.'

Cathy smiles at him and digs her hands deep into her coat pockets. She wonders what will happen to Kenny's boy in Easterhouse.

12: Way Out

'We're reaching a Rosa Parks moment,' Karyn says. John stands in front of her desk. 'We've tried everything. Stop and search thousands of people and it doesn't dent the murder rate. Encourage the kids to do sport, but the facilities shut down for the winter. Ban Buckfast, the sales go up.'

'What we need is something more radical.'

'Aye. Something that tackles the group dynamic. That's the really toxic thing.'

John nods thoughtfully and leaves. Karyn hunches forward over a stapled article, her fingers dug deeply into her hair. Her fringe sprouts through them. The title is 'David Kennedy and the Boston Miracle'.

She reads the opening and sits back, her eyes flitting round the room. Then she draws her chair up and turns the page. There is something different about this one.

In Boston in the early 1990s the teenage homicide rate was out of control. Kennedy, a researcher at Harvard, devised a programme that brought together cops, social-service providers and community leaders. It involved dramatic face-to-face meetings with the drug gangs. These meetings were named 'forums' and were usually held in a court room. The community leaders told them that they wanted the shooting to stop. The social-service providers offered them help and a way out. The cops warned them that the first gang that killed someone after the meeting would face the full might of the law. The police would crack down on anything illegal: drug sales, drug use, gun carrying, outstanding warrants, probation and parole violations. They would win and the gangs would lose.

The gang members left the meetings to spread the word amongst the guys they ran with.

This is radical, Karyn thinks, raising an eyebrow. Here is a method that turns the group dynamic in on itself. But does it work? A few pages in she finds her answer: following Kennedy's intervention, youth homicides in Boston went down by two-thirds in a few months. The pro- gramme had similar ground-breaking results in Chicago, Cincinnati and other inner cities in America.

•

After reading Kennedy's story Karyn vows to meet him, to see if they can bring his programme to Glasgow. She pays him a visit in New York, where he's now a professor. Karyn explains the challenges they are facing in the East End. Her concern is that Glasgow is not Boston. Boston's about control of the drugs market. The gang members are predominantly black. They've all got guns. It's not like that back home.

Kennedy reassures her that when his team goes to a new place people raise similar concerns. Everyone thinks it is different, whether it's West Coast, Asian gangs, or if the housing projects are high-rise not low-rise. People find every conceivable reason why it's different. But the violence is always tied to a superheated group. They walk across the courtyard and kill people they hate because that's what their dad did. They're trapped. They're terrified. They want a way out. No one is giving them a way out. No matter where he goes it's all the same.

To reassure herself Karyn goes down to Red Hook Community Court. There she sits on the bench as men come in front of the judge for a whole range of things. The majority of the murders and fights are about respect. They aren't about control of the drugs market. Fights about girlfriends. Fights about territory. Fights about disrespect. She realizes it's exactly what she has in Glasgow.

A few days later she strides through the transit lounge of Glasgow Airport, wheeling her case. John has come to pick her up,

'I met David Kennedy. His model will work here,' she says, pushing her sunglasses up her nose. 'Here's what you do. You speak to the gangs. You tell them to stop doing what they're doing and you give them an alternative.'

'Aha.'

'That's it.'

'You're joking.'

'No, the big threat is you give them the jail.'

'There must be more to it than that?'

Their first challenge is to build a coalition of the willing. Karyn and John start to lobby the partners to become involved. They stand in a room with a load of cops from Strathclyde Police. They've pitched them the Boston model, now they scrutinize the faces. The argumentative one with the shaven head and thick eyebrows puts his hand up for a question.

'It's not like Boston here,' he says. Karyn nods, she knows what's coming. She tells them what she saw at Red Hook Community Court. It is crucial they buy in. They also need to understand the enforcement.

'If they're not doing what they're told, if they're not changing, then we're going to do loads of stop-searches,' she says.

John is a powerful ally within Strathclyde Police. He goes to divisional commanders' meetings because he's known them a long time. He's a former homicide detective with a distinguished career in the Serious Crime Squad, the Drug Squad, as a hostage negotiator and on surveillance work in the Scottish Crime Squad. They all listen to him. The Chief Constable of Strathclyde Police agrees to commission the programme for 2008. It is funded for the first two years by the Scottish government and partners. It will cost £5 million.

Next they need to find ex-offenders who can mentor the boys if they decide to leave the gangs. Many will only really listen to an older member, someone who has run with the gangs, been in fights and got the jail. One of her partners introduces her to Iain. He has a gaunt face and a wiry, welterweight body. He is thirty-one but looks younger; prison has somehow preserved him. His voice is soft and firm.

'I can win a gang member's trust in ten minutes,' he tells Karyn. She asks him about his story.

"I killed my pal in a fight when I was twenty,' he tells her. 'He ran about with the same gang as me. My ma knew his ma. I'd got in a fight and he'd battered me. It was about my pride, my fear. I couldn't let it go. I was worried what my pals would think about me. '

As early as he could remember he was beaten by his alcoholic mum. It was random, explosive violence that he struggled to understand. His dad battered him with a belt when he was five for breaking into a house. He was always on the bad square at school for fist fights. Iain slashed a much older guy's face when he was fifteen, giving him eighteen stitches. By nineteen he had four pages of previous convictions. His pattern of offending is typical of the young boys she is targeting, Karyn notes.

'A lot of the time I was leaving the Sheriff's Court and walking over that bridge and thinking to myself, Why does this keep happening to me? Why do I keep getting the jail all the time?'

She knows Iain's words will resonate with young gang members; he will make a good mentor. She has him sit down with some police officers.

'We're sick of seeing young boys killing each other in Glasgow,' one cop tells him. 'We're sick of locking them up.'

They look him in the eye, treat him with respect. It feels strange to Iain. He'd grown up to think of the police as scumbags not to be trusted. He'd hated them. The officers seem to sense where his thoughts are taking him.

'We need to change your thinking.'

No police had ever spoken to him like that, like they care. He's the only one who has made it out of gang life: the rest are in jail or junkies; he's sick of the pattern. So he goes along with it. He starts helping in workshops with young gang members, telling them what it was like for him. They pick up on it. Slowly it gives him a sense of purpose. He does workshops on knife crime, gang violence, sectarianism.

The first Glasgow forum is held on 24 October 2008 at the Glasgow Sheriff's Court. The granite building has a stark futuristic facade, with revolving doors dwarfed by towering metal pillars. Sixty teenage gang members are escorted by cops in riot gear through a cordon of four mounted police to the entrance. They have been bussed in, some are down from Polmont. They look up to the deafening whomp of a police helicopter hovering overhead. A police boat cruises down the River Clyde

They are escorted into Court 8 and ordered to stay on one side in the public gallery. Facing them is a group sitting next to the judge on the bench. The judge tells them the court's in session, all mobiles off. Anyone who behaves badly will be dealt with severely. Karyn's surprised how well behaved they are. It's amazing that some of them can even be in the same room together without skelping each other. One by one members of the group opposite cross over to the boys' side to address them.

The chief of police is first. He rises in full uniform. Images flash on screens behind him. The kids have never seen anything like this before. They freeze in their seats as they recognize their own grainy faces in the intelligence images. They didn't know the cops did this kind of stuff.

'We know who you are. We know where you live, who you associate with, who you fight with,' he says. 'If we wanted to we could have all the police officers in that area outside your front door.'

An elderly plater from Clydebank, in a neatly knotted tie, black shirt and prescription glasses, crosses shakily to their side. His sharp joints show through his flannel trousers, his face is a mass of creases like brittle fractures. As he speaks his voice is shrill, warbly.

'Look, boys. Yous might not think you're causing us problems, but I'm going for my pension and I'm absolutely petrified of coming past you.'

Christine tells them what will happen when they end up soaked in blood in the emergency room. Behind her are graphic pictures of lacerations and massive slash wounds to the face. The damage a baseball bat and a knife can do. The atmosphere in the room is electric.

Then, the key moment, a mother goes up to them. She's the same age as their own mum, they think, looks a bit like her, with her gentle, measured voice.

'At the age of thirteen, my son was attacked by a gang with machetes,' she says. 'I did not recognize he was my child. He was so badly, badly attacked. Severe injuries to his face. He lifted his hands to protect himself and lost his fingers.'

When she stops talking some lads are blinking hard, trying not to let it show. Despite the macho swagger and bravado they love their mums. Another mother steps up. She tells them how she lost her son. She tells them the black cloud that went over her world that day. This is too much. Their faces show shock, fear and shame. There are tears now.

Finally Gary comes forward. An ex-offender who got the jail for eleven years for a murder he committed at eighteen when he was drunk, in a gang fight. He paid for it.

'I spent the whole of my twenties in a cell. Someone telling me when I can go to the toilet. When I can eat. There are no winners here. Carrying a knife, getting intoxicated doesnae make you a man.' The fight's gone out of him. He has such self-loathing that it speaks to them.

At the end, when the last speaker sits down, they are offered something unexpected. A choice. Chase rival schemes and get the jail. Or take this card, ring this number and people will help you get a job, training and housing. They are wary at first. They have never been offered a way out before.

A few days later one leaves a voicemail saying: 'Call me back if this shit's for real.'

A street worker comes out to see him in twenty-four hours, puts him on a programme. They meet St Mirren legend Tony Fitzpatrick and form a new gang with Big Craig, who ran with a gang in Penilee until he was twenty. He used to have wild fights in the Glasgow Viva Penthouse with open razors, knives and bottles. Whoever won the fight would ascend the stairs to claim his place on the big red seat overlooking the whole club. He tells them he gave his mother the worst four years of her life, then she died. Big Craig builds up trust with the boys. If the cops ask him for intel on them, he says no. He gets them to draw a circle of a safe area they can go where they live. They put the paper on the wall and they see how they've imprisoned themselves in a tiny space.

'A real man is one who gets up when it's bitterly cold and the wind is lashing and goes out and earns a crust for his family,' Big Craig tells them. One lad gets a job at Parkhead Forge Shopping Centre. But only Parkhead

Rebels can go there. Not Parkhead Wee Men. So he gets leathered. Another lad is a great artist, so Big Craig gives him money to start a mobile tattoo parlour and drive round Springburn in a minibus. The word goes out that something different is happening.

In Glasgow Royal Infirmary a midwife called Joyce Young hears about the programme. She lives in Black Hill, a deprived part of the city with high unemployment. She's an attractive blonde of thirty-nine in a fashionable mac and mini-dress. She used to do the labour wards but now only does pre-natal care.

A pregnant mum looks at her and asks, 'How many kids do you have?'

'Just one boy,' she lies. She can't say to a new mum, 'My son died.' The rapport will be gone. James was eighteen when he was stabbed in an unprovoked attack in the middle of the day, one Monday in 2007. His attacker was a drug addict, just out on bail. After James' death she looked into community violence and was appalled at the statistics. Sixty-two other young people died that year. She gets in touch with Karyn's office about educating teenagers. They meet up.

Karyn's spoken to a lot of parents who've lost their boys; she finds it really emotional. It is still the hardest part of her work. What really gets her about parents is that they don't want their sons to be forgotten. There is John Muir, for instance, who lost his boy Damien in a stab attack. He does loads of work campaigning on mandatory sentencing for carrying a knife, but he's getting older and it's destroyed his whole life. Karyn finds Joyce a really impressive person.

'When he was stabbed I was soon at his side,' Joyce tells her. 'He was in the Royal in resuscitation. There are things you should never have to see or watch. But you need to be there. There wasn't a minute that I thought, He's going to die. I thought, There are doctors and nurses, they save people all the time.'

Joyce does a lot of work with Karyn and the unit. She stands up at a forum and talks about James. The first time she feels sick, having to speak about him in the past tense. In her mind she's in denial, thinks he's gone away to Ibiza.

Another forum brings in eighty gang members. The motivational speaker Jack Black comes to address them. He has curly grey hair and lively dark eyes, in a smart open-neck white shirt and black suit.

'We got him to give us his time for nothing,' John whispers to Karyn, 'because he was once a social worker in Easterhouse.'

Jack Black bounds over to the kids, ready to work his audience.

'If yous were coming here you'd pay £1,000 to take this course. That's what I charge. I'm going to give it to you for nothing. So what is it you want out of today?'

One guy stands up at the back. He's the first guy to stand up.

'See that guy sitting down there.' He jabs his finger at a lad near the front. 'I've been fighting with him since I was eleven. I want to know why.'

Karyn and John turn and look at each other.

'Fuck. We all want to know why,' John breathes at her.

A year after the programme begins, the cops report that the large pitched battles in Easterhouse have gone. The East End is quieter. B Division now leave the Shettleston station early on Saturday afternoon and stop any teenagers heading home with carry-out.

One day Margaret pops her head round Karyn's office door.

'We're getting complaints from residents in Easterhouse.'

'Someone been battered with a machete?'

'No,' Margaret smiles. 'It's about dogs fouling the pavements.'

They exchange a look. Karyn crosses over to the coffee area, where the cop with the shaven head and thick eyebrows is. He looks up warily as she approaches.

'You know we've got a campus officer in St Mungo's Easterhouse now.'

He frowns at her. So what?

'We had twenty applications from kids there to join the police.'

They extend the model to a wider area of Glasgow.

By July 2011 they have been running the model for two and a half years. There is anticipation as they pore over the results. Karyn leans over a colleague's shoulder squinting at the screen. All those negative architects will be wondering if they have succeeded. So far four hundred gang members have signed up to the initiative. They have reduced their violent offending almost by half. It's had a real impact. For the ones who went through the intensive programmes, they've reduced their violent offending by 73 per cent. Karyn cracks into a smile and they set about releasing the stats. Soon the phones are ringing from the press. Karyn looks across at John. It's seven years since they set up the unit. All those people they have lobbied and debated with. At times it all seemed impossible. The guy who said: 'It's too big. Don't bother.' But there were loads who listened and helped out. Now the unit hands over the day-to-day running of the initiative to Strathclyde Police.

Karyn doesn't stop, she's relentless. She drives around in her battered Audi with rap music blaring. She likes Swedish House mafia. She's been into house music ever since university, listens to it when she's training for the triathlon. She likes the fast beat. She heads out to a pre-five nursery in Castlemilk, South Glasgow; it's called the Jeely Piece Club and it's been there thirty-five years. She's passionate about investing in the early years of a child's life. The evidence to the good is overwhelming and the costs are not high.

Maureen Douglass has worked there eighteen years. She is warm and instantly likeable, short and slight in jeans and an anorak, with neat brown hair and a ready laugh. Maureen sees toddlers arrive who have violent, drug-addicted or alcoholic parents. They manage to feed their child, wheel them about a bit in a pram and meet their basic needs. That's it. No smiles, cuddles or reading them stories. These toddlers can't play with others. She calls them floaters or butterflies. Given dolls, they show a father chasing a mother up the stairs, a mother hiding in a cupboard. It can start with two-year-olds: punching, slapping or biting. Maureen believes in these kids. Despite growing up in the worst possible environment they will make it.

She puts a dressing-up rail out for the older children. Two eleven-year-old girls put on dresses and handbags to act like grown ups. They come over to Maureen and give her a hard slap.

'You're f***ing grounded, get in the house,' one yells.

The trained workers at the nursery take time to undo the damage violence does to these kids. For toddlers there is a sensory room with tubes of calming lights, multi-coloured projections and music. They can go there to escape the chaos at home. In special playtime they develop the children's emotions and self-esteem. When the older kids leave the nursery they are called 'Jeely Weans'. They are angels who watch over the younger Jeely children in the community.

In Easterhouse the landscape is changing. The youths still shiver in their shell suits by Shandwick Shopping Centre, but a few yards away a brightly lit arts complex rises up like a spaceship. Walls of glass, angular wooden panels, silver chimneys. It cost £7 million and houses a pool, library, theatre and computers.

At first sight, things inside the Bridge look orderly. Teenagers are dotted around several banks of computers. A fresh-faced youth worker with a lip-ring goes amongst them telling them to keep down their language. But violence still lurks below the surface.

Red-haired, lanky Ross, fourteen, sits giggling with his pal Craig, twelve, shy and bespectacled. They are engrossed in their PC. Ross is a smart kid and wants to run for the Scottish Youth Parliament. His father put a double-barrelled shotgun against his head when he was three. He rammed it first in Ross's mum's neck, then as Ross screamed and his wee seven-year-old sister punched their father's back, he grabbed his daughter's throat and pushed the muzzle against her brother's fluffy temple. After that the alkie went to live in Parkhead. He turned up to Ross's thirteenth birthday but his mum locked Ross in a room with his PS3 while she was screaming outside. Dad yelling. Doors slamming.

Craig's mum is broke from supporting her brother Neil, a total waste of space. He's twenty-two, a railway labourer who sits at home in his Chelsea strip drunkenly heckling Craig on his PlayStation.

'You talking to the Americans, you dumb bastards!' Neil mumbles, lost in a beery fog, as Craig sets his PS3 voice-changer to high-pitched. At least he's brawn, Craig thinks, he'll protect the family. Craig's mum doesn't usually allow him out the house. He's asked for a treadmill for Christmas. He was third in the mini-Olympics in Glasgow over sixty metres. If you want to survive Easterhouse, you need to be able to run fast.

A chubby lad, Spoony, rushes up to them. A schoolmate with a cheeky dimpled grin, he boasts about a new samurai sword he's got, holds his hands a foot apart. They listen with awkward smiles. Spoony's daft but he's all right. Wide-eyed, excited, he tells his favourite story of a big gang fight last July between Drummy and Provvy, where a helicopter landed in a field, police were there in riot gear with German shepherds. 'Half the scheme were fighting,' he gasps wide-eyed. 'Fifty people. They'd been fighting every day for a month.'

He's so excited about it that Ross tries to muster a response, but as always he suspects Spoony's making it up. How do you hold a riot shield in one hand and a German shepherd in the other?

'You've been playing too much Saints Row II,' he says drily. The Aggro lads love that game, where two gangs battle for turf for the drugs market in an urban wasteland, hacking each other up with machetes and baseball bats.

'Their brutality is legendary,' Spoony croaks in a deep voice, as he walks off to the games room. He loves the film *Green Street* with Elijah Wood, especially the scene where they cut his mouth with a credit card.

Across the room are two other boys on the computers: Tam, seventeen, and his wee sister, both from a scheme near Easterhouse. They look sweet enough, harmless even. But the Bridge is a safe place to hide out if rivals are out looking for you. Saturday afternoon is the witching hour. Tam was charged with attempted murder at fifteen. He was at home watching Celtic v. Rangers when a can was skelped at the window, gave his wee sister a fright. So he picked up a pickaxe pole, gave chase, fractured the guy's skull twice, hospitalized him for months. Besides attempted murder he was done for permanent disfigurement and serious assault endangering life. He's in the Bridge because he's awaiting trial. Hallowe'en last year he was steaming on the Edinburgh Road and caught a belt buckle to the back of the head and had five stitches. He tinkers with his gang page on Bebo. Tam's dad broke his foot in a forklift truck injury a few years back and is now on painkillers, so Tam needs to stay out of jail to protect his sister. They are both bashful, a bit adrift.

The final group is a cluster of squealing fourteen-year-old girls from Aggro, chatting about jeggings, skinny jeans, crop tops and other Primark stuff. The youth worker tries to interest them in some certificates, but what they're after is sex education. One twelve-year-old's been grounded for smoking cannabis. Another's in loads of trouble for her drinking. Mel wants to go to uni and study modelling. She shares a room with her half-sisters and argues the whole time about make-up and the cats.

'Like drama, don't like my drama teacher,' she complains, tugging on a nail. 'She always picks on me.'

'Because of your big orange face. It's so noticeable.'

The Bridge shuts at five on Saturdays and they're out on the streets. To kill time they have a water fight in McDonald's, then off to buy three litres of Frosty Jack to drink with older boyfriends in the Den Toi, who they met in school. McDonald's and pickled onions cover the smell of the booze.

They walk out along the Easterhouse Road as the rain lashes down. It's still dangerous to be out on a Saturday night in Easterhouse.

A wee lad called Drew is referred to Karyn's gang programme by the cops. He's had twelve gang busts in one year and nine in the next. He is gaunt and undernourished, with wide, startled eyes. A thin red scar runs across his throat. He's seventeen so he may be at the age when he'll think about moving away. Drew took his first beating in a gang fight aged eight. They clipped his heels from under him, and battered him with bricks, bottles and coshes leaving him hospitalized for four weeks with a snapped ankle, broken ribs and a dislocated knee.

'I like being with my pals and getting mad with it,' he says. Karyn notices how self-conscious he is, trying to cover his mouth. His front tooth has been snapped clean off, just below the gum.

Later, she powers down the street next to Christine on the way to their Café for Contemporary Arts.

'I need a favour,' she asks. 'Can you fix this guy Drew's tooth? He's seventeen. '

In the open atrium of the café she orders coffee, banana cake and a bowl of chips.

'We need to get him a suit. He's going for interviews to be a joiner.'

'Tesco have good suits,' Christine says. 'My husband got his dinner suit there.'

John puts down the phone to his daughter Laura, a detective in the Easterhouse Murder Squad. It's good to talk to her. He's had a tough day with teachers, civil servants and social workers. Everyone protecting their budgets. All saying the same thing – it's just like this, that's the way it's always been, it's too bad. You'll never be able to fix it. He walks into Karyn's office and stares out the window, as the rain falls over Pitt Street.

'Sometimes I'm more angry than I'm happy.'

Karyn looks up at him. 'Anger's good,' she says. 'Anger's great.'

Afterword

The month after *Hood Rat* was first published in 2011, the inner cities erupted in the worst public disorder for a generation. Four consecutive nights of arson and looting left five dead, hundreds of police officers injured and thousands arrested. Riots broke out in Tottenham and other London boroughs then spread north to Birmingham, Manchester, Nottingham and Liverpool. The images that flashed around the world sent jitters through London's 2012 Olympic committee: a masked hoodie prowled past a burning police car; a woman jumped from a flaming building; shaken shopkeepers described their fear as kids as young as twelve smashed windows and plundered stores.

I'd spent two years talking to gang members and violent young men; I'd sat in patrol cars chatting with anti-gang detective units and been on dawn raids. So this inner-city violence came as no surprise. Cabinet ministers and columnists were quick to offer explanations, but if *Hood Rat* shows anything it is that the issue is complicated.

In the media frenzy following the riots, Swedish, Brazilian and Japanese press told me they were stunned by the images of Britain's streets. This is not the country that we are familiar with, they said. Why has this happened? But Britain has been two countries for some time now. There is the comfortable, middle-class economy. Then there's the inner cities. Decades of failed policies have left them abandoned and forgotten, like a Third World country or a war zone. These deprived areas have experienced the growth of teenage gangs, a rise in knife crime and terrible youth violence. The absentee father, the brutal stepfather or the depressed, harried mother crop up again and again when I talk to kids who live there. From a very early age, they are told that their lives will amount to nothing. They start to believe it, fall behind at school, truant, drift into delinquency and end up in a young offenders' institution at the cost of £60,000 a year. And the cycle continues. A quarter of young offenders are already fathers.

While Peter Oborne in the *Telegraph* chastised the British governing elite for two decades of moral disintegration – MPs stole and looted through their expenses, he reminded them, and the rich hid their spoils offshore – Michael Gove and right-of-centre red tops were quick to blame the 'feral underclass' for the riots. A popular conspiracy theory was that a network of organized gangs had called a truce in order to riot side by side in Tottenham. I refuted this idea in the *Guardian*: rival gang members entering Tottenham risked reprisals. 'If they saw someone who had done something to their family, they would not hold back just because a riot was going on,' Pilgrim told me. 'If senior gang members were involved, they would not be interested in just trainers and TVs. They'd take out the bank, the safes and tills from H&M and Foot Locker. They would break into the bookies.' He'd driven into the area with his family in his black BMW 4-by-4 and recognized local kids. The adrenalin and anger contorting their faces warned him off. He reversed out and away. 'It was only a matter of time before it all kicked off,' he sighed. To him there was nothing uniting the disparate groups involved except the chance for 'free shopping'. By October 2011 official Ministry of Justice figures confirmed that only 13 per cent of those arrested were identified as gang members.

Karyn McCluskey watched the CCTV footage of the riots with a sense of déjà vu. 'I've got copies of that CCTV in Glasgow seven years ago,' she told me. 'Young men fighting in the streets. You could see it in their faces. They were really enjoying it. Sensation seeking. Caught up in the heat of the moment.' All across England from Wolverhampton to Gloucester young men were kicking in windows and running off with electronic equipment. The Left focused on poverty and social exclusion, in an echo of Tony Blair's Social Exclusion Unit of '97. David Cameron, for the first time since he was elected, dusted off the rhetoric for 'Broken Britain'. Most rioters came from deprived areas with poor educational backgrounds; some were excluded from school. Yet no one rioted in Glasgow, which has some of the most chronic deprivation in Europe. In Shettleston, where I went out on patrol with the cops, the life expectancy of men is sixty-three, fourteen years lower than the national average, closer to Iraq or the Palestinian Authorities than the UK. One Glaswegian gang member phoned Big Craig, his mentor, to reassure him there'd be no trouble. Karyn told me that the youths on the Glasgow schemes don't aspire to have the latest mobile phones and flat-screen TVs. They also don't live side by side with ostentatious wealth that you see in Kensington and Chelsea. It's half an hour from Easterhouse in to the cappuccino bars of Glasgow's Merchant City, whereas in Hackney and Islington, rich and poor live side by side.

While poverty alone is not an explanation, there are tectonic pressures on young people from the two most powerful forces in Britain for the past twenty years: consumerism and celebrity. Songs tell them to make money, money, money. Superheroes flaunt bling. These forces have a dark side. Pilgrim was driven into crime in part because he was 'the last kid on the estate to have a Game-Boy'. He also wanted to be famous. When gang members talked to me about 'being famous' or 'making a name for myself' they meant acquiring a reputation for extreme violence. 'It's like *X-Factor*,' Detective Superintendent Darren Shenton from XCalibre told me, referring to the new gangs in Manchester.

The most dynamic, entrepreneurial kids in the inner cities are drawn into the £4.5 billion drug trade. The Olders who loiter at the school gates, sporting their jail muscle like a badge of honour, are more efficient and persuasive than any careers service. They groom boys like Troll, give them new trainers or £50 to draw them in. Pilgrim told me that young boys change when they realize the money they can make from dealing class-As. They move up from shotting, the drudge work, and start acquiring guns in the hope of earning £130,000 a year as a big player. The drug trade runs on violence, but drug policy hasn't altered in thirty years. The Misuse of Drugs Act of 1971 hasn't even undergone an independent assessment.

'Where are their parents?' became a popular outcry after the riots. Many of the kids I met in London, Glasgow and Manchester were fatherless, trying to be 'the man of the house', caught up in a warped, ultra-macho warrior code they'd picked up from Olders on the street. Again this is only part of it. Those fathers who stick around can be a malevolent influence; violent fathers create violent sons. Parenting is challenging when you are educated, in work, in a decent area with strong influences in your life and a stable marriage. Take away those protective factors and it's the toughest job society demands of you. Inexperienced, teenage mothers at risk need support, not demonizing. The Jeely Piece Club in Castlemilk is an example of a community nursery that has helped its depressed, at-risk parents and their toddlers over the course of thirty-five years. Could it be replicated elsewhere without that vital component: the dynamic individuals who run it?

This problem is no longer the sole responsibility of the police. I sat in the back of unmarked police cars with detectives who were underpaid, overworked, exhausted and frustrated by bureaucracy and form-filling. One of Svensson's colleagues was a forty-eight-year-old cop who tore a hamstring chasing a twentysomething gang member who was also a semi-professional footballer. Another had his leg run over by a gang member in a getaway car. They are weary that they keep arresting the same kids. 'For so long the police have taken on every problem,' Karyn said. 'And we can't do it. There's 50,000 cops in London and 12.5 million people.' It's time for other members of society to take an interest. There were encouraging short-term signs: The 'Broom Army' turned up in Clapham to clean up and 900,000 backed the Met on Facebook. 'I hope that's the beginning of their involvement and not the end of it,' Karyn said. 'I hope they go and join Chance UK and become a mentor. We have to use the assets in the community. What is it you want your community to be like? While it's criminal what happened, it'd be even more criminal if they don't seize this moment. Wouldn't it be great if people look back and say look what England did then. That would be a great legacy for us.'

Over two years I'd spoken to so many articulate, even charming young men, lost to a life on the streets. They felt abandoned. When no one cares about you, you are less likely to care about smashing a shop window. And in the end, street violence was always there; we just chose to ignore it.

•

If after reading *Hood Rat* you are interested in finding out more on these issues or becoming involved here are some good starting points:

www.chanceuk.com

www.actiononviolence.org.uk

www.xlp.org.uk

www.kidsco.org.uk

www.immediate-theatre.com

www.jeelypiececlub.org.uk